500 Reproducible Creative Classroom Techniques for Teachers and Trainers

Marlene Caroselli

Tomorrow's illiterate will not be the man who cannot read; it will be the man who has not learned how to learn.
—Herbert Gerjuoy

HRD Press • Amherst • Massachusetts

Copyright © 2015 by Marlene Caroselli.

The materials that appear in this book, other than those quoted from prior sources, may be reproduce for educational/training activities at a single site. There is no requirement to obtain special permission for such uses. We do, however, ask that the following statement appear on all reproductions:

Reproduced from 500 Reproducible Creative Classroom Techniques for Teachers and Trainers, by Marlene Caroselli, copyright © 2015. HRD Press, Inc.: Amherst, MA, www.hrdpress.com.

This permission statement is limited to reproduction of materials for educational or training events at a single site. Systematic or large-scale reproduction or distribution, or inclusion of items in materials for sale, may be carried out only with prior written permission of the publisher.

Published by: HRD Press
                22 Amherst Road
                Amherst, MA 01002
                (800) 822-2801
                (413) 253-3490 fax
                http://www.hrdpress.com

ISBN 978-1-61014-383-7

Cover Design by Eileen Klockars
Editorial Services by Suzanne Bay
Production Services by Anctil Virtual Office

Marlene has given us an astounding array of creative ways to handle all the nuts and bolts of participatory learning. This book will be an invaluable resource for anyone who wants to engage learners and help them understand, remember, and apply what you have taught them.

— Mel Silberman,
author of *Active Training* and
101 Ways to Make Training Active

500 Creative Classroom Concepts is a treasure of proven, as well as practical training tips. Whether you are a seasoned trainer or just starting out in the profession, you won't want to train another day without these precious gems at your fingertips. I only wish I'd had the wealth of ideas this book offers when I first started training. Thank you, Marlene, for a real prize!

— Elaine Biech
ebb associates inc
author of *Training for Dummies*

I have several of Marlene's other books and she has outdone herself in this delightful volume. The book has a wonderful format, great content, passionate writing style, immediate applicability—and brainteasers that keep my neurons, axons, and dendrites in shape.

Marlene has identified 20 critical tasks in a training classroom and provided 25 intriguing techniques related to each. You can mix and match the powerful ideas to create your personal training style. Use these techniques to improve your instructional and motivational effectiveness.

— Sivasailam "Thiagi" Thiagarajan, Ph.D.,
author of *Design Your Own Games and Activities*

Table of Contents

Introduction 1

An Investor's Guide 3

Chapter 1: 25 Ways to Have Participants Introduce Themselves 9

Chapter 2: 25 Ways to Test for Understanding 23

Chapter 3: 25 Ways to Add Humor 39

Chapter 4: 25 Ways to Give Feedback 53

Chapter 5: 25 Ways to Use Questions 67

Chapter 6: 25 Ways to Use Quotations 81

Chapter 7: 25 Ways to Have Groups Report 97

Chapter 8: 25 Ways to Get Through Printed Material 111

Chapter 9: 25 Ways to Choose Group Leaders 127

Chapter 10: 25 Ways to Fill "Odd" Moments 141

Chapter 11: 25 Ways to Deal with Reluctant Learners 157

Chapter 12: 25 Ways to Make the Subject Matter Relevant 173

Chapter 13: 25 Ways to Review 189

Chapter 14: 25 Ways to Encourage Participant Learning After the Course Has Ended 205

Chapter 15: 25 Ways to Encourage Managers, Principals, and Parents to
Continue the Learning 221

Chapter 16: 25 Ways to Develop Study Habits 237

Chapter 17: 25 Ways to Conduct Non-Threatening Competition 251

Chapter 18: 25 Ways to Make Take-Home Assignments Relevant 267

Chapter 19: 25 Ways to Think on Your Feet 281

Chapter 20: 25 Ways to Develop Self-Confidence 301

Appendix

Collective Nouns 325

Discussion Questions About Feedback 327

Sample Grammar Test 329

Sample Intuition Quiz 331

Selected Quotations on Leadership 333

Thought-Provoking Proverbs 335

Sample Letters of Commendation 337

A Training Checklist 339

About the Author 343

Introduction

This potpourri of pedagogical practices culminates a lifetime of teaching—in kindergartens, primary schools, middle schools, and high schools, in undergraduate and graduate school lecture halls, in corporate training rooms, on military bases, and in auditoriums before multi-thousand audiences. These experiences have created a very heavy "toolkit" that I am now eager to remove and turn over to others.

You, no doubt, already have a heavy toolkit of your own. If you bought this book, you are probably one of those exemplary instructors who is always experimenting, always discovering, always evolving. Like me, you are probably eager to share with others what you've done and what you've learned. Over the years, I have exchanged ideas with student teachers, with colleagues, and with readers of my other books, but nowhere have I presented 500 ideas all at once! (Actually, well over 1,000 when you add in all the options on virtually every page and add the Appendix ideas as well.) This book is a compilation of life-lessons for those teachers and trainers who are truly lifelong learners.

But the book is much more than tips and tools and techniques. It also provides information on various learning-situation elements—skewed information, perhaps, but as Søren Kierkegaard observed, "Education without bias is like love without passion." You'll hear my educational-beliefs coming through: I don't believe, for example, in long lectures. I'm opposed to death by PowerPoint. I think people have to get involved in order to get educated. I prefer table groups to lecture-hall seating.

I believe, too, that *someone* has made an investment in the learner—parents, managers, the organization, society, perhaps the learner himself. And investors want a return on their investment. This book has been written to maximize that investment.

An Investor's Guide

As a teacher or a trainer, you are investing in the learner—if only by way of the time and energy you exert to improve your teaching techniques. Throughout this book, you'll find improvement tips that will make your teaching and their learning fun, fast-paced, and functional. Before we get to those, however, here is a glossary of techniques and terms used in the book, as well as a checklist designed to advance your improvement actions.

Participant Assignments. In addition to individual tasks, I will suggest using pairs, triads, teams, and whole-group exercises to achieve various purposes. When the exercise calls for some type of revelation or personal experience, pairs or other small-group formations work well. When role-plays are used (or other exercises calling for an observer to note an interpersonal exchange), I suggest using triads. When an exercise merits full-group attention, the best method involves speaking to the class as a whole throughout a given exercise or for any one part of it. One option is to keep one-half of the class busy while you teach the others "up close and personal." Then reverse the process.

Quizzes. The element of surprise can be a powerful force in retaining new knowledge. Design quizzes that both elucidate and educate. By juxtaposing what participants knew pre-quiz with what they learned post-quiz, they can more quickly appreciate the width of the knowledge-gap. Other quizzes should be designed to test the degree of retention or to determine the degree of comprehension. (I recommend that you never ask any one participant how he or she scored on a given quiz. Additionally, never ask for a show of hands related to scores at the lower end of the continuum.)

Handouts. These are designed to supplement the intent of the exercise and to reinforce the main points being made. Handouts are also employed when participants need to have a common understanding of a situation, on the basis of which they'll take further action.

As you prepare your handouts, keep in mind their future value. What can you do to prevent them from being discarded as participants walk out the door? Design them so they will also be useful references or resources in the future. Consider what is most critical and how it can most easily be presented. By now, you know my biases regarding PowerPoint. Instead of handouts that are merely copies of your slides, put some effort into creating handouts that reflect the instructional flow of your presentation—handouts that contain summaries written in a conversational tone, perhaps, and exercises for future practice.

Case Studies. Case studies, due to their real-world nature, enable participants to correlate their own experiences with someone else's and to project possible outcomes. When the actual outcomes are compared to their projections, participants will then learn through discussion and analysis how best to handle comparable situations if and when they occur in their own lives. There's a safety net associated with case studies—they reveal pitfalls without making participants take the actual steps into those pits. By studying how someone else handled or should have handled a difficult situation, participants can derive benefit that can later be applied to their own personal and professional situations.

Buzz Groups. There's a definite "buzz" that emanates from a classroom filled with small groups working on the same assignment and probably approaching it from different perspectives. Trainers can optimize this excitement by establishing a few ground rules, among them the time element and the fact that groups should try to keep their voices down so others can work more easily. Additional factors to be considered include the following:

Selection of group participants. To avoid having people who see each other all day long sit together all day in a training session, here are several possibilities for grouping (or re-grouping).

- Have participants match well-known book titles with their authors. (In a group of 20 participants, you'd have 10 titles and 10 authors.) Distribute these assigned roles as participants enter the room and have the "titles" and the "authors" match up.

- As participants enter, give each person a different-colored candy kiss. Then assemble groups based on their colors.

- Write the name of the course on each of three large sheets of heavy paper or cardboard. Divide each sheet into irregular puzzle-pieces (seven or eight pieces for each puzzle if the class size, for example, is 22). Cut the pieces for each sheet and put them in an envelope. Shake the pieces up and then distribute one to each participant who enters the door. Have participants group themselves according to the color they selected.

Storyboards. Storyboarding, like so many other creative processes, started with the Walt Disney company. Today, the technique is used in meetings and training sessions around the world. You can use storyboards to lead discussions, and participants can use them to execute their project.

If you've never used them for instruction, now is a good time to start. If you use them often, you know their value in terms of focusing a group's attention in a visual manner and generating discussion. Typically, a four-foot by four-foot foam board is used with index cards and pins, but there are numerous variations on this basic theme. Storyboards are used to track a process, to generate creativity, to achieve clarity, to reach consensus, or to direct wandering attention to the problem at hand.

You (or the group's leader) will identify the purpose of the storyboarding task. Then provide relevant information using index cards pinned to the storyboard or taped to flipchart paper. Class participants or group members discuss the situation and jot down their ideas on cards, which are then arranged on the board. If possible, plan a break of some sort, if only a mini-mini-lecture or a brainteaser. Participants will need time for the ideas to settle and sink in before they return to the situation being storyboarded.

Then, have them go up to the board and rearrange the cards that are on it until they are satisfied with the answer or outcome.

Guided Discussions. You can design activities based on relevant articles or monographs that participants read in class. (Ideally, these should be distributed prior to the class so valuable class time is not taken up with background reading. The advance arrangement also prevents the "lag" that results from people reading at different rates.) Once the group has internalized the material, you'll discuss it using questions that have been prepared ahead of time.

Scripts. Scripts bring out the creativity in participants. They also help participants develop insights and convert theory to practical application. Scripts have a way of sharpening the distinctions between best-case and worst-case scenarios, and provide an interesting alternative to direct discussions of a given point. (Note: Scripts need not always be acted out. Often, the mere exploration of ideas on paper is sufficient to illustrate the point.)

Role-Play/Simulations. You'll find some participants naturally hesitant to engage in role-plays. It's important for you to overcome that reluctance, though, because role-plays provide an instructional value not afforded by any other method. Reluctance is usually tied to tension, a tension that results when individuals think about being someone or something other than themselves. If unchecked, tension can stultify creativity and can even block the natural flow of ideas.

One simple and quick way to relieve tension is to use the **Y-E-S** technique: Have the entire group engage in a deep, satisfying, collective **Y**awn just prior to the role-plays. Then provide **E**ducation about the value of role-plays (they help participants prepare for real-world encounters, they illustrate significant points, and they can actually be fun). Also provide education regarding the specific parameters of the roles and of the exercise itself. Finally, provide a few moments of **S**ilence, during which they can collect their thoughts (perhaps even jot down a few notes). Then . . . let the role-plays begin.

Another possibility is to refer to the activity without prefacing it with the words "role" and "play," which seem to concern some people.

Finally, provide guidance to the observers so that the debriefing sessions can have maximum benefit. Have three or four questions ready—perhaps even written on the flipchart so the observers can lead a discussion that benefits everyone.

For example, questions like these:

"If this role-play could be done a second time, what would you change?"
"Has a situation like this ever occurred in real life?"
"What other options/outcomes might have worked in this situation?"

Assessments. If it weren't for training opportunities, some participants would never introspect. The training environment is ideal for encouraging participants to take time to consider questions with potentially far-reaching implications. These assessments invite self- and organizational analysis.

Panels. An interesting variation on the theme of knowledge acquisition is to use panels. Panels can be composed of non-participants who are invited to the training room to present their views on a given topic. Following this presentation, a question-and-answer session will bring effective closure to the event. Panels, though, can also be composed of participants—volunteers or spokespersons selected by their table groups to present summaries of the work that groups have just completed. Panel members, representing the class as a whole, can exchange ideas on behalf of their groups. (An alternative would be to have participants write additional questions for panel members and to have a moderator collect these and present them to the panel for response.)

Fishbowls. This technique involves having one group work in the center of the room while the remainder of the class sits in a wider circle around them, observing their interactions. It's quite effective, for example, for those in the center to simulate a meeting while the outside group observes their interaction and effectiveness in dealing with the issue.

A Training Checklist

Included here is a list of responsibilities/recommendations that bespeak both professionalism and an ethical commitment to the profession. Even if you are only an occasional trainer, I think you'll find this list helpful.

- I know this subject well enough to be considered something of an expert in it.
- I get to the room at least half an hour early to set it up and to greet early arrivals.
- I do all I can to make participants feel welcome, such as putting a welcome sign on the door or writing the word "Welcome" on the flipchart.
- I make a sincere effort to learn about my participants, their work, their goals, their environments, and their strengths and weaknesses.
- I begin with an introduction to the course, and provide an outline of my objectives and my credentials for teaching the course. Then I follow with introductions of the participants themselves.
- I take care of "housekeeping" items at the beginning of class.
- I make participants aware of ground rules.
- I try to have all their names memorized before the first break.
- I am familiar with Howard Gardner's seven intelligences and/or J.P. Guilford's 124 intelligences and applaud more than the verbal or mathematical proficiency of participants.
- I work to learn (and post) participants' expectations for the course.
- I make sure there's a relevant reason behind all tasks.
- I try to structure courses according to a philosophy like Jesse Jackson's: "Put a floor beneath each learner and a ceiling above none." In other words, I make sure everyone possesses the basics before moving on to more-sophisticated concepts.
- I actively work to make the learning experience an enjoyable one.
- I can integrate their views into the course material.
- I try hard to keep discussions on target.
- I present an overview or agenda of what the course entails.
- I benchmark with other teachers/trainers to ensure that I am providing the most valuable information in the most relevant way.
- I am sensitive to diversity issues, including diversity in learning styles.
- I take pride in the professional look of my materials.
- I make deliberate efforts to structure activities to optimize the ABC's—the Affective realm, the Behavioral realm, and the Cognitive realm.
- I am aware of the "glazed-over" look characteristic of participants who are confused or overwhelmed by the material, and make adjustments when I see it.
- I debrief after content-rich activities.
- I use anecdotes and continuously refine my raconteur abilities.
- I actively work to make the learning environment one of comfort and inclusion.
- I seek feedback throughout the session—not just at the end.
- I frequently invite participants to discuss their real-world situations in light of the learning that is occurring.
- I make myself available to participants before and after the class, as well as during breaks.
- I periodically review the material or provide summaries.
- I consciously avoid sarcasm, vulgarity, inappropriate humor, and references that may be offensive.
- I anticipate questions that will arise and prepare responses to them.
- I employ anecdotes to illustrate points.

(continued)

A Training Checklist *(continued)*

- I assure participants that they will never be made to feel uncomfortable.
- I never lecture for more than 15 minutes at a stretch.
- I incorporate humor into the presentation.
- I include relevant news events and statistics in my presentation.
- I am "physical" with the information—i.e., I make dramatic gestures from time to time.
- I provide a change of pace on a regular basis.
- I consciously think about ways to make the presentations interactive.
- I encourage participants to meet and work with others in the room.
- I invite feedback about the presentation.
- I strive to relate the material to participants' jobs, goals, and lives.
- I schedule breaks as needed.
- I make sure that the screen and flipchart can be seen by every participant.
- I keep abreast of developments in the field.
- I am familiar with Bloom's Taxonomy and ask questions on all five levels.
- I revise my materials on a continual basis.
- I use media effectively.
- I have not stopped honing my communication skills.
- I employ a wide variety of methodologies.
- I evaluate learning comprehension in a variety of ways.
- I invite questions and feedback on my presentation.
- I invite (but put limits on) the telling of "war stories."
- I provide ways for participants to be continuous learners.
- I design effective closings.

Each of the twenty chapters that follow has its own Overview. For the sake of gender equity, the masculine and feminine pronouns will alternate by chapter. Each chapter contains a wide variety of tips, suggestions, options, cautions, F.Y.I tidbits, and recommendations. I've added brainteasers for a post-activity change of pace. The brainteasers can be used at the beginning of the class to provide an idea of the kind of brainpower amassed in the room; in the middle of a long activity, when you feel the class needs a mental break; when you want to get their "cerebral juices" flowing after lunch; when you have odd minutes to fill, and so on.

Note, too, that many of the techniques refer you to the Appendix, where you'll find a number of additional resources.

Einstein once said that love is the best teacher. I've loved preparing this compendium. I hope it teaches you in the best ways possible.

Chapter 1

25 Ways to Have Participants Introduce Themselves

Chapter Overview

The first few moments of class are fearful moments for some participants. For others, the introductions that take place at the beginning of a new program are sources of interest, of possibilities, of discoveries, of commonalities. While it's perfectly acceptable to ask people to give their names and tell a little about themselves, the process often lacks luster. You can enhance it by structuring the way you ask for atypical information.

What NOT to do: Don't try to be a comedian unless you are one. Henny Youngman got away with an introduction like this: "And now, the band that inspired that great saying *Stop the music!*" Don't try thinly veiled insults. They seldom work.

In this section, you will find 25 novel ways for students to share information about themselves, about their purpose for being in your classroom, and about the things they hope to learn.

1. Use the course title.

Print the name of the course on the board or flipchart. Leave space between the letters. Then ask each person to take one letter from the word and use that letter as the first letter of a word that explains why he is taking the course or what he hopes to learn.

Example: If the course is about supervision (S-U-P-E-R-V-I-S-I-O-N), you might take the letter 'I' and use it to introduce yourself in the following way: "I pride myself on being an intelligent person. Intelligence means always gathering new information. I'm here to learn as much as I can."

Brainteaser: There are eight learners in a room. Each one shakes hands just once with each of the other learners. What is the total number of handshakes?

Answer: 28. Gather seven other people and start shaking hands if you don't understand why the answer is 28.

2. Test their intuition.

Have each person give his name and make a statement about his confidence in his own intuitive powers or a statement regarding the degree to which he relies on those intuitive powers. Then tell the group you are going to give a quiz that will test their intuition. (Make up one of your own, or use the one provided for you in the Appendix.)

Chances are, they will do very poorly. If you use the Appendix quiz or one like it, go over the answers and then ask if anyone had a score higher than 60%. Very few will have so high a result. Use the opportunity to stress the importance of keeping an open mind and being willing to let go of preconceptions so new concepts can replace them.

Brainteaser: What is the first number starting with zero and continuing with whole numbers in ascending order that, when spelled out, has all the letters of that word in alphabetical order?

Answer: Forty.

---

3. Challenge them to tell why the course is important.

If the class is working in table groups, give them this assignment: "Come up with at least one situation or reason why the information in this course will be/can be important to you." They can speak in individual terms (e.g., to get a passing grade so they can graduate) or in more global terms (e.g., the better we are at communicating, the less chance there will be for discord).

Have each group start off their report by giving the names of the members. Then, as they present their situation or reason, list it on a flipchart. The totality of the responses will help reinforce your objectives for the course.

Option: On a flipchart or overhead, list as many concepts as you can. Have individuals or pairs select the one concept they'd be most interested in learning. Place a check mark beside each item as the responses are provided. Then make this promise: "I'll spend more time on the most popular than on the least popular. However, I reserve the right to drill, drill, drill on an unpopular-but-important (in my opinion) concept."

Chapter 1: 25 Ways to Have Participants Introduce Themselves

4. Assign partner-interviews.

Start by showing how a dull interview question generally elicits a dull answer: "How long have you been teaching?" "Twenty-four years." By contrast, a question such as "Of all the students you have taught over the years, who stands out in your mind the most?" is bound to yield the vivid memory of an obviously unforgettable character.

Allow a few minutes for participants to devise an interesting question. Once each person has had a chance to interview a partner, begin calling on them to tell two things only: the partner's name and the single most-interesting thing about him.

Brainteaser: What three letters can be used to spell three different words when the letter and the two missing letters are arranged like this?

```
____  ____  L___
____  L___  ____
L___  ____  ____
```

Answers: Pal, Alp, Lap.

---

5. Give participants a choice of questions to answer.

Demonstrate creativity from the get-go. Have a list of questions written on the flipchart or overhead. (PowerPoint them, if you must.) Then have each participant choose two and respond to one of them. (Note: Classes have a tendency to choose questions at the beginning of the list. To avoid monotony, insist that they answer their second question if too many responses are provided for any one question.)

Here are some interesting possibilities:

Of all your unforgettable memories, which one would you *like* to forget?
If your life were a television channel, such as a history channel, what would it be and why?
What famous person are you most like?
If you were principal of this school (or owner of this company), what one change would you immediately institute?
What is your favorite word? Why have you chosen it?
What correlations can you make between chefs and lions?
Other than picking teeth, what can a toothpick be used for?
What is one question you can't answer?

500 Creative Classroom Techniques for Teachers and Trainers

6. Have them explain why they're studying this subject.

As each student gives his name, he will also be asked to tell what he hopes to learn from the class or what his boss wants him to learn (or what his parents want him to learn, if the setting is a school setting). Stating their purpose for being there helps students to focus on the class and the learning they have a responsibility to acquire.

Brainteaser: What letter—clearly, visibly, obviously—is out of place?

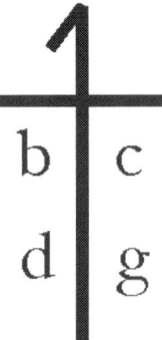

Answer: T. It is bigger and its lines are bolder than the other letters.

---

7. Make them think: What future use can they make of what they're about to learn?

This is an especially challenging assignment—so difficult, in fact, that you may want people to pair up to provide a response. Have each person give his name and then identify one *specific* future use for the information he will be acquiring. (Note: It's important for them to write their future use on a sheet of paper and then to read from that paper. Otherwise, you will find everyone parroting the responses of the first person.)

Leadership-class example: "I'm hoping to establish an Adopt-a-School program for the people in my department and a nearby elementary school. Given how busy people already are, I know the proposal and its acceptance will require real leadership. I hope this course provides me with effective ways to influence people to take positive action."

Brainteaser: What letter belongs in the blank?

O T T F F S S E ____

Answer: N. The letters represent the first letter in the spelling of the numbers from one to nine.

8. Let them critique you.

Education is all about change. All about moving from the darkness to the light. All about (literally, from the Latin) leading ourselves and others out of the present and into an altered state. Encourage your students to help you re-engineer yourself and introduce themselves at the same time.

Ask them to think about the best teacher they ever had, and to isolate one specific thing that teacher did that was memorable.

Then, call on each person to give his name and to complete this sentence: "I hope you will do what my favorite teacher did: he used to . . ."

Brainteaser: What letter belongs in the blank?

DJ FM AM JJ AS O__

Answer: N. The letters represent the first letters in the names of the months, starting with December.

---

9. Task the group with collecting knowledge.

A mind is a terrible thing to waste. So is time. By asking your table groups to record everything they already know about the subject, you'll learn what they've already learned. Thus you can make some quick, if subtle, adjustments to the plans for the day.

This activity will take at least 15 minutes, depending on the size of the group. Each person will tell what aspect of the course he has mastered. As they share their expertise, participants will have a chance to get to know others in their table group first. A spokesperson can introduce group members via a report that highlights the collective knowledge they possess. Poetry class example: "I'm Jerry. Among us, we have expertise in the haiku, the cinquain, the sonnet, and scanning techniques. And we have one person so enamored with Shakespeare that she even knows his birthday is April 23!"

Brainteaser: More of a brain-improver, this exercise develops both concentration and rapid thinking. Take five words (or ten, for a real challenge) of five letters each. Separate the letters in each word and combine them (first + first, second + second, et cetera), as shown below. Exchange with someone who has done the same thing. Time yourself, trying to better your "score" each time (the score is really the time required to figure out the words). Or assess yourself by comparing yourself to your partner: whoever finishes first is the "winner." (Note: The words can also be five letters each or seven letters each. I've chosen words of six letters for this exercise.)

(continued)

9. **Task the group with collecting knowledge.** *(concluded)*

Example: If I were to write the word "cat" with each letter bracketed on the left, you would have no trouble recognizing the word: [c [a [t. And if I were to write the word "dog" with the brackets on the right, you'd still be able to see "dog" quite easily: d] o] g]. But when I combine these two bracketed words, it's suddenly much more difficult to see them: [d c] [o a] [g t].

In the brainteaser that follows, two six-letter words have been combined the way "dog" and "cat" were combined in the example. Time yourself as you look for the ten words.

1. [c a] [a s] [r s] [p u] [e r] [t e]
   Words: _____ and _____.

2. [r p] [e e] [c n] [o c] [r i] [d l]
   Words: _____ and _____.

3. [d h] [a o] [n u] [c s] [e e] [r s]
   Words: _____ and _____.

4. [a f] [n i] [k n] [l g] [e e] [s r]
   Words: _____ and _____.

5. [c s] [o t] [u a] [p p] [o l] [n e]
   Words: _____ and _____.

Answers: 1. "carpet" and "assure" 2. "record" and "pencil" 3. "dancer" and "houses" 4. "ankles" and "finger" 5. "coupon" and "staple"

Brainteaser: Ready for more sports-team puzzles?

1. Artful ones from the city of Hispanic cherubs

2. Druids from a leguminous location

Answers: 1. Los Angeles Dodgers 2. Boston Celtics

10. Give one course-related word as a prompt.

Hone your own thinking about what you teach by pulling the gist of it from your gray matter. Choose a single word that encapsulates the course material. The word, ideally, will be a familiar one; use it to stimulate thinking about phrases that contain that word.

Example: In an art class, you might use the word "red," which is important as a primary color. Task table groups with creating lists of phrases that contain the word ("red-letter day," "seeing red," "Hunt for Red October," and so on). For a class in management or supervision, the word could be "lead." The related expressions might be "leading with your chin," "follow the leader," "You can lead a horse to water . . ."

Then ask groups to introduce themselves and share their lists. Encourage them to listen so carefully that the second (and subsequent) groups do not repeat any of the phrases used by preceding teams.

Note: if your chosen word does not elicit a long list of phrases or if there's too much repetition, have subsequent groups explain some of the terms or give examples of how one phrase might pertain to the course.

11. Tell them to find an object that symbolizes themselves.

If you will be meeting with the group more than once, just have participants give their names at the first session. For the second session, they are to bring some object that symbolizes who they are. At the very beginning of the second day, call on each person to use his self-symbol to introduce himself and explain why/how the object represents him so well.

Example: You could start the process by holding up a pencil and saying something like this, "Some of you will consider this pencil old-fashioned, compared to the speed with which you can produce words on a computer screen. And I suppose I am old-fashioned, but I still like this pencil as a self-symbol. Notice it's straight and narrow. I try to stick to the straight and narrow in my own life. Notice, too, that it has an eraser. This symbolizes mistakes I have made and my willingness to learn from them and move on."

Option: If the class is only being held for one day, ask participants to think of all the objects in their homes. Then, they are to select one and simply tell the class how the object reflects their personality, values, interests, et cetera.

12. Ask for truth and lies.

Each participant will tell three things about himself, one of which will be a lie. You, as the instructor and official lie-detector, can guess which is the lie. Every time you fail, award the participant a small knowledge-prize. The alternative is to call on various other class members to guess which statement is *not* true.

Option: Have participants tell a story regarding the subject matter and a time when their knowledge of the subject proved to be beneficial.

Brainteaser: What number does not belong with the others?

$$3810 \quad 6024 \quad 4816 \quad 1452$$

Answer: 4816. The other numbers within each number yield 12.

---

13. Use pennies as prompts.

Give participants a penny or two each, and then divide class members into groups. Each person will tell the group something about the year written on his coin—if only the fact that it was minted 20 years before he was born (as might be the case with young participants). The coins should stimulate some interesting discussion about American (or personal) history.

Then ask them to choose a name for their group, based on the most interesting year-information they heard (for example, "The Fabulous Forty-Niners"). Pass out a sheet of flipchart paper to each table group. Ask them to write their group name, the names of the group members, and then a statement related to history or to the group's personality. After 15 or 20 minutes, have each group report and then post the papers around the room.

Brainteaser: What three letters can be used to spell three different words when the letter and two missing letters are arranged like this?

$$\underline{\quad R\quad} \ \underline{\quad\quad} \ \underline{\quad\quad}$$

$$\underline{\quad\quad} \ \underline{\quad R\quad} \ \underline{\quad\quad}$$

$$\underline{\quad\quad} \ \underline{\quad\quad} \ \underline{\quad R\quad}$$

Answers: rat, art, tar

14. Provide examples of "try-umphs" and ask them to write their own.

Learning ain't what it used to be. The law school model of study groups has moved beyond the legal classroom. More and more learning situations today have students studying together—proof that the point is to gain knowledge (perhaps in order to pass an exam) and *not* to compete with one another.

To this end, ask participants to work with at least one other person. The teams are to come up with a three- or four-word statement that is a positive affirmation of the learning experience. The statement should suggest what they will try to do and add the "umph" factor to their efforts. They will use their try-umphs to introduce themselves.

Sample try-umphs:
- Just do it. (Nike ad)
- Just say "no." (Theme of an anti-drug campaign)
- Drive out fear. (Dr. Edwards Deming)
- Eliminate turf wars. (Dr. Joseph Juran)
- Never give up. (Winston Churchill)

---

15. Quote Drucker. Then ask them to ask questions.

Management guru Peter Drucker maintains that leaders know how to ask questions—*the right questions*. Ask each person to think of a question they'd like to ask you and to then introduce himself and ask his question.

If the class is large, divide the questions and the responding time in half by pairing up participants.

Brainteaser: What do these words have in common?

red, pink, gray, brown, black

Note: Participants will immediately respond that all the words are colors. Keep pushing them to find additional similarities.

Answer: The words are also all monosyllabic. They all end in a consonant. They also all start with a consonant. Each has only one vowel. Each has another word contained within ("Ed," "ink," "ray," "row," and "lack.").

16. Have them speculate about the agenda.

Have each small group make a list of what they think will be covered in the course on this day. Then have a spokesperson give the names of the people in his group and also the items on the group list. Wait until each group has provided its list. Then award a knowledge-prize to the group that comes closest to the agenda you have planned for the day. The group also wins the opportunity to put their list on flipchart paper and hang it on the wall.

Brainteaser: Which pair completes the analogy?

Note: The colons indicate the relationship. Instead of saying "short is to tall as small is to big," the analogy question would be written this way: "short : tall : : small : big."

    Note : Eton : :   a) school : dean

                          b) paper : pupil

                          c) message : school

                          d) time : emit

Answer: D, because the original (note: Eton) has two palindromic words, as does the last entry.

---

17. Activate change in their learning.

Write these letters and words on a flipchart, transparency, or PowerPoint slide.

    C = Concentrate   (What will they concentrate on learning today?)
    H = Habit   (What old learning habit do they want to break?)
    A = Attitude   (What attitude best serves knowledge acquisition?)
    N = New habit   (What new learning habit would they like to acquire?)
    G = Grow   (How do they intend to grow as a result of this course?)
    E = Educate   (Who else can they educate about this course?)

Then have each person stand, give his name, and respond to one of the questions.

Brainteaser: Which letter does not belong?

                N Y F M H K Z

Answer: M, because all the others require three strokes to make (M requires four).

18. Help them define the course.

Quality guru Phil Crosby once remarked that if you ask 100 different people in a given organization to define the word "quality," you might get 100 different definitions. To achieve consensus on an important course concept, ask small groups to define on chart paper a key word associated with the course.

Then ask a group spokesperson to give the names of each group member and then read the group's definition before posting it. Once each group has shared its definition, have the class vote on the one that best captures your intent (your vote is worth 50%). Then use that as the operative definition for the day.

Brainteaser: Which city is least like the others?

Seattle, Wichita, Dallas, Atlanta

Answer: Dallas, because it is a two-syllable word and the others have three syllables. Dallas is also the only word that does not have the letter "t."

---

19. Involve them in their own learning.

Ask table groups to prepare lists of what they believe to be the Seven Habits of Highly Effective Learners. Post the lists. Then have every participant circulate around the room to look at the posted lists and select one habit or trait that he possesses. When everyone has returned to their seat, call on each person to give his name and the specific habit he is proud to possess.

Brainteaser: What is the pattern in this arrangement?

86   11   4   90   1   7   16   12   28

Answer: The numbers are arranged in the alphabetical order of the spelled-out words.

20. Elicit a wish; make a promise.

Call on class members, one at a time. Ask each to give his name and one thing he wishes you would do during the course of the course. Then and there, make a promise to attempt to accommodate their needs. Ask them to alert you if you stray from your goal.

Brainteaser: What common word remains in the following grouping after you have removed six letters from it?

s i b x r o l c e c t o t e l r s i

Answer: Broccoli. You have to remove the letters that spell "six letters."

---

21. Provide lists of words.

You can hand out the lists or write the lists on flipchart paper and post the sheets around the room. The words can be related to hobbies, sports, current events, entertainment, cuisine, famous people, et cetera. Ask each person to select one word to which he is drawn. With their selected word in mind, participants find a partner who has a related word. The process of walking around and asking others if they share a common word helps break the ice. Having found another person with a similar word, the two participants will introduce themselves to each other and then to the class, providing a brief summary of their commonality.

Brainteaser: What number comes next in this sequence?

0 1 1 2 3 5 8 13 21 ___

Answer: This is the Fibonacci sequence: Each number is equal to the sum of the two numbers that precede it. Thus, the answer is 34.

22. Supply a list of metaphors.

Write a list of metaphors on the flipchart, such as these:

> My workplace is a bull ring.
> This school is an artist's palette.
> Fifth grade is a beach.
> The HR department is a shock absorber.

Each participant will select one metaphor and then explain his selection metaphorically by using at least one additional sentence that extends the metaphor he has chosen.

Participant examples: My workplace is a bull ring. If you turn your back for a minute, you'll be gored.

This school is an artist's palette. The diversity of styles, personalities, and backgrounds adds up to an unparalleled picture of productivity.

Fifth grade is a beach. And our teacher is a killer whale.

The HR department is a shock absorber. Without it, the corporate automobile would deliver a very bumpy ride, indeed.

23. Tape flipcharts around the room.

At the top of each, write one critical element of the course. As participants enter, ask them to circulate around the room, read the posted flipchart sheets, and then sign their name below the topic that most interests them.

Then read off the names of each person according to their signatures on the sheets. Form table groups on the basis of their interests.

Brainteaser: What word does not belong in this grouping? Why?

> father   brother   mother   aunt   cousin   uncle   grandmother

Answer: Cousin, because all the other words are gender-specific.

24. Ask each person to stand, give his name, and state one adjective that describes him well.

Ask the other participants to write down each name and related word. After every fifth person, stop the introductions and ask for a volunteer to repeat the names and adjectives—without looking at his notes. Continue the process until everyone has been introduced.

Award a token prize to the person who can recall the most names/adjectives.

Brainteaser: Can you think of a word that is used in combination with each of the other words in this list? Example: pad   church   hole   **Answer:** mouse.

1. cottage   cake   ball
2. bean   vault   north
3. pain   half   full

Answers: 1. cheese   2. pole   3. back

---

25. Prepare a list of incomplete sentences.

Examples: I know _____.

I have _____.

I believe _____.

I've discovered _____.

I learned _____.

I saw _____.

I came close to _____.

Then have participants select one statement and introduce themselves with a completed sentence.

Brainteaser: What holiday is represented by this combination of letters?

A B C D E F G H I J K M N O P Q R S T U V W X Y Z

Answer: Christmas, because there is no "l" (Noel).

Chapter 2

25 Ways to Test for Understanding

Chapter Overview

There's what *you* think participants learned. There's what *participants* think they learned. And then there's what *their bosses or parents* think they learned. These are not necessarily the same realities: in fact, they may not be realities at all. There are ever so many ways to assess what your participants are really learning. We detail 25 of them in this section.

1. Prepare at least ten questions.

Thirty questions would be even better. They should be questions that are answerable by "yes" or "no." Throughout the day, ask your questions in order to obtain quick feedback regarding their absorption of the new information you are presenting.

Ask participants sitting on the left-hand side of the room your first set of questions. Your second set of questions should be addressed to participants seated in the middle of the room. The final set of questions will go to people seating on the right-hand side of the room. This arrangement will help ensure that everyone has a chance to be tested for understanding.

Brainteaser: What is the smallest fraction containing the numbers 4, 5, and 6?

Answer: $\frac{4}{65}$

Brainteaser: Can you tell what number is missing?

3	5	8
1	7	6
11	4	5
15	16	___

Answer: 19. If you add the first three numbers in each column, you will get the number at the bottom. Add 8, 6, and 5 and the missing number is 19.

2. Excerpt ten key statements from the curriculum.

Write each in the largest print-size possible. Then post the papers around the room. Periodically, call on someone and ask her to stand next to the statement she likes best. Then have her paraphrase the idea in her own words.

Brainteaser: The letters "A," "C," "D," and "R" are used (not in this order, of course) to spell the word "card." These same letters appear in the list of words that follow. The number of blanks plus C-A-R-D letters represents the total number of letters in the word. A further clue is given in the synonym or describing phrase that precedes the word. Make a card game out of this brainteaser.

Example: Captivated by _ _ _ R A _ C _ D   **Answer:** Entranced.

Cannon or artillery :	_ R D _ A _ C _
Made a face, as if in pain:	_ R _ _ A C _ D
Teacher:	_ D _ C A _ _ R
Separated and distributed evenly:	_ A R C _ _ _ D
Comedienne's married name:	R _ C A _ D _

Answers: Ordnance, Grimaced, Educator, Parceled, Ricardo (Lucille Ball)

---

3. Have each person record an important point.

Ideally, she will note the most important thing she has learned to that point in the day. She will then teach that concept to a small group of three or four others. After approximately five minutes, have the next person in the group share what she has noted. (Note: If there are four people in each group, you'll need about 20 minutes to complete the exercise; five people, 25 minutes.)

Circulate around the room as the teaching sessions are going on. Offer to settle any confusion that may arise about the content.

Option: If it's a relatively small class, you can call on each person to teach her concept to the class as a whole.

Brainteaser: What number replaces the question mark?

5   3   10   6   15   ?   20

Answer: 9. Every other number increases by 5 (5, 10, 15, 20). The remaining numbers are increasing by 3 (3, 6, 9).

4. Have them prepare exam questions.

Then give each participant a number, starting with "1" and moving consecutively to the last person in the class. Next, ask people to write on a blank sheet of paper the numbers (vertically) from 1 to 23 (or whatever number represents the total number of people in the class.)

Now call on each person, starting with #1. She reads her question and the rest of the class answers the question on their papers next to the corresponding number on their answer sheet. Continue until each person has had a chance to read her question aloud.

Go over the answers together.

Brainteaser: What number replaces the question mark?

1   3   7   ?   31

Answer: 15. Each number is doubled, and then one is added ($3 \times 2 = 6 + 1 = 7$).

---

5. Form groups of five.

Their task: to write a group essay summarizing what has been learned thus far. (It's best to do this assignment after half the day (or more) has passed. Tell participants that you plan to use the information with future classes. Have each group exchange their essay with another group to ensure that there have been no glaring omissions.

Brainteaser: What familiar saying is captured with these sesquipedalian words?

> "Should an equestrian entity be made available to you without expectation of reimbursement, refrain from making an ocular foray into the oral cavity of that entity."

Answer: "Don't look a gift horse in the mouth."

6. Form groups of five again.

This time, they'll be responsible for preparing a group lesson plan to teach a key concept. (You'll need at least a half-hour for this.) They should consider what they will call their lesson, what its objectives will be, what the overview will contain, what the outline will look like, how they will begin the class, how long it will take to deliver, how they will end it, and how they will measure or test to ensure that learning has occurred.

If time permits, have each group make its presentation.

Brainteaser: What number replaces the question mark?

2   6   ?   54   162   486

Answer: 18. Each number is multiplied by 3.

---

7. Let them "pig out."

Ask participants to draw a pig. Give no other directions. Then have them look at what they drew as you read the amateur-psychological interpretations below. Have them introduce themselves by giving their names and then confirming or refuting the interpretations in relation to their own personalities.

- If they drew the pig near the top of their papers, they are positive and optimistic.
- If they drew the pig near the bottom, they are just the opposite.
- If they drew the pig in the middle, they are realists.
- If they drew the pig's face looking to the left, they believe in tradition, and are friendly people who remember birthdays.
- If they drew the pig's face looking to the right, they are innovative and active and tend *not* to remember birthdays.
- If they provided many details, they are analytical and cautious and tend to be distrustful.
- If they drew just a few details, they tend to be emotional and naïve risk-takers.
- If they drew the pig with four legs, they are secure and stubborn, and remain true to their ideals.

8. List ten key terms related to the course.

Do this in random order on chart paper, and post it. Then have groups prioritize the list in terms of what was most valuable to them. (The last item will be the least-valuable concept for a given team.) Finally, have them report and explain their selections (or at least the top two).

Brainteaser: Each of the words in this brainteaser has an A-T-O-M in it. Granted, the letters of the word "atom" may have other letters come in-between. In fact, wherever you see a blank space, that is where another letter (A, T, O, or M) will be placed. Your clues precede each puzzle word.

1. Whirlpool   _ A _ _ _ T _ O M
2. Marcel's expertise _ A _ T O M _ _ _
3. Capital of the Sudan _ _ A _ T O _ M
4. Robot   A _ T O M _ _ _ _
5. Cerebral squall   _ _ A _ _ _ T O _ M

Answers: 1. maelstrom 2. pantomime 3. Khartoum 4. automaton 5. brainstorm

---

9. Ask them to describe someone they know.

That "someone" would be an individual who really loves/excels at math, social studies, time management, or whatever the course topic is. Have them imagine what her days are like. What actions would she take? How would she be different from the individual with only a mild interest in the topic?

Then form large groups of at least eight people. Their job, step one: To share their descriptions. Step two: To glean ideas for ways to incorporate what they are learning into their lives after the class has ended. When possible, they should note the behaviors of the subject-matter experts they described earlier.

Brainteaser: What are the next four letters in this sequence?

A, F, H, I, ___ ___ ___ ___

Answer: K, N, Y, Z. These letters require three pen strokes in their formation.

10. Lead them in stating a mission.

To do this, begin by forming triads. Ask each triad to brainstorm a short list (three or four items) of the learning concepts that have been most valuable/interesting/significant in the course so far. Call on a spokesperson from each group to provide key words from the lists.

As they do this, develop a master list on the flipchart or board of the key words. Then ask the triads to formulate a mission statement for the class, based on some of the terms listed.

Helpful hint: A Google search ("examples of mission statements") will yield numerous examples for you to share with participants.

Enrichment option: Have your own mission statement prepared in advance.

Once the groups have written theirs, collect them and compare them to your own. Award a token prize to the triad that came closest to yours (or surpassed it).

11. Omit a key point from your summaries.

Prepare in advance four summaries—one list of key points for each quarter of the instructional day. Then go back and eliminate one key point from each list. After each two-hour block of instruction, have participants listen as you read your list. Award a prize to the first person in each group who is able to identify the missing point.

Brainteaser: Someone in your class will pride herself on her orthography skills. Challenge her and all others to spell the plurals of these words correctly.

phenomenon	octopus	manservant	man-o-war	oboe
sheep	Madam	deer	axe	teaspoonful
potato	ox	Mister	Jones	daughter-in-law

Answers: phenomena, octopuses or octopi, menservants, men-o-war, oboes, sheep, Mesdames, deer, axes, teaspoonsful, potatoes, oxen, Messieurs, Joneses, daughters-in-law

12. Help them stratify.

In an instructional setting, the word "stratification" is simply the process of listing items and then categorizing them. Here's how it works in a test-for-understanding situation. In the late afternoon of the day, ask small groups to list as many things as they can think of related to the learning they have acquired during the day.

The lists can contain statistics, quotes, and the names of famous people you've referred to during the session. They can also contain tools you've shown them how to use or rules to which they've been introduced, concepts you have presented, et cetera. They should strive to list 20–30 items, in no particular order.

Then have them stratify: They will find a heading or label for each of the classifications into which the course items could be divided. Each item will fit into one category (occasionally, more than one). In a management course, for example, the headings might be "Research," "Communication," "Resources," "Leadership," "Strategies," and "Skills." There might also be a category called "Miscellaneous," which would contain the few items that cannot be placed in any of the obvious categories.

Note that different groups might have different headings for their classifications and they could all be correct. The final step in stratification is to place every single item in one category or another.

Brainteaser: Match the speaker with the statement.

1. [Upon being asked why modern players have longer careers.] "Arabic exercises!"
2. "This planet is our home. If we destroy the planet, we've destroyed our home, so it is fundamentally important."
3. "The word 'genius' isn't applicable in football. A genius is a guy like Norman Einstein."
4. "Sure I've got an IQ. It's a perfect twenty-twenty."
5. "If the people don't want to come out to the park, nobody's going to stop them."

A. quarterback Joseph Theisman
B. baseball great Yogi Berra
C. linebacker Dick Butkus
D. halfback Duane Thomas
E. businessman Ross Perot

Answers: 1. C 2. E 3. A 4. D 5. B

500 Creative Classroom Techniques for Teachers and Trainers

13. Draw a body; use it for review.

You'll need large sheets of butcher paper or flipchart paper for this. Draw the outline of the human body. Label these parts: "Head," "Heart," "Hands," and "Heels." (If possible, have five of the same outlines drawn on five large sheets of paper—one for each group.)

Example:

Stop your lecture several times during the day and allow a few moments for the groups to discuss their learning to that point. Then have one person from each team go over to the drawing (or to her team's posted paper if you have one per team) and write one thing in the Head, Heart, Hands or Heels portion of the body. The "thing" would be an idea that intrigued them (Head section); a concept that they all really liked (Heart); a hands-on activity they worked on (Hands); or a possibility they'd like to get moving on or take back to the workplace right away (Heels).

At the end of the day, use these charts to summarize what was learned.

Brainteaser: If you don't have matches for these match tricks, you can always use toothpicks or even pens/pencils.

1. Turn ten matches into two.
2. Turn ten matches into a male cat.

Answers: 1. TWO 2. TOM

14. Have them create an alliterative phrase.

Zipf's Law asserts that we tend to look for the simplest, shortest way to express ideas. Of course, we cannot do this unless we understand the basics from which the shorthand will be derived. A thought-provocative way to ensure depth of understanding is to have small groups create an alliterative phrase that conveys the Zipfean-essence of the concept or entity.

Example: A course dealing with time management might be reduced to these few precepts: Omit, Organize, Objectify.

Allow time for the groups to prepare their alliterative reports. Then ask them to explain or give an in-depth rationale for one word they have chosen. To illustrate: "Omit" in a time management course could mean taking the advice of Mitchell Posner, who asserts that we have to be info-ecologists, discarding or omitting 99 out of every 100 bits of information that come our way.

---

15. Have them develop a rhyme.

Nearly everyone who has studied the way teams operate has heard the phrase "Form, Storm, Norm, Perform." But few people realize that Bruce Tuckman, the originator of the phrase (nearly 40 years ago), had to do extensive research on team operations before he could create this rhyme.

Have participants capture the essence of a learning segment in a rhyme, as Tuckman did with teams. Then have a spokesperson for the team share her team's work.

Brainteaser: Sequential letters in these sentences form the names of animals or birds. Can you find all three?

Example: The rat can bur<u>row l</u>azily if it chooses to.   **Answer:** Owl

1. She demanded, "Do gestures always have to signify hidden meanings?"
2. "Prestige," Raoul asserted, "is the result of attention to quality!"
3. It's often been noted that the head wearing a crown often feels a lack of ease.

Answers: 1. dog (Do g . . .)   2. tiger (. . . tige," R)   3. crow (wearing a crow . . .)

16. Convert them into teachers.

This test for understanding will require good organizational skills on your part. Distribute a 3 × 5 card to each participant. On the front, have them write down one concept they feel they have learned well. On the reverse side, ask them to note a concept they are still having some difficulty understanding.

Next, ask for a show of hands in response to this question: "Who is having trouble with _____?" While hands are still in the air, ask "And who wrote down that she feels she has learned this concept well?" Have the second set of handraisers work with the first to teach them what they know.

After a few minutes, move on to another concept and continue until everyone has had a chance either to teach someone else or be taught by someone else (or both). If an odd scenario arises (e.g., six people had difficulty learning a certain concept and no one seems confident about it), gather the group of six around you and re-teach it.

---

17. "Idol"-ize them.

The classroom version of the "American Idol" television talent competition can be presented in one of two ways.

1) You write a song that reviews the essential elements of the course.
2) Groups prepare their own songs that demonstrate their understanding.

Allow time for groups to prepare their renditions of the song, using whatever props they feel will add depth to the audience's understanding of their presentation.

As they are working, assemble a panel of three judges (selecting, if possible, those who bear some resemblance in appearance or personality to Randy, Paula, and Simon, the real "American Idol" judges). Then have the judges evaluate each group as they perform.

Brainteaser: Using only the letters in the word "r-o-a-s-t," make as many other words as you can. (At least 20 are possible.)

Answers: a, as, at, or, so, to, art, oat, oar, rot, sot, rat, tar, oast, soar, sort, star, tars, sat, rots, arts, taro, stoa

18. Develop their authoring skills.

If participants have a firm grasp of the fundamentals of the course, they should be able to express that grasp in writing. Ask them to write an article aligning their viewpoints with some of the course fundamentals. Give them some help creating a catchy title; putting a "hook" in the introduction; using subheadings; and concluding with some reference to the essential thrust of the article.

Submit the article for publication in the organizational newsletter, the local newspaper, or a publication such as Stephen Covey's *Excellence*.

Brainteaser: How many lines must be drawn in order to connect all the letters of the word "t-i-g-e-r" to each other?

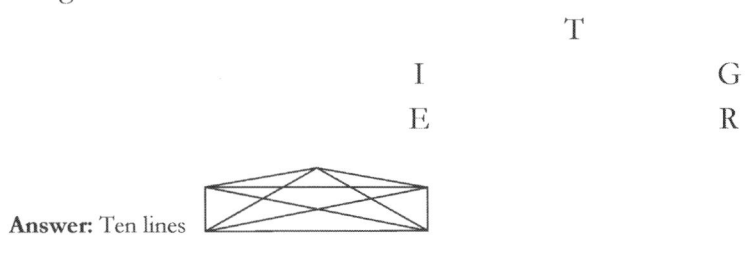

```
            T
    I               G
    E               R
```

Answer: Ten lines

---

19. Turn them into cartoonists.

Find a book of business clip-art and select several images. Paste them on a sheet of paper, and make enough copies so each participant has one. Then have pairs write the bubbled captions for one image. Their comments should reflect their comprehension of some aspect or theme of the course.

Brainteaser: Add a word in the first column to a word in the second and come up with a new six-letter word.

RAT	ART
KIT	LET
PAR	TON
BUT	FIT
COT	ROT
OUT	TEN
ERR	TAN
IMP	BOY
OUT	AND
COW	TON

Answers: rattan, kitten, parrot, button, cotton, errand, impart, outlet, outfit, cowboy

20. Have them develop a rhyme.

This test for understanding really *is* a test, but you will need an even number of groups in order for it to work. Have each group prepare a 20-question (neatly written) quiz. Make certain the groups are all moving along at approximately the same rate. (Issue warnings, such as "By now, you should have ten questions.")

Then have the groups exchange their quizzes. The answers from a given group will be returned to the group that wrote the exam. That same group will correct the exams and announce the scores.

Brainteaser: Without referring to a dictionary, can you find the five misspelled words?

consensus	caligraphy	filicity
accommodate	treacle	vocalization
fluorescent	imminence	vaccination
foreward	emminent	inoculate
geneology	flummox	immigration

Answers: foreward (foreword/forward); geneology (genealogy); caligraphy (calligraphy); emminent (eminent); filicity (felicity)

---

21. Appoint them the "de-terminators."

Initiate a discussion centering on this incomplete statement: "Someone who earns a passing grade in this class should be knowledgeable about . . ." Give the class one thing you believe is required to pass the class—one bit of knowledge that is a *sine qua non* needed for course-completion.

Ask them to work in small groups to determine what other knowledge-bits should be added as determinants of course success. Compile a master list and use it at the end of the class to review.

Brainteaser: How quickly can you rearrange the letters in the following words in order to form totally new words?

Example: C-A-R-E rearranged is A-C-R-E

1. B-A-T-T-L-E
2. S-C-A-L-P
3. S-H-O-R-E
4. S-I-R-E-N
5. D-I-E-T
6. C-H-A-R-M

Answers: 1 = tablet 2 = clasp 3 = horse 4 = reins 5 = tide 6 = march

22. Encourage group exam-preparation.

Mathematics professor Edward Dubinsky of Purdue University has had remarkable results with group self-education. In fact, students in his study teams score an average of 14 points higher on tests than students who study alone.

Give participants a choice between studying alone and studying as part of a group for your next in-class quiz. After they have taken it and you have gone over the answers, determine whether or not the solo study-ers out-performed the group study-ers.

Brainteaser: Can you figure out this famous saying?

DON
TGI
VEU
PTH
ESH
IP

Answer: "Don't give up the ship!" —John Paul Jones

---

23. Ask for a signature attesting to their learning.

Tell participants that they will be asked to sign a letter at the end of the class attesting to what they have learned. Emphasize the fact that it is their individual responsibility to make sure that they have in fact clearly understood the concepts. Tell them that if there is anything they do not understand, they should ask you to clarify or repeat it, because the letters will be sent to their parents (or managers, if you are a corporate trainer).

Then, at the end of the day, distribute the letters for their signatures. Collect them and distribute to the appropriate persons.

Brainteaser: Can you move only three circles so that there are four on the bottom, three on the next row, two on the next row, and only one at the top?

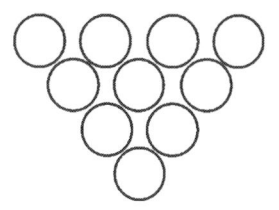

Answer: From the top line, take the extreme-left circle and the extreme-right circle and place them at the extreme-left and the extreme-right of the third row. Then take the circle in the last row and place it at the very top of the design.

24. Appoint a roving reporter.

Before the session begins, ask one participant to serve as a roving reporter. Work with her to prepare a list of five to ten course-related questions. Then introduce her to participants and begin the class by explaining that she will be gathering information about the learning in which they are about to engage.

Ask her to stand and introduce herself—perhaps she could even read a few of the questions. Once you have begun the lesson, the reporter will periodically go over to a table group (or various individuals) and ask questions regarding the course. Before she begins her relentless pursuit of truth and knowledge, though, have the class vote: Do they want a tape recording to be made of their answers? If so, the tape could be used for review, for sharing with future classes, or to demonstrate to the HR department, for example, that money spent on this training was money wisely spent.

Upon the completion of your presentation, ask the reporter to give a brief report regarding what she has learned.

---

25. Give them a choice of questions to answer in a group essay.

List ten essay questions related to the course content on a sheet of paper. Cut the sheet into ten strips of one question each and place the strips in an envelope. Have the group leader pull one from an envelope. If she thinks the question on the strip is too hard for the group to answer, she can put it back and choose another, but she can only do this exchange two times. She will briefly confer with her table mates, if necessary, to determine which of the three possible choices will guarantee them an "A" in the essay response they will then have to write.

Acknowledge that writing a group essay is harder than writing an individual essay, but also acknowledge that group projects are part of being a high school, college, or graduate school student. Further, point out that such writing is an important part of being in the workforce. Use the example of the multiple-author mission statement.

Allow up to a half-hour for essay completion. Then give the groups a choice: They can turn their essays in for your grading or they can read them aloud and have the grading done then and there.

Option: Each person writes three really tough questions related to the course material. Start by calling on one person to read her question. Select someone in the class to answer it. If the responder cannot answer the question, she (the responder) then has the opportunity to read *her* question aloud and call on someone else to answer it. However, if the responder *is* able to

(continued)

25. **Give them a choice of questions to answer in a group essay.** *(concluded)*

answer the question, the original question-asker will go on to her second question and then her third. If the same responder can correctly answer all three questions, she will deserve some reward—a round of applause, at the very least.

Brainteaser: Here are examples of "Pronounced Oddities."

> Polish furniture needs someone—no matter what ethnicity—to polish it.
> Lead if you can get the lead out of your feet.
> Produce produce on your own farm.
> He will refuse to remove the refuse.
> Entrance me with your entrance.

Try to come up with comparable sentences of your own.

Brainteaser: What letter belongs in the empty space?

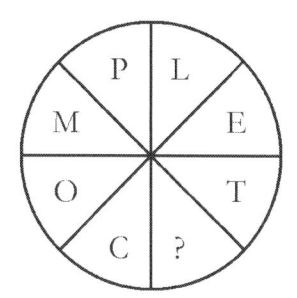

Answer: The missing letter is "e." If you start with the letter "c" and move in a clockwise fashion, you will get the word "complete."

Chapter 3

25 Ways to Add Humor

Chapter Overview

Humorist William Arthur Ward once observed, "A well-developed sense of humor is the pole that adds balance to your steps as you walk the tightrope of life." To be sure, the microcosmic classroom has tightropes all its own. The effective instructor, though, can add balance to the classroom by injecting appropriate forms of humor. Surprise is one of those elements. So is a sense of relief. So is the sense that what we are experiencing is a common theme in the circus of life.

This chapter contains 25 ways to help steady those tightrope-learners before you.

1. Incorporate a humorous bit of information.

Find a humorous fact. Use it to segue into your instructional point. For example, in a course on time management, you could use information about "resistentialism" to introduce the importance of setting deadlines. "Resistentialism" is a term coined by humorist Paul Jennings to describe the feeling that an inanimate object (copy machine, computer) somehow knows when you are under tremendous stress and so decides to break down at exactly that time.

Brainteaser: "Kangaroo" words are larger words that have smaller words contained within them. (The two words have similar meanings.) The smaller word contains letters from the larger word in the proper sequential order, but there may be other letters in-between that will have to be ignored. For example, we know that the word "d-e-c-e-a-s-e-d" means "dead." The four letters of the word "d-e-a-d" appear in the word "deceased" in the right order, but not right next to each other.

Do you see the kangaroo words in these two words?

1. facade   2. satisfied

Answers: 1. face 2. sated

2. Find fodder in the familial.

Search through your own experiences for a time when something funny happened to you at a family gathering. Use that experience to illustrate some of your objectives for the class.

Example: An older friend of our family, too vain to wear her glasses at social gatherings, once mistook the banana cream pie on the buffet table for dip. With each mouthful of potato chip-laden-with-cream, she'd nod her approval of the taste. Finally, she announced, "This dip is delicious, but it doesn't taste like the dip I buy at Wegmans. Where did you ever find it?"

I use this example to illustrate the fact that in interpersonal relationships, we always have choices: we can correct people's behavior, tolerate it, mock it, or graciously ignore it.

Brainteaser: Do you see the kangaroo words in these words?

1. deliberate (used as a verb)   2. precipitation

Answers: 1. debate   2. rain

---

3. Use cartoons.

Cartoons are great classroom devices, but be mindful of copyright laws. In some instances, you will need permission to reproduce them, which will take some time. (Passing around a political cartoon from the Op Ed page of your local newspaper falls within legal boundaries.) You can also use clip art, or draw a simple cartoon of your own. More choices: you can use a complete, related-to-the-course cartoon as a springboard to discussion, or reproduce just the illustration and have students add the verbal bubbles to explore some aspect of the class.

Brainteaser: How quickly can you find the words that start with the letter "s" and that mean the *opposite* of the given word? (More than one word may be acceptable.)

Example: tall   **Answer:** short

1. body   3. meaningless
2. vague   4. plentiful

Answers: 1. soul or spirit   2. specific   3. significant   4. sparse or scarce

4. Use drama.

If you have a bit of the ham in your DNA, it will be easy for you to enliven the subject by changing your voice, impersonating a character, doing a little dance, or adding some other histrionic flourish to the material from time to time. If such dramatics are not comfortable for you, at the very least you can move your arms or wave a ruler to emphasize a given point.

Brainteaser: Can you identify the missing letters in these words, from which only the repeated letter remains? (Clues are provided in parentheses.)

1. T _ TT _ _ T _ _ _   (a snitch)
2. _ _ L L _ _ L L _   (member of the Clampett clan)
3. F _ F _ _ - F _ F _ _   (so-so odds)
4. _ E E _ E E _ E _   (one who has an apiarian interest)
5. K _ _ _ K K _ _ _ K   (trinket)

Answers: 1. tattletale 2. hillbilly 3. fifty-fifty 4. beekeeper 5. knickknack

---

5. Ask a question that reveals something about you.

I often startle participants prone to grammar-complacency (or worse yet, syntactically boring sentences) by asking them "Do you think it's possible for a 62-year-old woman to have feelings of attachment for marks of punctuation?"

Typically, they are caught off-guard by the question, and their hesitation seems to make everyone else curious about what their response will be. Once I get that response, I emphatically declare, "You're right! I *have* those feelings. I LOVE the semi-colon because it is so pure, so pristine. Unlike the comma, which does so many things and therefore is so hard to teach, the semi-colon has only one purpose in life: to separate big chunks of information."

You'll find questions of your own related to the subject matter.

Brainteaser: Even if you are not a sports fan, you can figure out the teams being referred to if you use the verbal clues.

1. Whitney's fans seeking black gold
2. Nordic explorers from the land of 10,000 lakes

Answers: 1. Houston Oilers 2. Minnesota Vikings

6. Self-deprecate.

Self-deprecating humor—that is, poking gentle fun at one's self—is a wonderful way to win over audiences at your own expense if you are confident enough to spend emotional currency in this way. (Later in this book, you will see how this communication tool was used by the Great Communicator himself—Ronald Reagan).

Example: In my business writing classes, I often say: "I would rather write than do anything else in the world." Then, in a sotto voce aside, I'll add: "Which may explain why I haven't had a date in fifteen years."

It may take a while to recall them, but surely there are some things about you that you can self-mock.

Brainteaser: Here are more sports teams for you to name.

1. the Empire State's damned ones
2. the Lone Star State's forest personnel
3. the native residents of Grover's city

Answers: 1. New York Yankees 2. Texas Rangers 3. Cleveland Indians

---

7. Invite participants to share their relevant jokes.

Don't even think of trying this without first issuing several warnings regarding offensive jokes and language. Then appoint an "Appropriate Officer" in each group, whose responsibility will be to make sure that the jokes are not targeted at any group and that they make no references to sex, politics, religion, or ethnicity. The second "appropriate" standard the joke must meet is that it is relevant to the course material.

Once the Appropriate Officer has deemed the jokes suitable for sharing (on two bases: suitability and relevancy), call on each group to present its joke-teller and joke.

Note: You may wish to have ready a few jokes of your own in case a given team is unable to come up with anything funny.

Brainteaser: Here's another sports team for you to name.

Ancient ones from a Puget Sound site

Answer: Seattle Mariners.

8. Give a list-example; then ask for a list.

The Internet is filled with humorous lists of definitions or examples. (If you cannot find such an e-list or cannot obtain permission to use such, buy a book on the subject and read the list aloud.) Here's one I found on the Web:

Five Reasons Why It's Better to Be a Woman

1. We get off sinking ships first.
2. We know how to celebrate sports victories without taking a champagne-bath.
3. Doors are held open for us.
4. When we dance, we look graceful.
5. We can watch the Super Bowl without swearing, spitting, or stuffing ourselves.

Once participants have seen or heard an example, have small groups compile funny lists of reasons why it's better to know about the subject of the course or presentation than not know.

Brainteaser: And yet another sports team for you to name.

Leaders from a city of crazy little women

Answer: Kansas City Chiefs.

---

9. Show examples of typo-bloopers.

No matter what subject is being studied or profession is being pursued, people who can express their ideas about that subject will always fare better than those who cannot. (Research shows, for example, that doctors who communicate well with patients are less likely to be sued by them than are doctors who are abrupt or who do not inform patients sufficiently well.)

Having established the importance of communicating well (if only for essay exams, college entrance, job interviews, et cetera), show course-related typographical errors and discuss the impression created by statements such as this sampling from job applications. (Statements like these are ideal for courses on career development or interviewing skills.)

Examples: "I am a rabid typist."

"I am young and have no bad habits. I am willing to learn."

"I have prepared annual fudgets in excess of $1 million."

"I would prefer to be ballroom-dancing, but it doesn't pay enough."

"I left my last job when they stopped paying my salary."

10. Show them how to refute criticism humorously.

Cognizant of rumors concerning his macabre nature, author Stephen King once attempted to reassure his fans. "I have the heart of a little boy," he asserted. Then he added this macabre twist: "It sits right on my desk in a jar of formaldehyde."

After this opening, share a few sentences pertaining to the subject—sentences that reflect the stereotypical thinking about that subject. "History is boring" or "Accountants are dull people" or "Thanks to e-mail, we don't have to worry about grammar any longer."

Example: History is boring. And those who don't study it may not live long enough to fall asleep!

Ask small groups to refute the so-called "wisdom" by writing a sentence with a twist, in Stephen-King style.

---

11. Find a relevant, funny line.

There it is again, the word *relevant*. I don't endorse using humor merely for the sake of humor—that's a waste of instructional time. But if the humor can be tied to a concept being presented? Now *that's* a different story. Let's say you are telling participants to trust in their own ideas and not depend on the approval of others. You could use this wonderful line from Dolly Parton: "I am never offended by dumb blonde jokes. [Pause.] That's because . . . [Speak slowly and with emphasis on each word] . . . I know I'm not dumb. [Pause, then say conspiratorially] I also know I'm not blonde!"

A little research will help you find other examples that pack a special punch for the subject matter you are teaching.

Brainteaser: Here are more of those "c-a-r-d" games you saw earlier. (Remember, the clue can be found in the synonym inside the parentheses.)

1. A _ C _ _ R _ D   (Nautically fixed in place)
2. D _ C R _ A _ _   (Reduce)

Answers: 1. Anchored 2. Decrease

12. Develop your own funny lines.

And when you see that they evoke giggles, grins, and/or guffaws, use them repeatedly. To illustrate, I tell my students, "Let me tell you a little about myself. I like to ask questions. Questions make people nervous. And in a classroom setting, a little bit of nervousness is a good thing. But remember: This is America. You don't have to do anything you don't want to do. So, if I call on you for an answer and you don't have it, or you have it but you don't want to give it to me, look me right in the eye and say, 'Pick on somebody else, lady.'"

Of course, if you've discovered a certain gimmick or prop or dance step that makes people smile, by all means use that as well.

Brainteaser: Can you fill in the missing letters quickly?

1. C _ _ _ R A D _   (Home of the avalanche)
2. C _ _ _ _ A R D   (Place for dishes)

Answers: 1. Colorado 2. cupboard

---

13. Use your own experience.

You can help break down the barrier that separates instructor from learner by showing your human side, as well as your academic side. (Again, be sure your experience has a direct relationship to the course you are presenting.) Think about all the funny things that have happened to you over the years (some will seem funny only in retrospect). Call upon friends, family, and co-workers to jog your memory. Then write down a few amusing experiences that will illustrate a point you are trying to make.

Example: When explaining the various kinds of intelligence, I emphasize that we each have our own special set of intelligences that differ, thank goodness, from person to person. I then confide that I have verbal skills, but I am very limited when it comes to mechanical things. From that admission, I proceed to tell about the time I carried my fax machine down three flights of stairs and then to the repair shop, returned three days later, and paid a $75 "repair" bill—only to learn that the fax machine had simply run out of paper.

14. Capitalize on in-class humor.

There's one in every class—one class clown, that is. When this individual makes a funny comment, encourage future funny contributions by telling him that he can earn money with his one-liners. Comedians are always on the lookout for fresh new material. So are greeting card companies.

To back up your claims, get thee to a library. Take a look at the *Writers Digest*. Copy down the names of a few people or organizations willing to pay for witticisms. Then, when the class cut-up comes out with his choice words, you can come out with *your* list of paying opportunities.

Brainteaser: Here are the beginnings of famous sayings. Your job is to complete the sentences in your own words.

1. Better safe than . . .
2. The pen is mightier than . . .
3. A penny saved is . . .

Possible answers: 1. Better safe than punching a fifth-grader. 2. The pen is mightier than the pigs. 3. A penny saved is not much.

---

15. Create two diametrically opposed outcomes.

And make them course-related, of course. Then have participants come up with their own amusing twists.

Ronald Reagan example: "Politics is not a bad profession. If you succeed, there are many rewards. If you disgrace yourself, you can always write a book."

Language Arts example: "Poetry is a good thing to study. If you are really good with it, you can become a poet and win the hearts of future boyfriends or girlfriends. And if you are not very good with it, you can always use prose."

Brainteaser: More famous sayings for you to complete. Make them amusing if you can.

1. You can lead a horse to water . . .
2. Two's company; three's . . .

Possible answers: 1. You can lead a horse to water if you have eight people helping you pull. 2. Two's company; three's the Musketeers.

16. Give them a common saying, and call for a response.

Collect a number of familiar sayings. Have participants relate each saying to some aspect of the course or their contribution to it. If necessary, ask an extended question to add even more sparkle to their responses.

Example: "You've heard it said that in negotiations, it's important to know what each person brings to the table, so to speak. What do *you* bring to the learning table?"

Extended example: "Do you bring a knife, a fork, or a spoon to the learning table? Tell us exactly *how* you use the piece you bring."

Brainteaser: More A-T-O-M words for you to figure out. Again, the clues are in parentheses.

1. _ A T _ _ O _ _ _ M   (love of country)

2. _ _ A _ T O M   (ghost)

Answers: 1. Patriotism 2. Phantom

---

17. Encourage their cartoon-ability.

Ask for cartoon representations of some aspect of the course. (Stick figures are perfectly acceptable.) If you're teaching a biology class, for example, and the unit is on reptiles, it would be fairly easy to draw two snakes facing each other, one with an obvious bulge in his throat. It is this snake who says to the other, "Excuse me, I have a frog in my throat this morning."

Brainteaser: The word we are looking for in this puzzle will be used in three places, but the letters of that word will be reconfigured in each place to spell a new word.

Example: T-R-A-C-E the exact route to the last place you saw the C-A-R-E-T. Don't R-E-A-C-T to your fears.

1. I need to _____ you that it may be _____ than you think to _____ your lifestyle!

Answer: alert later alter

18. Have them create a saint.

Sisyphus, who relentlessly pushed a rock up a mountain despite the fact that it rolled back down each time, has been called "the patron saint of workaholics." Have teams use/create figures—real or mythical, alive or dead, famous or just plain familiar—as designated representations of some element of the course.

For example, who could be considered these "patron saints"?

> The patron saint of those who are always learning
> The patron saint of those who do extensive research
> The patron saint of those who are never back from break on time

Brainteaser: Here's another of those one-word-spelled-three-different-ways puzzles. You'll note that there are some clues embedded in the original sentences.

_____ to be a more moderate human _____. Don't _____.

Answer: Begin   being   binge

---

19. Use animal phrases.

In deference to any members of PETA who are present, you'll probably want to avoid a phrase like "beating a dead horse." But you could use any number of other analogies. Compile the list at the flipchart as participants throw out their animal-phrases. Then distribute a marking pen and card-stock paper to each table group. Ask the groups to select a favorite phrase, copy it, and hold it up as various classroom situations warrant.

Example: "Memory like an elephant's"

If you call on a member of the group to repeat, without looking, the objectives for the class, his group mates would be fully entitled to hold up their "elephant" sign commending the memory power of the person who had answered the question correctly.

Brainteaser: The letters in the word "A-T-O-M" also appear in this other word. All you have to do is figure out the missing letters. (Your clue is in parentheses.)

_ A T _ _ O M _   (tomb)

Answer: Catacomb.

20. Type, copy, and distribute proverbs.

Prepare a list of proverbs and have triads paraphrase them in relation to the course.

Example: "Three may keep a secret, if two of them are dead."

Paraphrased example: "Triad members won't fight to be spokesperson for the group if two of the members are not present when the spokesperson is needed."

Note: A list of proverbs has been included in the Appendix for your convenience.

Brainteaser: One word spelled three different ways will fit in the blanks of this sentence.

Ed _____ _____ millions as a television star, but even he can _____ a rabbit when he goes hunting.

Answer: Asner   earns   snare

21. Make collective nouns a source of humor.

The phrases "a pride of lions" or "an exaltation of larks" carry weight and power; they evoke wonderful imagery. Collective nouns can also evoke the wry humor derived from the double entendre, such as the phrase "a mess of Army cooks."

Depending on the nature of your course, you could ask small groups to come up with some collective nouns of their own—"a wisdom of CEO's," for example, or "a foie gras of French students."

Note: Be sure to check out the list of collective nouns in the Appendix. They may prompt some further humorous noun-making.

Brainteaser: Here's our final one-word-with-three-spellings puzzle. I hope it won't leave you feeling that you just want to be left alone.

As _____ as _____ was, she could occasionally _____ on your nerves.

Answer: great   Greta   grate

22. Spend $10 and get guaranteed laughs, forever.

There's no doubt about it: Laughter is contagious. When the group needs a break (but not an out-of-the-room break), play a few minutes of a laugh track. You'll get smiles at the very least, and people falling out of their chairs at the most. The sound track will lessen classroom tension and leave learners refreshed and renewed. You can purchase one of these CDs at HeyUGLY.org.

Brainteaser: Can you find the typographical errors in these science-student responses to exam questions?

1. To collect sulfur fumes, hold a deacon over a flame.
2. The pistol of a flower is its only protection against insects.
3. Blood vessels are arteries, vanes, and caterpillars.
4. Water is composed of two gins: hydrogin and oxygin.
5. When you breathe, you inspire. When you don't, you expire.

Answers: 1. "Deacon" should be "beacon." 2. "Pistol" should be "pistil." 3. Arteries, veins, and capillaries. 4. Hydrogen and oxygen 5. "Inspire" should be "inhale," and "expire" should be "exhale."

---

23. Imitate Jay Leno or David Letterman.

This assignment will require some preparation, but once you have it ready, you'll be able to use it whenever you teach a particular course. First, the next time you don't have to get up early, watch Jay Leno or David Letterman. Take notes on what works with the audience and what does not.

Incorporate appropriate elements of the monologue into a monologue of your own to introduce the course you are about to deliver. You don't have to be a comedian, but you *do* have to be able to deliver a funny line with a straight face.

Brainteaser: Give seven matches or toothpicks to each person or group. Challenge them to form a powerful word (an abbreviation, actually) by moving just three matches to a new location.

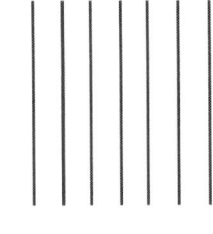

Answer: TNT

Chapter 3: 25 Ways to Add Humor

24. Start with a funny greeting card.

Try to find one that is related to the class. White-out the punch line. Make copies and distribute the verse-less cards to pairs. Ask each pair to come up with a punch line of their own. Have them share what they've done and award token prizes to the pair whose punch line is voted the most clever. (Rubber noses would be in keeping with the spirit of the assignment.)

Brainteaser: This is a tough one. You need to find a word that can be put in the middle of this verbal string of letters. Once your word has been written in parentheses, it will complete the first word on the left of your parenthetical insertion. It will also *start* the second word, which ends on the right of the parenthetical insertion.

Take S (_ _ _) E, for example. When the word "top" is placed inside the parentheses, it joins with "s" on the left to create the word "stop" on the left. When this parenthetical word—notice three blanks are there for the three letters of the word—is added to the "e" on the right of the parenthesis, you have another word: "tope." (A "tope" is a small shark.) For S (_ _ _) E, then, TOP is the inside answer, creating S+TOP and TOP + E.

1. S (_ _ _) T

Answer: 1. (tar) to create "star" on the left and "tart" on the right.

---

25. Draw on their television viewing.

On an overhead transparency, write the names of all the television channels. Display the list and ask, "If this class were a television channel, which would it be? Give reasons for your selection." Have small groups make their selections and discuss their choices. Advise the group to be prepared to tell their reasons when called upon.

Brainteaser: Here are more of those tough puzzles. You need to find a word to put inside the parentheses. Note that the number of blanks is equal to the number of letters in the word. Your "inner" word will create two new words—one when your word is combined with the letter(s) on the left, and a second word when your word is combined with the letter(s) on the right. (More than one answer is possible.)

1. BROW (_ _ _ _) NIK
2. C (_ _ _) X
3. GOLF (_ _ _ _) GAME
4. DE (_ _ _) CH (the canine)

Answers: 1. beat 2. ape 3. ball 4. bit

Bonus:

What do Amelia Jenks Bloomer, Luigi Galvani, and George Josef Kamel have in common? They have all given their names to words we use every day ("bloomers," "galvanize," and "camellia.") You will have at least one person in your class who is well-known for a particular behavior. Create an eponym in his honor. Refer to it as often as you can.

Example: In a recent class for employees in the state comptroller's office, four people happened to sit together: a man named Todd and three women. When I called for their report on a class assignment, I off-handedly said, "Now, let's hear from Todd and the Todd-ettes." Other students picked up on the newly created name and used it for the rest of the session. It's not quite eponymous, but you get the idea.

Brainteaser: Let's move toward the end of the alphabet now for the group vocabulary test. Place a check mark next to the words you know. However, you must be prepared to defend what you think you know. The group with the largest number of defendable checkmarks will be declared the winners.

__ ubiquitous	__ ululate	__ umbrage	__ unabated
__ unadulterated	__ unassailable	__ unbridled	__ unctuous
__ underling	__ undue	__ undulation	__ unembellished
__ unequivocal	__ unflappable	__ unfrock	__ unicameral
__ unimpeachable	__ unipetalous	__ unipolar	__ unscathed
__ unseemly	__ unwieldy	__ urbane	__ urchin
__ uric	__ usurious	__ usurp	__ utopian
__ utilitarian	__ uvular	__ uxoricide	__ uxorious

Brainteaser: Look at these "W" and "Y" choices. By now, you know that you have to put a check mark next to the words you know. Other teams may challenge you, so be sure you know the words you have checked. The group with the largest number of defendable checkmarks will win this challenge.

__ waddle	__ wallow	__ wampum	__ warbler
__ warily	__ warranted	__ waspish	__ wheedle
__ whelk	__ whelp	__ whence	__ whet
__ whimsical	__ whim-wham	__ whinny	__ whirligig
__ willful	__ wily	__ wistful	__ woebegone
__ wrathful	__ yak	__ yammer	__ yawp
__ yearling	__ yeoman	__ yeti	__ ylem
__ yogi	__ yokel	__ yore	__ yucca

Chapter 4

25 Ways to Give Feedback

Chapter Overview

We've grown a lot more sophisticated in our collection and distribution of feedback, but in the early days of our country, politicians had a unique (and less-refined) way of obtaining feedback from their constituents. Since they had no telephone, television, radio, or internet, politicians did their own polling by sending their assistants to local taverns. The underlings were told to "go sip some ale." Of course, as they did so, they were tasked with listening to the concerns of the (drinking) public. Over time, the two words "go sip" were combined into one: "gossip." Although the word has a negative connotation today, its original meaning was a synonym for "feedback."

In this chapter, I'll show you 25 ways to give feedback in the most positive of ways.

Note: If you'd like to explore the role of feedback in personal growth, be sure to look at the list of discussion questions in the Appendix.

1. Prepare critique sheets.

Word the sheets so that they engender astute observations in the gentlest of ways. Include a few yes/no questions; a few 1–5 ratings (low-to-high); and a few fill-in-the-blank questions. Use them following individual or group assignments. Mix your own feedback in with the other responses and collect the sheets. Hand them to the individuals and groups that have made presentations.

Option: Ask participants/groups beforehand if they wish to receive feedback. Of course, you will honor their requests, but I suspect you will find that everyone wants feedback, especially if you assure them that it will be delivered kindly and anonymously.

Brainteaser: Figure out the "total" of the numbers between 1 and 100. In other words, if 1 is added to 2 and then that total is added to 3, and the new total is added to 4 and so on (all the way to 100), what would the grand total be? Try to find a shortcut.

Answer: The traditional method does work, but it works slowly. A more efficient method is to break down the components into 50 parts, each formed by adding the last number with the first, sequentially. For example, 100 + 1 = 101. 99 + 2 = 101. 98 + 3 = 101. 97 + 4 = 101. 96 + 5 = 101, and so on. The result of this continuation would be 50 combinations of 101, a much easier calculation. The answer is 5,050—a calculation that can actually be done without paper.

2. Give them a choice: Invite them to one-on-one meetings with you, or with a partner of their choosing.

Most people prefer their feedback to be delivered privately. If you give an intensive/extensive assignment to the class, you will have time to meet individually with those who want your feedback. A few suggestions for engaging in those sessions:

- Try to avoid using absolute terms, such as "always" and "never."
- Don't overload the recipient with too many observations about needed improvement.
- Give the individual time to respond.
- Ask probing questions.
- Work hard not to interrupt.

They can choose, if they wish, to receive feedback from a partner whom they trust to be "gently honest."

Brainteaser: Remember those tough parenthetical word-in-the-middle word games? Here are more, should you dare to tackle them.

1. B (___) O W
2. S P (___) E A R

Answers: 1. ALL (ball + allow)   2. END (spend + endear)

---

3. Make it a group thing.

Sometimes there will only be two or three individuals who will benefit from corrective feedback. However, isolating those individuals and pointing out the areas needing improvement is counter-productive. Instead, address your remarks to the whole group.

Comments like these are good: "I've noticed several of you are. . . ." or "This is a common mistake. I see it all the time." or "Very few people can avoid . . . but most of us are doing it, thus minimizing our effectiveness." Such diplomatic remarks help the mistake-makers save face. (This non-obvious approach is bound to gain you respect, too; the non-targeted students will come to realize that they can trust you not to embarrass them.)

Brainteaser: Students came to class on Monday morning, expecting to be given the test their instructor had promised. Instead, they were told that they would have the test two days after the day before the day after tomorrow. When will they take the test?

Answer: Thursday.

4. Comment on a paper they have written.

This will be hard to do in a one-day class (unless you give up your lunch), but it works well with participants whom you will see on more than one occasion. Have them record their thoughts, individually or collectively. Then provide feedback in any color ink but red on the papers they have written.

Brainteaser: Class participants were given a choice regarding the number of homework questions they could answer. Peter answered more than Shirley. Connie answered fewer than Pam. Pam answered fewer than Shirley but more than Robert. Which class member did the second-largest number of homework questions?

Answer: Shirley did the second-largest number of homework questions. Peter is the one who answered the most, because all the others are described as doing fewer than someone else. Shirley comes in second because she does more than Pam, who does more than either Robert or Connie.

---

5. Correct publicly.

A good alternative to "for your eyes only" comments on paper are the "for everyone's eyes" comments on paper. Give an assignment requiring a collective essay response. Have groups draft a copy and then write the polished essay on flipchart paper.

Next, with a brightly colored marker, make your comments on each paper. This way, everyone will benefit from your incisive and insightful remarks, and no one person will feel singled out.

Brainteaser: Elizabeth not only holds a full-time job working for the government, but she also has her own business boarding cats and canaries. If the creatures she is caring for over the weekend have between them a total of 17 heads and 56 legs, how many cats and how many canaries does she have to feed?

Answer: Elizabeth is caring for 11 cats and 6 canaries. Of course, each creature has two hind legs, so 17 heads means 34 hind legs total. The remaining 22 legs have to be the front legs of 11 four-legged cats. Thus, 11 heads belong to the cats and the remaining 6 heads have to belong to the canaries.

6. Implement peer evaluations.

Teachers do it. Police officers do it. Even bird-watchers and bee-keepers do it. No reason why class participants shouldn't do it! The "it," of course, is peer evaluation. The easiest way is to have table groups make a report or presentation as an ensemble cast or individually as solo performers.

After the work of the group has been displayed or demonstrated, you will meet briefly with the group to provide your own feedback. Meanwhile, the other groups will prepare short assessments of their own. These can be written, collected, and given to the group that has just finished delivering its report, or a spokesperson from each group can present them orally.

Brainteaser: The local high school is holding a chess tournament. Eighteen students have signed up for the competition. How many matches must be played before there is a winner to be declared?

Answer: 17. Look at it this way: Every match will have one loser. Every person other than the winner will lose once and only once. Eighteen players means that there will be seventeen losers. And so, there will have to be 17 matches in order for a champion, the only person never to have lost, to be crowned.

---

7. Invite an outsider in.

To add a bit of drama to an ordinary classroom day, invite an outsider in to serve as a judge of sorts and to give her feedback regarding various projects in which the groups have been engaged.

Brainteaser: What common word connects the three words in each line?

Example: Marshall   pincher   saved

Answer: Penny, as in Penny Marshall (the star of "Laverne and Shirley"), "penny pincher", and a "penny saved"

1. salad   head   roll
2. opera   house   fixture
3. clause   artist   fire
4. ugly   fire   drain
5. ware   foot   "B"
6. basket   foot   base

Answers: 1. egg 2. light 3. escape 4. plug 5. flat 6. ball

8. Go Greek: Use the Delphi Technique.

Dating back thousands of years, this feedback method evokes total honesty by asking feedback-givers to write their anonymous comments on a small sheet of paper. Once they have done so, ask a volunteer to collect the papers and then leave the room. She will analyze the responses in terms of patterns: What strengths did most people mention? What recommendations appeared repeatedly? What usual comments appeared? Ask the analyzer to be judicious as she prepares and then delivers a short report that is helpful but not hurtful.

Brainteaser: More "Find the Common Word" puzzles

1. nap   sup   burglar
2. mouse   technician   Sally
3. church   pad   Mickey
4. hopping   none   prison
5. cut   tiger   bag
6. job   chair   top

Answers: 1. cat 2. field 3. mouse 4. bar 5. paper 6. desk

---

9. Ask participants to prepare a self-evaluation.

The ancient Greeks believed that the unexamined life is not worth living. By extension, work that is not evaluated by someone at some time has little chance of being done better. Ask participants to create an evaluation form they can use to evaluate their performance.

Options: Ask participants, if they evaluate themselves, to keep a log in order to determine whether or not improvement is occurring.

Before participants actually use the form in self-assessment, ask them to compare their form with the form a partner prepared for herself. (This comparing can also be done in triads or groups of four.) Participants should revise their forms, if necessary, to include ideas they picked up from others.

Ask participants to select one or two other people whom they feel they can trust (or one or two other people with whom they have not yet had a chance to work). They can then ask these trusted advisers for feedback on their own performance, using the evaluation form they themselves prepared.

10. Use the old standby: give feedback yourself.

It's been used ever since teachers began teaching: the one-to-one feedback response. And it works, assuming it's used carefully. There are more than a million words in our language; you can always find the ones that will permit you to build, to develop, to construct through your critiques.

Option: To add a little spice to the feedback soup, ask the participant if she would like either a one-word response or more-detailed feedback. Remain true to their request. If they only want one word, say "Good" or "Better" or "Perfect."

Brainteaser: Here are more team names. This list, though, is easier because the cities are not part of the names.

1. hibernators
2. iron men
3. ewes' mates
4. midnight snackers

Answers: 1. (Chicago) Bears 2. (Pittsburgh) Steelers 3. (Los Angeles) Rams 4. (Los Angeles) Raiders

---

11. Give a private audience; prepare unique comments.

This technique works best in a class that extends beyond one day, where there is enough time for you to give a private audience, sooner or later, to every member of the class. Have your comments prepared in advance so you don't say the same things over and over. (You can be sure there will be some participants who will share notes. It can be devastating if they discover you are providing the same or similar feedback to everyone. They are unique individuals; your commentary should reflect that uniqueness.) Encourage participants to respond to your feedback. Listen carefully as they do so.

Brainteaser: In the problem below are words that have two things in common. First, they are all words related to the vocations or avocations people pursue. Second, the people who hold those positions are all familiar with one word that is common to their occupations. Your job is to find the word that pertains to *all* the positions.

Example: baseball player   spelunker   cricket player

Answer: Bat, used by the two athletes above and often seen by spelunkers or cave explorers.

1. surgeon   seamstress   writer

Answer: thread

12. For the confident, ask groups to provide feedback.

The confident individual can meet with group members and obtain their feedback. This small-group setting also allows the individual to ask questions, ask for advice, or explain why she chose a particular course of action.

Brainteaser: The preceding brainteaser asked you to find a word familiar to the people listed in the question. The questions that follow are more of the same.

1. musician — police officer — cook
2. artist — cosmetologist — baker
3. florist — basketball player — farmer
4. rancher — orthopedist — aerobic instructor
5. machinist — farmer — maternity-ward nurse
6. court judge — musical artist — journalist

Answers: 1. beat 2. brush 3. basket 4. calf 5. crib 6. record

---

13. For the super-confident, ask the whole class to provide feedback.

This feedback method is not for the faint of heart, so always make it a volunteer decision. There will probably be some participants in your classroom with a "bring-it-on" attitude—people who will actually enjoy standing before the total group and learning ways that they can improve their performance. Applaud their courage, and then ask the groups as a whole for feedback. Caution: Always encourage participants to use kind-but-honest words.

Brainteaser: Among the papers in Boston's John F. Kennedy Library is evidence of a game the President used to play to amuse himself. Although the conditions he established for himself were very difficult, you can make accommodations based on the nature of the students you teach. Kennedy would have categories across the top of a page. Down the left-hand side, he would have letters. He would then allow himself only 12 seconds to come up with a word to write in each box. We'll do a simple box here, with only two categories and one letter.

	Famous Romans	French writers
R		

Answers: Romulus and Rousseau

14. Provide reality-TV judges.

Thanks to Mark Burnett and the reality show "The Apprentice," television viewers in the U.S. are used to seeing judges provide feedback to wannabes. With spin-offs and imitations, we've seen feedback judges for models, fighters, survivors, chefs, scholars, fashion designers, dancers, singers, comedians—you name the category, and you're bound to find "expert" judges providing feedback to contestants in that category.

If you follow the "Apprentice" format, you can have one older, experienced George; one hard-driving Donald; and one very capable Carolyn—all in fun, of course. But to be on the safe side, have those receiving feedback appear as a group so that no one person will have to face the criticism alone.

Brainteaser: Can you think of a small, four-letter word that ends in "eny"?

Answer: Deny

---

15. Have them select their own feedback.

As you review student papers or performance, make a list of your comments and note for your own records the papers or individuals on whom those comments are based. (Your list should have as many comments as there are participants or groups, so that each person can select at least one they believe pertains to them.) Then write the list on the flipchart or an overhead transparency. Do *not* write the names of the people or groups on whom the comments were based.

Have each person or group claim one feedback comment they think describes them. Have the individual or group explain why she or they "own" that comment.

Option: Ask the individuals or groups if they wish to know if the feedback-comment they selected was the one intended for them. If not, don't provide the match. If so, you can tell them which comment was originally intended for them.

16. Tape-record their presentations.

Each time an individual or group makes a presentation, tape-record it. Then hand one group at a time a tape player and the tape. Ideally, there will be a breakout room available for them to play back their presentation and critique it among themselves. At the very least, they can stand in the corridor for a few minutes while they listen and probably learn from their mistakes.

Brainteaser: You're already familiar with the JFK brainteaser in activity #13. This time, though, you'll need to supply three answers for each category.

	Famous Romans	French writers
L		
S		
P		

Answers: 1. Lucullus, La Martine 2. Seneca, Stendal 3. Publius, Proust

---

17. Do a mini-force field analysis.

Kurt Lewin's analysis tool is a simple "T." At the top of the "T" are two words, written one below the other. The words are "Ideal" and "Current." Have participants make their "T" by asking who or what presents the "Ideal" in terms of a Subject Matter Expert (SME) for the course you are teaching. (The identified person might be a member of the class or a respected figure known in the field.) The "Current" would be the individual herself, or her group if people are working together.

On the left-hand side of the T are the Driving Forces (represented by a plus sign). These are the actions participants can take to achieve the Ideal status in order to become more like their Ideal. In the right-hand column are the "Restraining Forces" (shown by a minus sign). This is where participants write the things that prevent them from reaching the Ideal or prevent them from developing their strengths. (Note: The two columns should not be mirror reflections of each other.)

Brainteaser: Here's a good test of your spatial reasoning ability. Picture a round of cheese. How can it be cut into eight equal pieces with only three straight cuts?

Answer: First, cut the round of cheese in half as you would if you were splitting a cake into two layers for filling. Keeping the two halves on top of one another, make two more cuts so that you have four quadrants. You will then have eight pieces.

18. Lift sentences.

"Lifted" sentences are sentences you have taken from each of the papers submitted to you. Select sentences that contain an error. Without identifying any authors, make sure there is equal representation among participants. (In other words, don't take all the error-sentences from one paper.) Distribute copies of the lifted sentences and invite the class's input or feedback on each of the statements. Try to point out something positive if you can, but always and gently point out the error(s) the sentence contains.

Brainteaser: Here's another test of your spatial reasoning. Without using paper or pencil, can you identify the familiar object?

> Imagine the letter D. Rotate it 90 degrees to the right. Put the number 4 above it. Remove the horizontal segment of the 4 to the right of the vertical line. What do you have?

Answer: A boat.

---

19. Have them introspect.

Following their submission of work (i.e., reports), hand each person a small sheet of paper. They will have to check one of two statements.

1) ___ This was the best I could do.
2) ___ This was not my best. If you will teach me how to _____, I can make this better.

Collect the sheets and take appropriate action.

Brainteaser: Here's another test of your spatial reasoning ability.

> Imagine the letter B. Rotate it 90 degrees to the left. Put a triangle directly below it that is the same width, and point it down. Remove the horizontal line. What do you have?

Answer: A heart.

20. Admit that turnaround is fair play.

Here's their opportunity to give *you* feedback. In the process, they will probably learn something about themselves. If you're brave, hold a five- to ten-minute discussion asking for ways you can improve the class. The information participants provide will tell you a little about them and a lot about yourself. (For example, someone who says you need to control class discussions better is probably someone who learns best in quieter settings.)

Option: Don't wait until the course is over to hand out evaluation forms. Obtain feedback halfway through, or even several times during the course of a day. The evaluation could consist of a single question: "In relation to the concept I just taught, how confident are you that you have learned it well enough to teach it to someone else?" (Suggest that respondents evaluate the extent of their learning by using increments going from 10% to 100%.) If the average of the percentages is lower than 70%, you have a lot more work to do.

---

21. Ask if they are confident enough to have their grade publicly posted.

First, announce that you will only provide grades that range from B– to A+ on an assignment or test. Anything lower than that will be returned to the participant with your written comments, but no grade. Second, ask if participants want to have their work posted for the benefit of others.

Those who opt for privacy will have their papers corrected and returned directly to them. Those who don't mind sharing will have their papers posted around the room. Allow about 15 minutes for participants to walk around. Circulate with them, answering questions as they arise.

Brainteaser: A final test of your spatial reasoning ability:

> Imagine the letter K. Place a square next to it on the left side. Put a circle inside the square. Now rotate the figure 90 degrees to the left. What familiar object are you looking at?

Answer: A television (the old kind, with "rabbit ears").

22. Use a scoreboard.

At the very beginning of the class, divide participants into teams and ask each one to come up with a team leader and a team name. Then have everyone vote on whether or not they want to have a low-key competition. Have token prizes ready, and display them at this time. (In a multi-day class, the prize might be exoneration from homework.)

If they opt for competition, write the team names on a scoreboard and keep a tally throughout the day. Stress repeatedly, of course, that the important thing is not who has the highest score, but whether or not they are learning.

Brainteaser: Mrs. Smith lives in a culturally diverse apartment building. All but two of her neighbors are Spanish, all but two of them are Egyptian, and all but two of them are Turkish. How many other residents are there in her apartment building?

Answer: Three others. Two of her neighbors are not Spanish, though one is. Two are not Egyptian, but one is. Two are not Turkish, but one is. That adds up to three neighbors, one from each of the representative countries.

---

23. Have pairs critique other pairs.

Divide the class into pairs. Each person in the pair will give feedback to her partner based on what she has observed, heard, and/or read of the partner's contribution and/or work thus far in the class. Then, the partners will reverse their roles so that each person will have had a chance to critique and be critiqued.

In the next stage, you will elicit from the group as a whole the names of well-known people whom they admire—from any field. Aim for as many names as you have participants. Have each person then select one name and jot down a few notes specifying ways that she is like the person she has selected.

Then have the same individuals work in pairs, as they did before. (By now, a certain level of comfort should have been established.) Each partner in the pair will continue the critique-discussion, this time using the famous figure as a prompt. In this round, however, participants will assess themselves instead of having their partner assess them, as was done in the first round. They will tell how the famous figure in some way resembles them, their philosophy, their approach, et cetera. The final stage has pairs joining pairs to share selected feedback with the new members of the foursome.

24. Create a list of attributes, and have participants use it to deliver feedback.

Here are some you may wish to use:

____	hungry	____	aware of priorities
____	direct	____	rebellious
____	self-confident	____	honest
____	analytical	____	ambitious
____	intelligent	____	able to work within established time frames
____	funny		
____	decisive	____	energetic
____	interested in challenges	____	sincere
____	willing to explore possibilities	____	stressed
____	high-achieving	____	honorable
____	irreverent	____	able to express a vision
____	articulate	____	realistic
____	enthusiastic	____	unwilling to waste time
____	proud to be affiliated with the organization	____	problem-aware; solution-oriented
		____	bold
____	able to listen intently	____	fact-oriented
____	verbal	____	creative
____	reliable	____	willing to take risks
____	one-directional	____	easily defeated
____	trustworthy	____	rewarding
____	opinionated		

Distribute several copies of the list to each participant. Then, as various groups make their reports, ask remaining participants to listen to the reports and provide feedback by placing a checkmark next to the attributes they feel most apply to the presenter or presenting team.

Collect the feedback sheets and give them to those participants who have made reports during the break. (Note: These forms could also be used by observers who are watching teams work.)

Brainteaser: An instructor has decided to reward an exceptional class. She heads to the grocery store with $60. If she spends ¼ of her money on beverages, $40 on snacks, and 10% of the original amount on paper plates and napkins, how much cash will she have left?

Answer: $9.00.

25. Collect pictures or drawings of animals.

Put six different ones on a single page, with a blank line for the presenter's name beneath the image. Write a positive feedback statement beneath three of the pictures and a negative feedback statement beneath the remaining three. Leave room for additional comments if participants choose to write them. For example, if the picture is of an eagle, the positive description could read, "Your presentation soared." If the picture is of a giraffe, the positive description might say, "You aimed high and reached your mark."

On the negative side, a picture of an elephant might read, "The presentation plodded along; add more excitement to your voice." For a pig stuck in the mud, the description might be, "You were stuck in the mud of too many details." (Be kind with the negatives.)

Make twenty copies of the page. (Assuming that you have a class of 30 students, each person will receive 30 positive-comment images and 30 negative-comment images. Then, as each student makes his or her presentation, the audience members will decide to use either their positive-comment image or their negative-comment image as feedback for the presenter.) Then, cut up the pictures so that each image includes the blank line for the presenter's name, along with the comment you wrote and more blank lines for any comments audience members choose to write.

Each participant should have one positive image and one negative image for each of the presentations that will be given.

Collect the images after each report and give them to the individual (or team) that made the report, with the request that they not read their feedback until the break. (Otherwise, they will not be paying attention to the next presenter.)

Brainteaser: See how quickly you can figure out synonyms for each of the following words. Note: Each answer must begin with the letter "s."

A. fast
B. fake
C. fashionable
D. fable
E. faith

Answers: A. speedy   B. synthetic   C. stylish   D. story   E. spirituality

Chapter 5

25 Ways to Use Questions

Chapter Overview

Ask the typical adult, "How do you get to heaven?" and the answers will sound strikingly similar: "You do good deeds." "You lead a virtuous life." "You live by the Ten Commandments." Ask the typical child, though, and you'll receive answers that diverge: "You have to take the God elevator," or "You go to Hell and take a left," or "When all the bad has been spanked out of you, then you're ready for heaven."

Had the question been framed differently, would the adult answers have been more creative? I believe so. Unfortunately, we teachers and trainers tend to ask questions quickly and want responses just as quickly. Consequently, we often fail to frame questions in ways that elicit thoughtful, creative, rich responses.

To help you elicit those rich responses, try the techniques in this chapter. They're designed to improve both the "how" of your questions and, consequently, the "what" of your answers.

1. Use questions for discussion.

No doubt you are already doing this, but here's a variation on a familiar theme: Have your questions about a given module ready in advance—10–20 of them. Distribute the list and use it in any number of ways:

1) Have groups select the question they think is hardest. Then have them select another group they want to answer the question. In return, they take that group's question, whatever it is.

2) Have each person rank the questions in terms of the intelligent exchanges they are likely to elicit. Then call on a few people at random to tell which was their top-ranked question.

3) Appoint a scorekeeper to check off the questions as you ask them during the course of the day. At 2:00 or 3:00 in the afternoon, ask him to read all the questions that remain. Answer them then.

Brainteaser: What is one-twentieth of one-half of one-tenth of 10,000?

Answer: 25.

2. Use questions for review.

At the end of a given segment, ask for a volunteer to explain the main concepts conveyed in the segment. Ask questions of the volunteer if he erred or omitted an important point. For example, "Wasn't there a third choice on Fiedlfer's continuum?" You can also quiz participants at the end of the segment to make sure they understand what was taught.

Brainteaser: This time, you'll have to rely on your reading ability rather than your spatial reasoning ability to answer the question. (Note: The puzzle can also be read aloud to test students' listening ability.)

> Henry's mother Mabel had four children—that is all.
> The first one's name is Summer.
> The second one's name is Fall.
> The third child is Winter—
> That leaves one more.
> Can you guess the name of the last child she bore?

Answer: Henry.

---

3. Use questions for homework.

I like giving choices. One of the choices for homework is to answer a certain number of questions from a list of questions I have included in the curriculum materials. Then, first thing the next morning, I assemble groups (based on the common question they chose) to share their answers.

Brainteaser: Here's another chance to work on the Kennedy brainteaser. You'll need three answers for each category.

	Russians	Jazz Musicians
C		
M		
P		

Answers: 1. Chekov, Coltrane 2. Mussorgsky, Monk 3. Pushkin, Parker

4. Use questions to reinforce.

It's up to you to probe beneath the surface of statements, because most participants will opt for easy ways out and will give "surface" answers. For example, at the end of nearly every class I teach, I ask participants to stand and explain their action plan for implementing what they have learned.

If someone says, "I'm going to use the K-I-N-D approach," I will ask questions to reinforce their intent:

"Can you tell me what the acronym stands for?"
"How often will you use it?"
"In what situation will you use it?"
"Whom will you tell about your plans to use it?"
"How will you gauge the effectiveness of your new behavior?"
"Who will help keep you on track?"
"What other tools can you use to supplement the K-I-N-D approach?"

Don't overlook opportunities to ask questions to deepen the learning experience.

5. Use questions to encourage introspection.

Training gives adult participants time to think about the larger questions. When they are at work, they are too busy to introspect. (The average American employee has 37 hours' worth of unfinished work on his desk at any given time.) In the relative comfort of the classroom, away from the pressing demands of time clocks and bosses, participants can think about the "mega" questions.

I often post the questions that follow and tell participants at the very beginning of the day that before the day is over, they must have an answer to at least one. (Be certain to call on everyone before the class is over.) These questions can easily be modified, if necessary, for school situations.

1) How will you use your new knowledge?
2) Whom will you tell about what you have learned?
3) How can the organization benefit from what you have learned?
4) What new behaviors will you engage in as a result of this training?
5) What is different about you as a result of this training?
6) How will the organization get its return on the investment it has made in you?

6. Use questions to ascertain the ability levels within the group.

It is surprising that so many instructors don't bother to learn *something* about the group's experience/expertise before beginning to instruct them. Questions can help you uncover what you need to know so that you can calibrate your intended course of action.

Example: I begin a Language Arts or Business Writing class by calling on each person with a question, such as "What aspect of grammar has plagued you up until now?" "What would you like to master before this day is over?" "Why did you sign up for the class?" or "What is your boss hoping you will learn?"

I write their responses on a flipchart. Once the list is complete, I review it. The responses that fall outside the scope of the class (*"I want to improve my handwriting,"* for example) are addressed. Those that were cited by numerous participants will probably require more time than I had planned to spend, but I can make adjustments as I go along.

As always, ask participants to write their answers down before you begin calling on people. Otherwise, you will get "parroting."

---

7. Use questions to increase participation.

The easiest way to increase participation this way is to ask participants to raise their hands if they fall into a category you're asking about: "How many of you have wished you could think faster on your feet?" This, though, is a fleeting kind of participation.

I prefer the longer-lasting participation that can be achieved by asking the *right* questions. To illustrate: "Can you find three other people in this room who use humor to defuse potentially explosive situations?" or "What do you do to help yourself think faster on your feet?"

Brainteaser: Remember the earlier exercise that called for a common word that tied together people in three different occupations? Here are four more teasers:

1. poet   tennis player   romantic comedy writer
2. travel agent   author   police officer
3. meteorologist   seamstress   optician
4. manager   musician   shepherd

Answers: 1. love 2. book 3. eye 4. staff

8. Use questions to compliment.

Here's a partial list of questions designed to encourage, to develop confidence, to acknowledge effort. Use them in response to responses given by participants.

"You've taken other management classes, haven't you?"

"Was your mother an English teacher? Is that why you know so much about gerunds?"

"Has anyone ever told you that you have a real aptitude for this?"

"Did you know you could be making money on the side with the sense of humor you possess?"

Brainteaser: A clothes dryer is filled with 22 red socks and 39 blue ones. If you pulled out one sock at a time without looking, how many would you have to remove before you could be certain you had a matched pair?

Answer: Three—the third will definitely match one of the other two.

---

9. Have groups choose their own question.

Post your most challenging questions around the room. Ask groups to select the question they feel they have the most collective knowledge about. Have them work on their group response for a written or oral presentation. Then grade their efforts.

Brainteaser: (Note: This problem should be done first by individuals and then by members of a group.) "Read through this problem by yourself. Then write the missing word on a sheet of paper and turn it in to the instructor. When the rest of the class has also done this, then work on the same problem with members of your team. You will have five minutes as a team to come up with one answer."

> The slskjdfjd eikchvhed bkehly biekkdh the slkeh wcord. Then the slskjdfjd _____ bhxldly down the xhnbkd.

After you've learned the correct answer, consider this: If you had the right answer working as an individual, were you able to persuade your team of the correct answer?

a. eivhedlsk   b. ejsleked   c. ylkcjs   d. vkgjshf   e. pooasodf

Answer: b. A past-tense verb ending in "ed" is the only word that fits this syntax.

10. Use questions to stimulate creativity.

Having participants consider possible consequences of various scenarios is an excellent problem-solving/strategic-planning tool. As a prelude to such heavy-duty thinking, post a generic list of "What if . . .?" questions (several follow) to spark their creative embers. Have them formulate and share their answers. Then, ask about what-if consequences in relation to issues impacting the learning.

Examples: What if teachers earned as much as rock stars?
What if women ruled the world?
What if elephants could fly?
What if no one were allowed to earn more than $100,000 a year?
What if all students were free to choose their own course of study?
What if all celebrities had to donate five hours a week to a charitable cause?
What if all politicians had to sign an ethics pledge?
What if war were declared illegal?
What if there were no music in the world?
What if leadership had to be shared?
What if the driving age was restricted to ages 20–60?
What if America had to "adopt" another nation?

11. Engage partners in questioning each other.

The instructor is not the only source of knowledge in a classroom. Nor should the instructor be the singular source of questions that test participants' understanding of the course material. Have individuals or small groups prepare questions covering what has been taught. Then call on each, in round-robin fashion, to ask their questions of others in the room. Continue until all participants have had to answer at least one question and/or until all questions have been asked.

Option: Organize the session into a competition that ends when only one team is left standing. Appropriate prizes could be awarded to the winning team. (See the Appendix for a copy of a letter to managers. It could easily be adapted to send to parents.)

Brainteaser: You have only five seconds to figure out the answer to the sample problem. (Others will follow on later pages.) Look at the sample now and try to solve it.

Which of the five possible answers makes the best comparison? "Meat" is to "team" as 7892 is to:

(a) 2987   (b) 9872   (c) 8278   (d) 2897   (e) 2978

Answer: d (2897). If "meat" is a 1-2-3-4 sequence, then "team" is sequenced 4-2-3-1.

12. Allow them to stump the teacher.

Participants must have at least a basic understanding of the subject matter in order to formulate a question regarding it. Allow them to ask questions of you. If one question goes so far beyond "basic" that it truly stumps you, reward the asker accordingly.

Brainteaser: As promised, here are more of those word/number combinations.

Allow yourself only five seconds for each.

1. "Real" is to "Lear" as 3968 is to:
   (a) 8336   (b) 3698   (c) 3896   (d) 6983   (e) 8963

2. "Kant" is to "tank" as 1743 is to:
   (a) 3741   (b) 4137   (c) 3714   (d) 1347   (e) 7314

3. "Part" is to "tarp" as 7352 is to:
   (a) 7235   (b) 2357   (c) 5732   (d) 2735   (e) 2753

Answers: 1. e   2. a   3. b

---

13. Obtain questions from others.

Before the start of class, hold brief interviews with managers, executives, principals, school board members, parents, and other appropriate people. Learn what questions they would like to have answered by participants, and pose these at appropriate times during the course of the instructional day.

Brainteaser: At the end of the school day on Friday, five students rushed out of the building. John was not the first one out. Charles was neither first nor last. Jocelyn pushed out immediately behind John. Priscilla was not the second one out. Zoe was the second person after Priscilla. In what order did the students race from the building?

Answer: Priscilla was first. Charles was second. Zoe was third. John was fourth. Jocelyn was last. Noting the wording of the question, we can determine that John, Charles, Jocelyn, and Zoe were not first. Therefore, Priscilla was. Right away, that tells us Zoe was third. If Jocelyn was right behind John, then they must take the only two adjacent spots—fourth and fifth. Charles then must move into the only spot that remains: second place.

14. Ask the "eternal questions" related to the course.

It was Sigmund Freud who posed one of the most enduring psychological questions: "What does a woman want?" This assignment has triads creating an enduring question of their own—one that will probably be asked long after the course has ended, one that may have an answer that changes with time, one that can continue to challenge future students who are struggling with the very same issues.

For example, in Language Arts or business writing classes, I am repeatedly asked why there are so many different ways to spell the simple "ew" sound (as in "new").

Ask each group to come up with at least one such question. Then call on them all in turn to pose their question and invite the class to respond to each.

Brainteaser: Check the words known by at least one person on your team. Be prepared to define those words if you are challenged.

abash	aberration	abet	abeyance
abject	abjure	ablution	abnegate
abominate	abrade	abrogate	abstemious

15. Tell the famous "Why?" story.

Participants will enjoy the story (perhaps an urban legend or campus truth) of the psychology professor who had only one question written on the board for the final examination: "Why?"

Students went to great psychological depths to respond. All except one, that is—the only one who received an "A" for the course. He was the student who wrote a one-word answer: "Because."

This assignment capitalizes on that story. You will ask a series of two-, three-, or four-word questions. Participants must reply using the same number of words in their answer as you used in your question.

Brainteaser: More spelling challenges. Decide as a group which words you know. Compare that number to what other groups know. Warning: Be prepared to correctly define the words, if challenged, or else face the embarrassing consequences.

| abstruse | accede | acclivity | acerbity |

16. Force the questions.

Here's what I do. First, I tell them (more than once) that questions are a sign of intelligence. There are no stupid questions. What's "stupid" is sitting there wondering about something, but not asking.

I remind them that in a classroom, as in real life, they are *supposed* to ask questions. Then, I warn them fairly early in the day that if I don't get questions from them later, I will force them to ask their questions.

Periodically, I will ask, "Any questions?" If there are none, I'll say, "I'm old enough to know that total silence does not necessarily equate with total comprehension. You have three minutes to come up with a question in your table group." (Restrict the questions to the subject matter.)

Then call on each table group to ask their question. Answer accordingly.

Brainteaser: If the day before two days after the day before tomorrow is Monday, what day is it today?

Answer: Sunday.

---

17. Ask, "What have I not made clear?"

A little humility in a classroom goes a long way. When you place the onus for misunderstanding upon yourself, you make it easier for others to ask their questions. By asking what you have not made clear, you suggest that if they are confused, it is *your* fault—not theirs.

If the group tolerates playfulness, you can then segue into a quiz: "Now that I have made everything perfectly clear, you should be ready for this quiz."

Brainteaser: More spelling challenges. Decide as a group which words you know. See if you know more than the other groups, but be prepared to correctly define the words or else face the consequences.

abstruse	accede	acclivity	acerbity
acolyte	acquiesce	acrimonious	actuary
acumen	adage	adduce	adipose
adjure	adroit	adumbration	adventitious
adverse	affinity	affluent	agglomerate

18. Draw up a list of questions.

Permit them to choose any ten to answer, rather than every question. This should build their confidence and show you that they at least understand *some* of what was taught. For overachievers, you can give bonus points for additional questions answered.

Brainteaser: We're still on the A's for the group vocabulary test. Again, decide which words you know by placing a checkmark in front of them. But . . . be prepared to defend what you define. The group with the largest number of defendable checkmarks will be declared the winners.

agnomen	agronomy	akimbo	alacrity
alchemy	allay	allegory	alleviate
allude	alluvial	altercation	altruism
amatory	ambergris	ambulatory	ameliorate
amenable	ampersand	amulet	anachronism
analogy	anathema	aneroid	aneurysm
animadversion	animalcule	annotate	anomalous
antecedent	antediluvian	antipathetic	antithesis

---

19. Use the old questions in a new way.

Everyone knows the journalistic five W's and one H. Post them in a visible place. After teaching a particular concept, call on someone to tell you which of the six words is most relevant to the concept. Then have him explain why he chose that particular word and tell its relevance to the course content.

Option: If they prefer, they can ask a question that starts with a "W" or "H" word, but that word cannot be "Who," "What," "Where," "When," "Why," or "How."

Brainteaser: Consider this scenario: You drove to a meeting 50 miles away at a speed of 50 miles per hour. On the way back from the meeting, however, you ran into highway construction. As a result, you only averaged 25 miles an hour for the trip back. What was your average speed for the round trip?

Answer: Thirty-three and a third miles per hour. It took one hour to get to the meeting, but two hours to return (50 miles, traveling at a speed of 25 miles an hour). That's 100 miles traveled in three hours, an average of 33 and one-third miles per hour.

20. Use questions to make them "bloom."

Nearly 50 years ago, Dr. Benjamin Bloom from the University of Chicago found that more than 95% of the questions instructors ask students elicit responses that require little cognitive effort. He subsequently devised a taxonomy of questions, the lowest level of which is simple recall. Here are the six levels and sample verbs within each. For each of the key concepts you present, have questions on all six levels.

1. Recall (Repeat, Name, List)
2. Comprehension (Describe, Discuss, Report)
3. Application (Choose, Dramatize, Illustrate)
4. Analysis (Analyze, Compare, Experiment)
5. Synthesis (Compose, Organize, Write)
6. Evaluation (Assess, Predict, Defend)

Brainteaser: When George and Laurene were married 21 years ago, George was three times as old as Laurene. Today, he is twice as old as she is. How old was Laurene on her wedding day?

Answer: 21. He was 63 at the time. Today, she is 42 and he is 84.

21. Use quotations about questions.

There are some fascinating ones around. Explore them with your participants in relation to the material being presented.

"I'd rather know some of the questions than all of the answers." (James Thurber)

"When you ask a dumb question, you get a smart answer." (Aristotle)

"The way you ask a question has a lot to do with the answer you get." (Glenn Varney)

"The uncreative mind can spot wrong answers, but it takes a very creative mind to spot wrong questions." (Antony Jay)

"There is this faculty in the human mind that hates any question that takes more than ten seconds to answer." (Norman Mailer)

"By the judicious use of questions, you can easily secure immediate attention, maintain interest in the item under discussion, and direct the course that you want the conversation to take." (Gerald Nierenberg)

"Leaders don't need to know all the answers. However, they need to know how to ask the right questions." (Helm Lehman)

"Someone who continually asks probing questions may appear to be holding up progress but may be ideal for leadership." (Mary Frances Winters)

22. Have a Q & A session after every big module.

There are numerous ways to run the Question-and-Answer session. You can provide all the answers and participants have to come up with the questions (or the reverse). You can assign table groups for each learning module and have the groups answer the questions posed by the rest of the class. You can even invite a reporter in from the organizational or school newsletter/newspaper to pose questions to the class. (Ideally, he will also write an article about the class.)

Brainteaser: A student burning the midnight oil had the television on in the background. The weatherman on the midnight news program gave this forecast: "It is raining now, and there will be rain for the next two days. However," he assured the audience, "in 72 hours, it will be bright and sunny."

In disgust, the student said aloud, "Wrong again." How did he know he was right and the weather forecaster was wrong?

Answer: Because 72 hours from midnight would be midnight once again. It could not be bright and sunny.

---

23. Compile a list of questions for those in authority.

Go beyond the classroom. Have participants draw up a list of questions they'd like to pose to school administrators, company executives, or local politicians. Make certain the questions are related, if only peripherally, to the subject matter at hand. Then invite the authorities in or compose a class letter to be sent *out* (mailed to the appropriate person).

Brainteaser: Before you jump at these answers, take a moment to reflect.

1. What fruit did they eat that led to Adam and Eve being banished from the Garden of Eden?
2. Who said, "Everybody talks about the weather but nobody does anything about it."?
3. In what year was Christ born?
4. Boris Karloff is known throughout the world for the frightening character he played in the movies. Who was that character?

Answers: 1. It is not known what fruit. The Bible merely refers to the fruit from the tree of the knowledge of good and evil. 2. It was not Mark Twain who made the comment, but rather his friend Charles Warner. 3. The actual date was somewhere between the years 8 and 4 B.C. 4. Frankenstein was the name of the scientist who created the monster, who was not named.

24. Prepare a list of questions from popular songs.

Then have participants answer the questions in relation to the course. Depending on the age of your audience, you will choose questions accordingly. Here's a sexagenarian's list of possibilities.

"Why can't you behave?"
(For courses in interpersonal relationships, psychology, conflict management)

"What's love got to do with it?"
(For courses in career management, supervision, art history, ethics.)

"Doesn't one and one make two?"
(This Ella Fitzgerald romantic query could be combined with a line from Donella Meadows, who asserts, "You think because you understand *one* you must understand *two*, because one and one makes two. But you must also understand *and*." Both could apply to problem-solving and leadership courses.)

Brainteaser: How much dirt is there in a hole two feet by two feet by two feet?

Answer: None.

---

25. Use questions from the world of sports.

The sports section of any given newspaper on any given day will yield questions that can be applied to the subject matter at hand. Here are two examples from the Rochester, New York *Democrat & Chronicle* for June 19, 2005:

- Torii Hunter, center fielder for the Twins, was asked if he'd rather take a Randy Johnson fastball to the head or play for Tampa Bay. His reply: "Randy Johnson. If he hits me, it's over with. But if you play for the Devil Rays, you're stuck." (With some revision, a similar question could be used for a course on decision-making or even for strategic planning.)

- Quarterback Tom Brady of the Boston Patriots was asked to comment on the size of the new Super Bowl rings. His reply: "If they get any bigger, you'd have to wear it on your belt." (Could be used in a Language Arts class to show the lack of agreement in the pronouns, or in a speech class to show the use of hyperbole.)

- Other questions, more legendary in nature, can be found in any number of books or articles. Here's an example from *Body Slams!* by Glenn Liebman: When asked what he expected his opponent to say after losing, pro wrestler Kurt Angle responded, "It was an honor just being in the ring with you." (Could be used in courses dealing with civility or sales.)

(continued)

25. **Use questions from the world of sports.** *(concluded)*

Option: To stimulate creativity or to add some quick comic relief, pose questions reporters actually asked of sports figures. Have participants guess what the answers were. Then tell them what was actually uttered. For example, Jimmy Piersall, a major league outfielder and father of ten children, was asked how to change a diaper. "You cross first base," he explained, "over to third and home plate over to second."

Brainteaser: What's your interpretation of the proverb "Brevity is the soul of wit"?

    a. Those who are witty have a special soul.
    b. Long-windedness can spoil a funny story.
    c. Witty people are rare, even though funny people abound.
    d. Brevity and longevity are essential elements in a joke.
    e. A witty remark is different from a joke.

Answer: b.

Brainteaser: These mixed-up words all belong in the same category. (The first word names the category.)

    SGMEA
    OIGNB
    PLOOOYMN
    NNSETI

Answers: games, bingo, monopoly, tennis

Chapter 6

25 Ways to Use Quotations

Chapter Overview

There is nothing quite like a quotation to lend credence to your opinion, to suggest you are a well-read person, to show off your memory, and to help sway others to your point of view. To illustrate, if you are arguing for simplicity in a process, who could argue *against* Einstein's assertion that we "make everything simple but not simpler than it has to be"?

Quotations in the classroom provide vitality, verve, and verbal magic. Here are 25 ways you can use them to bring life and light (and sometimes even laughter) to your classroom lessons.

1. Post the quotations around the room.

During breaks, encourage participants to view and discuss them. If you don't have the wall space or can't put anything up, compile a list of relevant quotations. Distribute copies of the sheet to participants. Have them circle their favorite and then form a group with others who circled the same quote. Allow some time for them to discuss their selection.

Options: Periodically during the training day, call on someone to share her favorite quote and to tell why it resonated with her. You can also pair participants off and have them explain their selections. If you have selected complex quotes, ask for volunteers to share their interpretations of the quotes.

Brainteaser: You'll need to devote some of your analytical powers to solving this problem. It starts with Anamay, who likes music but not books. She does have a cat but refuses to get a goldfish. She'd move to Utah in a heartbeat but would never move to Michigan. She favors bacon but would never eat toast. Does she drink water or tea?

Answer: Water. She likes things that are spelled, like her name, with vowels and consonants alternated.

Brainteaser: What number is missing from this sequence?

4   9   15   22   30   ___

Answer: 39. The difference between 4 and 9 is 5. Each time, you increase the separating number by one (5, 6, 7, 8) so that the missing number in the sequence is 39.

2. Ask group leaders to choose a favorite quote.

If you have posted the quotes around the room, this activity lends some excitement to the day because the leaders have to rush to remove their favorite from the wall before some other leader takes it. Have each group leader then bring her selection to her group, which will prepare a report correlating the quote to what they have learned so far. (Note: Make certain to select quotes from both men and women and from various ethnic leaders.)

Option: If they wish, participants can take part of a quote and complete it by adding their own course-relevant ideas. Poet Donald Marquis, for example, maintains that there are two kinds of people in this world—those who are able to share the secrets of the universe with you and still not impress you with how important those secrets are, and those who can tell you that they just bought paper napkins and make you thrill and vibrate as you listen. (His poem is ideal, by the way, for a presentations, train-the-trainer, or teacher education course.) Participants, no matter what the course, can use the Marquis beginning: "There are two types of people in this world: those who . . . and those who . . ." They can then fill in the omitted words with ideas of their own, related to the course content.

3. Use an especially pertinent quote to generate discussion.

Write a quote on the flipchart (or put it on a transparency) and use it as a stimulus for whole-class discussion. Elicit examples of the point the quote is making.

Example: In Management, Supervision, and Leadership classes, I like to quote General Patton, who advises, "Give direction—not directions."

Option: Scatter relevant quotes throughout your curriculum material, and ask participants to choose their favorite quote and discuss its relevance to them or to the material.

Brainteaser: Imagine that you have been given nine golf balls but only four different-sized boxes or bags. You've been asked to put all the balls in the boxes in such a way that there is an odd number of balls in each box. In other words, the boxes can only have 1 or 3 or 5 or 7 or 9 balls in them. How would you do this?

Answer: You really have to think *inside* the box (or bag) for this one—quite literally. The only way to do it is to put at least one box or bag inside the other. There are several ways to do this. You could, for example, put three of the smaller boxes or bags inside the largest box or bag, and then put all the golf balls in that one box or bag.

4. Present opposing viewpoints.

To really stimulate discussion, take two diametrically opposed quotes from two well-respected figures and explore both viewpoints with the group.

Example: Stanford professor and best-selling author Jim Collins (*Built To Last*) endorses the need for BHAGs: Big, Hairy, Audacious Goals. Contrast that with Mother Teresa's assertion: "We can do no great things—only small things with great love."

Brainteaser: What letter is missing from the sequence in the third row?

1	2	3
E	H	M
D	H	O
P	S	___

Answer: X. Look at the letter in the last column of row one. There are twice as many letters separating it from the one preceding it than there are letters separating the first two letters in the row. Row two has the same pattern. In other words, TWO letters are in between E and H (F and G). But FOUR letters are in between H and M (I, J, K, and L).

---

5. Assemble familial wisdom.

Ask table groups to share advice or aphorisms passed along by their family elders. Then have them choose one that has particular relevance to the course and share it when called upon.

Examples: "One day you'll thank me for this." (Could be used in a course dealing with financial management, foreign language, or goal-setting.)

- "Just because everyone else is doing it doesn't mean you have to."
  (Could be used in courses dealing with leadership, ethics, or whistle-blowing.)

- "Out of the frying pan and into the fire."
  (Could be used in courses dealing with decision-making, problem-solving, or history.)

- "Don't use that tone of voice with me."
  (Could be used in courses dealing with confrontation, sales, music, or presentations.)

- "Do you think I work for the electric company?"
  (Could be used with courses dealing with creativity, science, ecology, or the environment.)

- "Do you think I was born yesterday?"
  (Could be used with courses dealing with relationships in the workplace, human resources, science, or financial investing.)

6. Use quotations as examples of what *not* to say.

You've seen them—the books and calendars that contain the most foolish things ever said. To be fair, a lapsis linguae could, of course, be attributed to fatigue or confusion. The foolish things that come out of people's mouths are part of the slippery verbal slope we climb every day. No one is immune from the trouble that can be caused by spoonerisms or malapropisms.

You can use quotes that poke gentle fun at public figures as examples of what to avoid or as examples of the lack of understanding shown by those supposedly "in the know."

Caution: Make certain your examples are diversified: men and women; Republicans and Democrats; numerous different ethnic groups; corporate, legal, and entertainment figures; and so on.

Caution: Choose examples that relate to the subject matter you are presenting. Here is an example that can be used for a stress management class that emphasizes the need for physical exercise. When asked why one of his players failed his physical exam, San Diego Chargers manager Steve Ortmayer responded, "John didn't flunk his physical. He just didn't pass it!"

For a political science class or to provide an example of a tautology [phrase containing unnecessary repetition], you might quote Dee Dee Myers, former Clinton press secretary: "Democrats did very well in Democratic primaries."

For a drama, literature, or performing arts class: When Cheryl Crawford declined to produce *Death of a Salesman*, she said to Elia Kazan, "Who would want to see a play about an unhappy traveling salesman?"

Brainteaser: Every minute, an amoeba splits in two. Each half grows immediately to the same size as its parent. In one hour, the number of amoebae in a pond completely cover the bottom of the pond. To the nearest minute, how much time was needed to cover half the bottom of the pond?

Answer: 59 minutes. Keep in mind that the amoebae double in number every single minute. So, the bottom of the pond would have been half-covered one minute before it was *completely* covered. In the space of the one minute between minute 59 and minute 60, the creatures doubled their number. And, accordingly, the pond went from being half-covered to completely covered.

7. Have them decide quote-attribution.

A great way to generate discussion about the subject matter at hand is to provide a quote and then ask participants to decide whether or not it was actually said by a figure prominent in the field. In a leadership or ethics class, for example, you could ask them to decide whether or not author/consultant Tom Peters actually said, "If you have gone a whole week without being disobedient, you are doing yourself and your organization a disservice." Explore as well what he might have meant by the statement. (He actually did say this, and the quote provides excellent fodder for discussions on such topics as innovation and whistle-blowing.)

Brainteaser: How would you interpret this Laotian proverb?

"Rich together; poor if separated."

a) "Money is the root of all evil."
b) "A single bamboo pole does not make a raft."
c) "United we stand; divided we fall."
d) "It takes a whole village to raise a child."

Answer: c.

---

8. Have them match quote and quotee.

Find at least ten quotations that relate to the course you are presenting. Then type two mixed-up columns: one listing speakers, and the second listing statements. Distribute and ask triads to match the speaker and the comment they believe she made. Award a token prize to the triad that has all the correct answers, and ask them to explain the thinking that led to their decisions.

Brainteaser: Can you think of a scenario in which the following circumstances could easily be true?

Paul has not yet learned to read. Accordingly, he cannot write either. In fact, he is unable to feed himself or dress himself. At this stage, he is clearly unable to earn his own living. And yet, he is given an official, highly regarded, and extremely well-paid position. What are the circumstances?

Answer: Paul, while still an infant, has been made a crown prince, due to the unexpected death of his father, who had been the king of the country.

9. Have them match a quote with an era.

Not only can quotes give people something to think about, they also help develop awareness of the universality of certain values. You'll prepare two columns and ask triads to match the saying with the century (so to speak). Use the quotations as discussion prompts relative to the course being taught.

Example: Match the quotation on the left with the era in which the statement was made.

1. "We are what we repeatedly do. Excellence, then, is not an act but a habit."   A. 1800's

2. "Be a Columbus to whole new continents and worlds within you."   B. Contemporary

3. "I am indeed a king, because I know how to rule myself."   C. Before the birth of Christ

4. "We can no longer wait for the storm to pass: we must learn to work in the rain."   D. 1500's

Answers: 1. C (Aristotle)   2. A (Thoreau)   3. D (dramatist Pietro Aretino)   4. B (Peter Silas, former CEO of Philips Petroleum)

10. Find quotable material within the class.

Have five sheets of flipchart paper hanging on a wall. Ask each person to think of an original observation or summary about something in the course material. It should be a statement that provides a profound insight about the course. Then give the magic marker to one participant and ask her to neatly print her profundity (but not her name) on one of the sheets. You will continue teaching while the wall-writing goes on.

Once the first participant has finished, she gives the marker to a second person, who will write her personal observation or insight. The pen-passing and statement-writing will continue until everyone has had an opportunity to record her thoughts. Then pass out small adhesive dots, one per person. Two at a time, participants will go over and decide which of the statements they feel is most profound. Each person will "vote" by putting her dot next to her favorite.

When you see that the voting is completed, finish your lecture and determine which statement garnered the most votes. Ask for the author to identify herself and acknowledge her effort with a round of applause, at the very least.

11. Have them quote you on that.

Decide in advance what unalterably true statements you can make about the content, the class, the conditions under which you operate. Then, several times a day, with great flair, make your pronouncements. In time, these statements will become a source of mild humor by which you will be known.

Example: If you have discovered counterintuitive bits of information that will surprise their scholastic sensibilities, say something like, "You may think knowledge is power. Knowledge is *not* power. If it were, librarians would rule the world! The real power comes from putting the knowledge to action. And you can quote me on that."

Brainteaser: You may have heard the riddle about never dying in the dessert because of all the *sand which* is there. In a similar vein, the answers to these riddles lie in food-related words.

1. It's a special experience watching Fred and _____ dance.
2. If you _____ a dead man, he can tell you no lies.

Answers: 1. Ginger 2. berry (bury)

---

12. Go from the familial to the curricular.

Have group members share their all-time-favorite quotes. The choices can be quotations they've picked up from family members; they can be quotes from a holy book; they can be something one of their heroes has said. Then, each group will decide which of the quotes shared by members of that group is the group's favorite.

In the second phase of this process, groups exchange their quotes. They then discuss ways to correlate the quote they have been given to the content of the course.

Example: In a Teambuilding class, the saying "All's well that ends well" could be related to the four stages of team development (Form, Storm, Norm, Perform) identified by Bruce Tuckman.

Brainteaser: A manager and her subordinate are involved in a heated exchange.

> "I'm the manager," says the one with gray hair.
> "I'm the subordinate," says the one with blonde hair.
> If at least one of them is lying, which one is?

Answer: You'll need your logical powers to think this through. There are four combinations possible here: true-true; true-false; false-true, and false-false. The first combination (true-true) is not possible, because we know that at least one person is lying. It can't be the second or third combination either, because if one person is lying, than the other one could not be telling the truth. The only possible combination is false-false.

13. Use ad agency talent to elicit student talent.

Find interesting remarks or statements in newspapers or magazines, such as the statement appearing in an ad for Rockwell International that was designed to lure retired engineers back to work: "Bring a lifetime of experience to the experience of a lifetime."

Without using the same words or ideas—just the syntactical structure—have participants create one-sentence ads relevant to the course.

Brainteaser: Intelligence is sometimes defined as the ability to discern patterns among seemingly unrelated things. Analogies ask you to do such discernment by giving you the relationship between two items and then asking you to find a comparable relationship in two other items. So, "agreement" is to "consensus" as:

a) puzzle: solution
b) treasure: hunt
c) peacefulness: tranquility
d) oven: stove
e) circle: geometry

Answer: c.

---

14. Let them paraphrase a famous quote.

Their cerebral juices should flow with this assignment: Take a famous quote and ask them to change it by adding, subtracting or paraphrasing so that the final sentence has significance for the course.

Example:

Original: Early to bed and early to rise makes a man healthy, wealthy, and wise.

Revision for a course in stress management: Early to bed and early to rise may not yield you health, wealth, or wisdom—not if you are letting worry keep you awake!

Brainteaser: The local grocery store, alas, has an employee fond of playing practical jokes. One day, he mixed up the signs on the tea containers. They used to read "Green only," "Lemon only," "Green and Lemon." Now they are all wrongly labeled. He will let you pull one tea bag from any container and look at it. Using only the knowledge gained from your "pull," how can you return the signs to their rightful places?

Answer: You have to start with the container that says "Green and Lemon." You know that it has the wrong label, so it cannot contain both types of tea bags. Whichever one you pull out—let's say "Green"—you know all the other bags in that container are "Green." So you will take the "Green" label and put it here. Then ask what bags are in the container labeled "Lemon." They cannot be "Green," as you know. Also, they cannot be "Lemon," because if they were, the container would have the right label. So, they must be "Green and Lemon."

15. Use participant-created chiasmus statements.

Sentences that take words from the first half of the sentence and turn those same words around in the second half to create a related but "twisted" meaning are known as *chiasmus* sentences. Depending on the nature of what you are teaching, these sentences can provoke interesting discussions. In a class for senior citizens, for example, a delightful chiasmus from LeRoy Satchel Paige could be used: "Old age is a question of mind over matter. If you don't mind, it don't matter!"

In a class dealing with reaching one's potential, you could use Jesse Jackson's wonderfully inspirational chiasmus: "I was born in the slums but the slums were not born in me." A final chiasmus example for history teachers comes from President Jimmy Carter: "America did not invent civil rights. Civil rights invented America."

Brainteaser: What number belongs in the blank space?

14	9	5
21	8	13
28	9	___

Answer: 19. The third number in a row equals the difference between the other two.

---

16. Take quotations from popular music.

You can provide the lines, they can provide the lines, or you can present a combination of both possibilities. The assignment remains the same, though: They are to take the quotation and show how it explains some concept or precept associated with the course you are teaching.

Example: The line from a Ray Charles classic "It's a sad, sad situation and it's getting more and more absurd" can be applied to any number of situations: declining test scores, environmental problems, the rise in the number of children born with autism, and so on. In this case, participants discuss things that they consider to be "absurdities." Of course, they will have to be knowledgeable about the situation in order to express and perhaps defend their point of view.

Option: Depending on the makeup of the group, how well they know one another, how musical they are, what the course content is, and so on, you might opt to have them write a song—and even perform it—using their words sung to an old, familiar tune.

17. Synthesize the course in a single quote.

You'll have to do some research to find these bon mots, but they are out there. Once you've found the perfect one for the program you are presenting, use it as part of your opening remarks. Then call on participants repeatedly to repeat it.

Examples: For a problem-solving course in which you emphasize the need to make careful and deliberate decisions, you could use this famous line by H. L. Mencken: "For every complex problem, there is one solution that is simple, neat, elegant,—and *wrong*!"

In a program dealing with management, supervision, or interpersonal skills, you could use this powerful but brief observation by the former head of Ford Motor Company, Don Petersen: "Results depend on relationships."

Brainteaser: When it first came out, only a few people could afford this book. Now, nearly everyone has it. Yet you can't buy it or get it from a library. What is the book?

Answer: The phone book.

---

18. Encourage diversity through quotations.

Given my great admiration for Native American culture and traditions and the amount of work I do in the Southwest, I like to incorporate Indian quotes in my classes. They cannot stand in isolation, of course; they need to be woven into the content being presented. Proverbs from any and all cultures can serve, of course, but here are a few of my personal favorites.

Examples: Max DePree, author of *Leadership Is an Art* and a former CEO, talks often about the need for tribal storytelling in organizations. A great segue into his philosophy for leaders could be this quotation from Geronimo, Chiricahua Apache Chief: "When a child, my mother taught me the legends of our people."

For courses dealing with values, the words of Sioux Chief Red Cloud carry great import: "I am poor and naked, but I am the chief of the nation. We do not want riches but we do want to train our children right. Riches would do us no good. We could not take them with us to the other world. We do not want riches. We want peace and love."

19. Use titles or phrases that have numbers in them.

The most famous is probably "the Ten Commandments." But there are numerous others: *The Seven Habits of Highly Successful People* or Miguel Ruiz's *The Four Agreements*. Other examples might be the *"4 C's of diamond value"* or *The Seven "S" Words in Leadership Language*. Have participants take one such phrase or title and prepare a comparable statement that captures the essence of the course. If participants prefer, they can take one set of lessons and make them relevant to the course content, using "numbered" principles of their own.

Examples: Here are Ruiz's four "agreements":

> Be impeccable with your word.
>
> Do not take anything personally.
>
> Do not make assumptions.
>
> Always do your best.

The four agreements for an art course might be these:

> Be impeccable with your technique.
>
> Do not permit critics to destroy your creative spirit.
>
> Do not fail to seek new inspiration.
>
> Always experiment.

Brainteaser: Can you write a number that equals 100 by using only 9's?

Answer: $99 + \frac{99}{99}$

---

20. Debunk myths or prevalent wisdom.

It's best to have your collection ready ahead of time, so start assembling quotations that seem to capture truth. Present your list to the class. Have them select one popular mindset and play devil's advocate in relation to it and in relation to the course.

Example: "Attitude is all." A stress management instructor might insist that good health—not attitude—is all. She might assert that without it, you have nothing: "Your attitude doesn't matter, your bank statement doesn't matter, your relationships don't matter. You need to be physically well in order to maximize the other aspects of your life: mental, financial, personal, attitudinal, and so on."

(continued)

20. **Debunk myths or prevalent wisdom.** *(concluded)*

Brainteaser: If a duck and three-quarters lays an egg and three-quarters in a day and three-quarters, how many eggs do seven ducks lay in a week?

Answer: You have to do some mind-stretching to figure this one out. Imagine a super-duck that can lay an egg and ¾ of an egg in one and ¾ day. So, it's laying 1 egg per 1 day and 7 eggs in 7 days. Now, figure out how many super-ducks are there in 7 ducks. To find out, divide 7 by 1 and ¾ and you get 4 super-ducks, which is the same as 7 regular ducks. Multiple 4 super-ducks (the same as 7 of those regular ducks) times 7 eggs a week and the answer is 28 eggs a week.

---

21. **Have them stratify the course content and then recall quotes related to the stratifications.**

We've already talked about stratification—the process of breaking down a broad topic into several categories or subheadings. Divide participants into groups of five or six, and have them decide on 6–10 topics they believe the course is based on (or should be based on). Have one representative from each group meet in a breakout room or in the corridor to reach agreement on a final list of 6–10 stratification categories.

When they return to the room, stop your lecture and ask them to write the categories on the flipchart. Then ask each team to choose two categories and write as many famous quotes regarding that category as they can think of. (It will help to have several books of quotations available for classroom use.)

Have a roving recorder listen in and do some swapping. If a team seems stuck finding quotes on one of their two topics, they can do an exchange using the recorder as a broker. She will give another group a quote they can use for *their* list, but that group will have to give up a quote needed by the group that was stuck.

---

22. **Use multi-quote lists as stimuli.**

Some people are known for one memorable and quotable statement. Others, for a number of them. (You'll see from the examples that a single expert can provide considerable verbal fodder for classroom use.) If yours is a specialized topic (such as quantum physics), you may have to do some reading to come up with your lists. (I strongly recommend Meg Wheatley's *Leadership and the New Science*.) Biographies are an especially good source of relevant quotes from a single-person source.

Distribute the list of quotes and have participants circle the one that most piques their interest, for whatever reason. Then form groups based on their selections. Ask them to discuss and then summarize their insights.

(continued)

22. Use multi-quote lists as stimuli. *(concluded)*

Stimulating Words of Wisdom

From Oscar Wilde:
- To know everything about oneself, one must know all about others.
- When people agree with me, I always feel that I must be wrong.
- The tragedy of old age is not that one is old, but that one is young.
- The old believe everything; the middle-aged suspect everything; the young know everything.
- I can resist everything except temptation.
- Education is an admirable thing, but it is well to remember from time to time that nothing worth knowing can be taught.
- Experience is the name everyone gives to their mistakes.
- Nothing succeeds like excess.
- Discontent is the first step in the progress of a man or a nation.

From Aristotle:
- We are what we repeatedly do. Excellence then, is not an act but a habit.
- To understand the metaphor is the beginning of genius.
- Art consists in bringing something into existence.
- A beginning is half the whole.
- Character is the result of our conduct.
- The greatest crimes are caused by surfeit, not by want. Men do not become tyrants in order that they may not suffer cold.
- Democracy is where the poor rule.
- Fear is pain arising from the anticipation of evil.
- A fool contributes nothing worth hearing and takes offense at everything.

From anonymous sources

On genius:
- Genius is that which generates heat and progress.
- Genius is a fugitive from the law of averages.
- Genius is something you can't be by trying.

On happiness:
- Happiness is enjoying doing and enjoying what is done.
- Happiness is not what we have, but what we enjoy.
- Happiness is not created by what happens to us, but by our attitude toward each happening.

On ignoramuses:
- An ignoramus is someone who despises education.
- An ignoramus is someone who can't explain what he doesn't like.
- An ignoramus is someone who doesn't know about what *you* learned yesterday.

On money:
- Money is the fringe benefit of a job you like.
- Money is the only true aristocracy.
- What gives value to money is work exchanged.

23. Use quotations to end the class on a high note.

In most courses, the instructor hands out certificates of attendance at the end. Instead of just passing them out, try having participants give them to one another. But they cannot just thrust the certificate in the hand of another participant—they have to give a little speech along with the certificate. (I typically leave the "wrong" certificate at each person's seat—the certificate does not have that participant's name on it, but rather someone *else's* name. This is the participant to whom she will deliver the certificate and the speech.)

Explain that the speech can and should be short, and tell them that you will make it easy for them: You will provide a list of quotations that contain positive remarks. They are to choose the one remark they think best describes the person to whom they will be delivering the certificate of completion.

Note: Make certain you have more quotes than class attendees.

Examples of quotes and short speeches:

For a Nursing, Stress Management, or Psychology class:
- "To array a man's will against his sickness is the supreme art of medicine."
 —Henry Ward Beecher, preacher and writer (1813–1887)
- *"John, when you told us about the nutrition classes you hold for cardiac patients, you showed us how to use will against sickness. You are supreme."*

For an Environmental Science class:
- "Few are altogether deaf to the preaching of pine trees. Their sermons on the mountains go to our hearts; and if people in general could be got into the woods, even for once, to hear the trees speak for themselves, all difficulties in the way of forest preservation would vanish."
 —John Muir, naturalist, explorer, and writer (1838–1914)
- *"Maria, it's clear that you have heard the trees speak, and you've made them speak to us. Thank you."*

For virtually any class:
- "Knowledge comes, but wisdom lingers."
 —Alfred, Lord Tennyson, poet (1809–1892)
- *"Antonia, we've all acquired knowledge in this class, but it's clear from the way you lead our group that you came in with wisdom and you're going out with even more wisdom."*

For a class in Science, Art, Reading, Time Management, or Writing:
- "The ability to simplify means to eliminate the unnecessary so that the necessary may speak."
 —Hans Hofmann, painter (1880–1966)
- *"Takeesha, it's necessary for me to say that you're terrific!"*

Chapter 6: 25 Ways to Use Quotations

24. Use quotations as the basis for role-plays.

To emphasize key points, have participants devise skits that incorporate a quote. For example, if you are working with adults, you can use this naughty-at-first-glance quote by Bette Reeve: "If you think you are too small to be effective, you have never been in bed with a mosquito!"

The skit could center on an exchange between two people, one of whom is trying to encourage the other to be more empowered. The skit could conclude with the encourager quoting Bette Reeve.

Brainteaser: What do you think is meant by this Ethiopian proverb: "Do not hold the leopard's tail, but if you do hold it, don't let it go"?

a) Be cautious.
b) Stay away from dangerous situations.
c) Avoid threatening circumstances, but if you find yourself in one, protect yourself.
d) Leopards don't like human beings.

Answer: c.

---

25. Assign quote-discovery for homework.

If the class is going to extend for longer than a day, ask participants to find relevant quotes as they watch the evening news, read the newspaper, or do some online research. The next morning, call on each person to share her quote. Record the quotes and their sources in a classroom quotebook, which can be used with future classes.

Brainteaser: What word, phrase, or familiar saying is shown in the box?

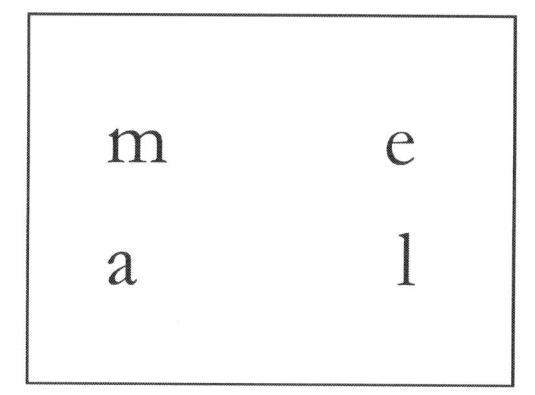

```
┌─────────────────┐
│                 │
│   m         e   │
│                 │
│   a         l   │
│                 │
└─────────────────┘
```

Answer: Square meal.

Chapter 7

25 Ways to Have Groups Report

Chapter Overview

There are few things duller than listening to someone read a speech. On a less-grand scale, there are few classroom things duller than listening to a group spokesperson read his report. And yet, if you don't call on groups to share reports about the work they have done, they are likely to feel slighted or feel that they did "all that work for nothing."

Don't despair. There are ever so many ways to get the reports from the groups without causing educational ennui in the others as they listen. Here are 25 of those ways.

1. Challenge them to condense.

Condensing lengthy reports will certainly make them more digestible. Encourage a one-sentence summary. Call on the first group to report. Members of the other groups can ask questions of the reporting group after they have given their condensed report to make sure that nothing important has been overlooked. Continue in this fashion until all groups have had a chance to give their reports.

Brainteaser: Professor Donald Gorham of Baylor University found in his research studies that personality can be identified by the choices people make when given an array of interpretations for proverbs. Those who consistently chose specific interpretations were found to be either practical, scatterbrained, or deeply moral. Try this example and see what it reveals.

Proverb: "Beauty is only skin-deep."

a) All woman share traits that make them virtual sisters.
b) Women can make up their faces, but their inner beauty is untouchable.
c) Pretty on the outside does not always mean pretty on the inside.
d) Inner character is more important that what appears on the outside.

Answer: There will be more of these. A c) reveals a logical nature, and an ability to perceive subtleties in expression. An a) answer indicates that you have a practical streak. A b) indicates a scatterbrained approach to life. A d) suggests that you have rigid moral principles.

2. Have them identify five key points.

To encourage brevity in a report of substance, ask for bulleted points (on a flipchart), rather than whole sentences. This makes it easier for the other class members to take notes and to maintain their interest in the information being shared.

Brainteaser: Can you tell what phrase, saying, or word is contained in the box below?

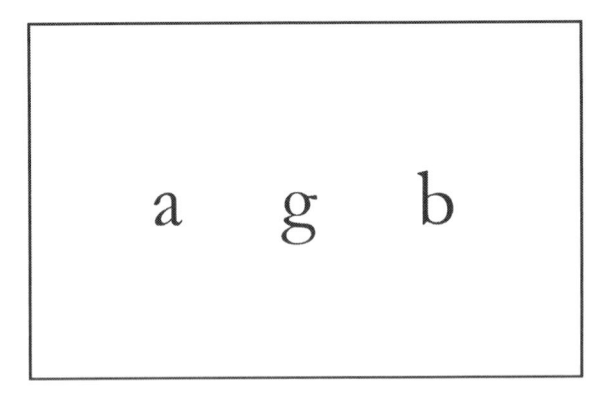

```
a     g     b
```

Answer: Mixed bag.

---

3. Alternate the groups that report.

Chances are, you'll have several assignments in a given day that require group reports. For the first assignment, just call on half the groups to share their report. For the second assignment, call on a spokesperson each time from the groups that did *not* give their reports the first time around. If there is a third task calling for a group report, go back to the first half once more or divide the reporting sections into thirds. Choose different groups to report each time.

Brainteaser: This brainteaser has two parts. First, you have to add a "Y" to each word that is given to you. That's the easy part. Then you have to rearrange all the letters (including the Y) to form a new word. For example, "thou" + Y, when rearranged, yields "youth."

1. BASS
2. GRIND
3. IDLE
4. DRONE
5. RUBE

Answers: 1. abyss 2. drying 3. yield 4. yonder 5. buyer

4. Call on groups at random.

If a given group knows they won't be called on, they will be tempted to do a superficial job preparing their report. To offset the temptation to be cursory, call on different groups at random to share their reports with the class. Keeping them "off balance" will usually yield more balanced reporting.

Brainteaser: On tests such as the Scholastic Aptitude Test, students are given only about 30 seconds to ponder each question. Here are eight questions. You should try to answer them all correctly in a mere four minutes. Good luck.

What word is the antonym of the boldfaced word in capital letters?

1. **OBVIATE**   a) alleviate   b) sweeten   c) propel   d) retain   e) fill
2. **DEMURE**   a) long   b) complex   c) irate   d) harmful   e) loud
3. **SOLICITUDE** a) illness   b) disregard   c) optimism d) jealousy   e) ire
4. **PREVALENT** a) uncommon   b) popular   c) musical   d) fantastic   e) high
5. **JUDICIOUS** a) wise   b) legal   c) foolish   d) scholarly   e) tiny
6. **HILARITY**   a) politics   b) sorrow   c) religion d) geography   e) push
7. **CHRONIC**   a) temporary   b) angular   c) swift   d) incorrect   e) full
8. **HABITABLE** a) uneasy   b) unlivable   c) unhappy   d) unlucky   e) taut

Answers: 1. d 2. e 3. b 4. a 5. c 6. b 7. a 8. b

---

5. Ask them to report to each other.

You'll need an even number of groups for this reporting exercise. Have group #1 give their report to group #2 and then #2 will report to #1. The same procedure will be followed with the remaining groups, who will report to each other at the same time.

Brainteaser: Can you meet the SAT-specification of 30 seconds per analogy?

1. DESIGN : PATTERN : :
   a) flight : airplane
   b) motorcycle : car
   c) artist : palette
   d) plan : program
   e) idea : execution

(continued)

5. **Ask them to report to each other.** *(concluded)*

> 2. PROMISE : GUARANTEE : :
> a) warranty : product
> b) pledge : allegiance
> c) agreement : contract
> d) honor : word
> e) ethics : honesty

Answers: 1. d   2. c

---

6. Post their reports around the room.

A simple but effective alternative to the monotony of having groups report is to have them post their reports around the room. Then allow time for participants to read what has been written. The whole group can circulate around the room to read and make comments on the posted reports, or different groups can be assigned to different wall reports.

Options: Have participants circulate around the room as a group to look at the reports. As they do so, encourage them to write questions or make comments on the posted papers.

Invite someone in from the school or organization to review the reports posted around the room. Have him comment afterwards on what he read.

Brainteaser: You've probably watched the dog shows on television. If so, you've seen the photographers snapping away. Alas, one photographer aimed only at the ground and recorded a total of 196 feet and paws. A ceiling camera, though, had an electronic scanner that counted 126 eyes. How many people and how many dogs were in the competition?

Answer: 28 people and 35 dogs.

Brainteaser: What number belongs in the blank space?

2	5	29
3	4	25
2	7	___

Answer: 53. The third number in each line equals the sum of the squares of the first two numbers.

7. Have group leaders make a collective report.

Once the groups have finished preparing their reports, ask a spokesperson from each group to meet in a breakout room or in the corridor. Once assembled, the group will prepare a synthesis of their respective reports and then return to the room to deliver just one report (instead of one report from each group's spokesperson).

Brainteaser: Can you identify what popular expression, person, place, or thing is expressed by the letters and numbers in the box?

```
1 d   2 r   3 a
4 c   5 u   6 l
       7a
```

Answer: Count Dracula.

---

8. Have group leaders decide which report the class most needs to hear.

Assuming that the groups have prepared reports on a similar topic, have each one appoint a spokesperson or advocate when they have finished. The advocates will then meet in a separate place (even a corner of the room will do, if there is no breakout room available). Once assembled, the advocates must analyze the various reports and then decide which one contains the most valuable information for the entire group to hear. The "winning" group report will be delivered once the spokespersons have returned to the classroom.

Brainteaser: You've seen the questions that call for food-word answers. Here are more of the same. The words needed for the blanks are actually food-related terms.

1. You're probably not old enough to remember _____ Jeff.
2. If you don't come indoors where it's air-conditioned, you'll _____ the sun.
3. Typically, her leading man is a _____; _____ Ryan likes them anyway.

Answers: 1. mutton (Mutt and) 2. bacon (bake in) 3. nutmeg (nut; Meg)

9. Ask group leaders to report to different groups.

Once the groups have completed their reports, have a spokesperson from each group move to another table and share his group's report with the new group. If time permits, you can continue with this group reporting until every group has had an opportunity to receive the report from every other group.

Note: To ensure that everyone has had a chance to serve in a leadership role, rotate group leaders and/or team spokespersons.

Brainteaser: What do you think this Japanese proverb means?

"The world belongs to the whole world."

a) Advocates of free trade will ultimately prevail.
b) All nations should be taking better care of the environment.
c) Terrorists will never succeed.
d) There should be universal visas and passports.
e) American products are enjoyed all over the world.

Answer: b.

---

10. Involve all group members in the reporting.

Tell the groups in advance that only one person at a time will stand and report one key fact. Ideally, you will have the same number of people in each group. Tell them to figure out who will go first, second, third, and so on, based on the alphabetization of their first names. So, in a five-person group, Andrea would be #1; Bob, #2; Consuela, #3; Dimitri, #4, and Evangeline, #5. It's generally more interesting to have person #1 from group #1 give his fact and then move on to person #2 from group #2, then #3 from group 3, and so on. Continue in this round-robin fashion until every person has had an opportunity to report on one key fact.

Brainteaser: S-C-R-A-P-B-O-O-K

Use any of the letters in the word "scrapbook" to spell the synonyms for these phrases.

1. To punch someone _____
2. Public land where picnics are often held _____
3. A dishonest person _____
4. A crustacean or a curmudgeon _____
5. A wild pig
6. What Emeril knows how to do so well

Answers: 1. sock 2. park 3. crook 4. crab 5. boar 6. cook

11. Request the definitive definition.

Poet Robert Frost has defined love in this way: "Love is the irresistible desire to be irresistible to the desired." Not only is it an amusing play on words, it pretty well captures the meaning of romantic love. Challenge your participants to define the essence of their report in a similarly succinct yet word-playful statement.

Brainteaser: You will multiply long and hard to get this answer, or you can do it the easy way. Here's the problem: "Red" and his sister "Rose" are multiplying by four. Red starts with the number 4. Rose multiplies it by 4 to get 16. Red then multiplies that to get 64. Rose then does her thing and comes up with 256.

After doing this for a while, one of them comes up with the number 1,048,576. Was it Red who reached this number, or Rose?

Answer: It was Rose. Notice that all Red's numbers ended in 4, while all hers ended in 6.

---

12. Have them haiku it.

You no doubt remember the structure of the haiku: three lines of text, with five syllables in the first line; seven in the second; and five in the third. Give participants the option of working alone, in pairs, or in triads. They will write a haiku poem to reflect some aspect of what they have learned. Once they are ready, have each writer or writing group present their haiku. They will read it twice to allow others time for reflection. Afterwards, award a token prize to the individual or group with a haiku that had the most captivating capture of the course ideas.

Brainteaser: How good is your intuition? Without using a dictionary, choose the correct meaning for the word in capital letters. Your five choices are written beneath the word.

PHLYCTENULE

a) the white bark of certain fruit trees
b) vascular tissue
c) the state of being stolid
d) a blister
e) hardening of the walls of veins

Answer: d.

13. Stimulate report-thinking via vocabulary.

An interesting way to stimulate thinking about the subject and to simultaneously teach a new vocabulary word is to give each group an unusual word and its definition. Then, have them incorporate that word into their report. Ask for volunteers to share their results.

Possible word:

quidnunc	=	A gossip (from the Latin word meaning "What now?")
ennui	=	boredom
ergo	=	therefore
remuneration	=	payment (Point out that many transpose the second syllable and then incorrectly pronounce the word "renumeration.")
verbiage	=	wordiness (This is new to those who mispronounce it as "verbage.")
oral	=	spoken; the opposite of written (Again, not a new word, but perhaps a new realization: The opposite of a written contract is not a verbal contract. It's an *oral* contract.)
verisimilitude	=	the appearance of being real or true (literally "similar to the truth")
intromit	=	to allow to enter; to insert

14. Provide the rubric.

You provide the structure. They provide the report, which must conform to the structure. And, because this assignment is so structured, give them a choice: Let them select any structure they like, and choose whether they want to work alone or with someone else.

Examples of Structures:

"We will provide three reasons why . . ."
"This report describes cause and effect."
"Two different perspectives are contained in this report."
"A brief history of _____ will be revealed in this report."
"Our report will show you how to _____."
"Ever wonder why _____? You'll learn why in our report."
"Two major points are made in this article."
"A problem is presented in this report, as well as _____ possible solutions."
"One truly amazing fact will be shared in this report."
"Our report covers _____ from a historical viewpoint."
"You'll hear a paradox in our report."
"This analysis may surprise you."
"We promise you'll know _____ by the end of our report."

Chapter 7: 25 Ways to Have Groups Report

15. Have them decide whether or not to report.

This possibility is a tad threatening—for you! Give participants the option: They can either say, "We decline to make a report because we came up with nothing worth repeating" or "We've learned something really interesting. Here's what it is."

If you are brave enough to face the possibly of a roomful of non-reports, this option can be fun and critical-thinking-sharpening.

Brainteaser: A three-letter word, in parentheses, can be combined with the letters on the left to create a new word each time. Can you figure out what word is needed in the parentheses?

(_ _ _)
ST
BR
S
L
GR

What is the three-letter word that fits in the blanks?

Answer: a-n-d.

---

16. Have them present a wordless report.

The founder of National Cash Register, John H. Patterson, researched the mind's receptivity. He learned that the optic nerve is 22 times stronger than the nerves that control our hearing. How did he use this knowledge? He used visuals to sell cash registers at the company's new showroom in Paris—even though he spoke not a word of French! Was he successful? So much so that he was able to get a lucrative foothold in the European market.

The challenge for your participants? Present their report without uttering a single word.

Brainteaser: There are four lines below. Can you add five more to get ten?

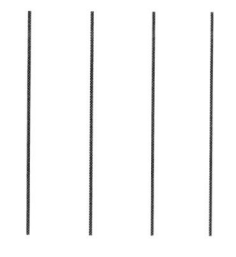

| | | |

Answer: TEN

17. Select a reporter by popular choice.

Have groups prepare their reports. Afterwards, distribute small sheets of scrap paper. Ask participants to write on them the name of the one person in the room whom they feel would make the best reporter—not the person they like best, but the person who is most likely to make the best report. To avoid popularity-contest thinking, suggest that they decide on the basis of who will be shortest (or the funniest, most articulate, most mellifluent, et cetera).

Collect the papers and ask for a volunteer to take them into the corridor and tally them.

When he returns and announces the name of the chosen reporter, hand all the reports to that person and ask him to either select one he'd like to deliver, or prepare a composite of the reports. When he's ready, have him do his thing.

Brainteaser: How good is your intuition? We're certain you've never counted to get the correct answer to these questions, but what's your best guess?

1. How many ridges are there on a quarter?
2. How many on a dime?

Answers: 1. 119   2. 118

---

18. Call for the creation of a headband or bumper sticker.

You can make this reporting assignment more interesting by providing basic art supplies, but essentially, you're asking this: "Design a headband that captures the essence of your report. If you wish, you can create a catchy bumper sticker slogan instead."

Brainteaser: This event actually happened: A young man at a boarding school needed money. Instead of requesting it from his parents, he wrote to his doting grandmother and asked for a small contribution. She wrote back, but instead of giving him money, she lectured him on being more frugal and condemned his extravagance. The boy was thrilled. Can you figure out why?

Answer: The boy's grandmother was Queen Victoria, and her grandson knew that the letter had value—the equivalent of about $20 at the time that he sold it!

Chapter 7: 25 Ways to Have Groups Report

19. Have them punctuate the report with sound effects.

This option calls for imagination, but the participants will have fun, and in all likelihood, their reports will be remembered longer than those delivered in the traditional fashion. Ask participants to add sound to their reports. (Groups work better than individuals on this assignment.) They can do the usual (hand claps, feet stomps, whistles, hums, giddey-up clicks, finger snaps), or they can burst into song at certain intervals. The choices are theirs.

Brainteaser: How good is your vocabulary? Can you match these six words with the correct meaning? In 60 seconds? Give it your best shot, and then compare your speed and accuracy with the rest of the class.

1. Abase
2. Abate
3. Abeyance
4. Abhor
5. Abject
6. Abjure

A. Miserable
B. To hate, to regard with horror
C. To renounce
D. Temporary suspension
E. To degrade
F. To decrease

Answers: 1. E 2. F 3. D 4. B 5. A 6. C

20. Challenge them to create a portmanteau.

All you want for this report is a word—a single word. The challenge is that the word doesn't exist. It's one they have to make up by combining the first part of one word with the second half of another word. This newly created "portmanteau" will reflect the basic meaning of the report they have to make.

Everyday examples:

smog (smoke and fog)
brunch (breakfast and lunch)
spork (spoon and fork)
dramedy (drama and comedy)
Eurasian (European and Asian)
simulcast (simultaneous and broadcast)
ammeter (ampere and meter)
craze (crack and glaze)
limon (lime and lemon)

Leadership example:

executary (secretary handling some executive functions)

21. Have an individual do a collective report.

Appoint one person to circulate among the groups, sitting in just long enough to gain a sense of their discussions. The reporter then gives a brief overview of each group's discussion, allowing limited input from the groups to update or amend any of the reporter's comments.

Brainteaser: Can you figure out what letter is missing from the following?

Answer: The letter "l" will create the word "silkworm," spelled in a counter-clockwise direction.

22. Read their written, flipcharted reports.

Have each group prepare a one-paragraph report on flipchart paper. Post the sheets around the room and then read each aloud yourself, allowing a brief period for discussion or comment.

Brainteaser: Insert the correct numbers in those lines that have no numbers, and you will find that the rows, the columns, and the two diagonals will, when added, all yield the same number.

32	19		8
10	25		
9			
35	16		11

Answers: Line one: missing 27; Line two: missing 17 and 34; Line three: missing 26, 28, 33; Line four: missing 24. Insert these and you'll see everything adds up to 86.

23. Play devil's advocate to their advocacy.

Tell them they will be preparing a report, but that they will have to advocate a particular course of action or thinking as part of their preparation. Warn them in advance that it behooves them to be ready to defend their point of view.

Then call on a spokesperson from each small group to share the group's "advocacy." You will respond, trying to puncture the metaphorical balloon of their beliefs.

Brainteaser: A popular Russian proverb warns that if you chase two rabbits, you will not catch either one. What is the meaning behind this proverb?

a) A bird in the hand is worth two in the bush.
b) A rabbit will always be faster than a tortoise.
c) Better to let animals come to you than to try and chase them down.
d) Do one thing at a time.
e) Some things were simply not meant to be.

Answer: d.

24. Gather supplies and have participants make storyboards.

Whether or not they possess artistic talent, groups are perfectly capable of using storyboards to present their reports. (Storyboarding, by the way, is also a novel but effective way to solve certain problems.) They will probably need about ten frames to express their ideas. Their storyboard, of course, should have a title. When they finish, post the storyboards around the room and allow time for participants to circulate and read them, or ask questions as they move around.

To make sure they are reading the work of others, give each person a scrap of paper and ask him to write the title of the storyboard he found most informative.

Brainteaser: You know what centipedes and millipedes are? Insects with 100 and 1,000 legs, respectively. Multipedes are insects with an unspecified number of legs. Assume that two multipedes are courting each other. One says to the other, "If you could give me two of your legs, we'd have the same number."

To which the other remarked, "And if I had two of yours, I would then have three times as many as you!" How many legs did each of the two multipedes have?

Answer: One had six and the other had ten.

25. Ask them to design a logo for their report.

Have small groups prepare their reports as they usually would. When they are ready, tell them there is a second phase to their report: They are to assume that their report is an organization or an entity of some sort. What logo could they design to represent their report-body? They are free to use words as well as images. Once these have been drawn, ask a spokesperson from each group to stand, present the logo, and briefly explain its significance.

Reducing-conflict example: Our logo is a queen. Beneath her face, you'll see the words of a Norwegian proverb: "Inside every woman is a queen. Speak to the queen and the queen will speak to you." We've chosen this logo to represent our belief that when people are treated respectfully, royally even, conflict can be reduced. It's also our belief that just as there is a queen inside every woman, there is also a king inside every man.

Brainteaser: If you can unscramble the four words and then combine the first letter in each word, you will get a word that stands for a valuable metal.

BBGLOE
VSLOIE
HNUCL
NNREID

Answer: Gold. The words are gobble, olives, lunch, dinner.

Chapter 8

25 Ways to Get Through Printed Material

Chapter Overview

It's a persistent pedagogical problem: how to review pages of important information in a textbook or curriculum without inviting the sleep-gods to visit. You can solve the problem with the techniques on the following pages—a total of 25 novel ways to keep participants awake and involved as they interactively respond and react to the material before them.

1. Tell them key words to underline.

I try to avoid asking the whole room to read several pages while I wait for them to finish; the slower readers will feel some pressure to catch up (and thus are not likely to ingest as much as they should), and the faster readers always wind up waiting for the slower ones (and thus become bored).

A good option is to work together as a reading orchestra, with you as the conductor. Tell them which words/sentences/passages are most important, and have them underline or highlight those. As you proceed, raise questions. (You could assign for homework answers to questions you've raised; point out correlations to other material already covered; make projections as to what they will encounter in the next section, and so on.)

Brainteaser: Can you think of a two-digit number that is one more than a squared number and one less than a cubed number?

Answer: 26. It is one more than 25 (5×5) and one less than 27 ($3 \times 3 \times 3$).

Brainteaser: What number belongs in the blank space?

234   225   216   207   198   ___

Answer: 180. Add the digits in each number and then subtract it from the number itself to get the next number. For example, when you add $2 + 3 + 4$, you get the number 9. Subtract 9 from 234 and you get 225.

2. Let them stop after finding two gems.

Tell them the pages you want them to read, but ward off the groans by tempting them: Tell them that as soon as they have located two instructional "gems," they can stop reading. Encourage them to scan and skip and make their selections from the middle portion and the end portion—not just from the beginning portion.

If time permits, call on several people to share their verbal jewelry, asking them to identify the page, paragraph, and line so others can note it.

Brainteaser: Let's try more vocabulary words. How quickly can you match the words to their meanings?

1. Apogee
2. Appall
3. Append
4. Apprehend
5. Archetype

A. Original model
B. To add or attach
C. To understand, to arrest
D. To horrify
E. Highest point

Answers: 1. E   2. D   3. B   4. C   5. A

---

3. Have the group isolate the most important point.

There's an adage that tells us that misery loves company. To be sure, the misery of reading a long passage in isolation can be alleviated if you ask the group to identify the most important point in the passage. Encourage the group leader to divide the passage any way she feels is most expeditious: by page; by beginning, middle, end; by headlines; by scanning; and so on. They will then share what they have learned with each other.

Once they know what they collectively know, their job as a group is to decide which fact was most valuable. Call on each group leader to share that fact. When other class members oppose or disagree with a group's most-important selection, have the leader of that group defend her group's choice.

Brainteaser: A pen and a bottle of ink together cost a total of $2.50. The pen costs $2 more than the ink. What is the cost of each?

Answer: The pen costs $2.25 and the ink costs $.25.

4. Catch them off-guard.

Tell them the pages you'd like them to read. Then tell them you will be calling on people at various stages to answer a question—most likely bespectacled people. Invariably, someone will discreetly take off her glasses to avoid being called on. Bring humor to the action by pointing out that you are not as dumb as you look (if you don't mind self-deprecating humor).

After a few minutes, call on someone wearing glasses to tell you what she remembers most from what she has read thus far. She will tell the group how far she has read, and then share the most salient point. Make a comment or two, and then tell the class to resume reading from the point at which the respondent left off.

Again, wait a few minutes. This time, interrupt them by asking if they feel that an instructor has the right to change her mind. (If you are a woman, you can take adage-advantage by prefacing this question with another question: Ask them if they know what a woman's prerogative is. Most will have heard that a woman's prerogative is to change her mind. Then dramatically say, "That's right! I can change my mind! And I just have.") Tell them you've changed your mind and for this section, someone *not* wearing glasses will be called on.

Repeat the process of asking the second person how far she has read and what stands out in her mind from those pages. Comment. Allow a few more minutes of reading from the finish-point cited by the second respondent. Then call on someone either bespectacled or not to share the third point of interest.

Because they are not certain whom you will select for the third input, they are more likely to be ready and well-read.

Brainteaser: These mixed-up letters spell the names of towns and cities. Can you tell which is a town in England?

> RINBEL
> RETHISCEHC
> DADIMR
> MORE

Answer: It's Chichester. The others are Berlin, Madrid, and Rome.

5. Divide the material into sections.

Pre-read and decide how the material can be chunked—ideally to equal the same number of table groups. Then, when the class is underway and you get to the section of the book or handout that will be read, ask for five volunteers (assuming there are five table groups)—one from each of five groups. Once five hands go up, loan their owners your instructor's guide so they can mark off the five sections in their own manuals. Or have five sheets of paper ready, each telling the passage-boundaries for each of the five volunteers.

Then have them decide among themselves which of the five sections will be theirs. The volunteers also get to choose the group they'd like to lead for this assignment. They go to the group and tell the group members the section to be read. Group members read the material and prepare brief reports on it. If no one volunteers or not enough people do, simply assign five group leaders and continue with the plan.

Brainteaser: It is the concensus of opinion that their are three errers in this sentence. Can you find them? (Can you find more than three?)

Answer: Two you will spot readily. "Their" should be "there," and "errers" should be "errors." But "concensus" is also spelled wrong. It is also redundant or tautological to say "consensus of opinion," because a "consensus" really is a collection of opinions. And the statement that there are three errors is wrong, because there are actually five.

6. Let there be contrapuntal movement.

Begin by dividing the material to be read in half: men take the first half, women the second. Other options: Those under a certain age take the first half, and those equal to or above it, the second half; those who like football, the first half, and those who do not, the second half. Any division will work. Then assign the reading, telling them to select their three favorite points as they read. (In the meantime, post flipchart paper around the room—use one wall for the men and one for the women, or for whatever two divisions you have created.)

When it seems that most people have finished, hand a magic marker to one person. Ask her to record her favorite learning point from the three she selected. When she has finished, she will pass the pen to someone else who will record hers on the appropriate flipchart page.

After everyone has recorded, appoint a "duplicator" and give her a heavy magic marker. It will be her job to cross off duplicated points of information.

Finally, read both lists to the class, providing commentary as appropriate.

7. Assign reading for homework.

Not only will this assignment eliminate the tedium of classroom reading, it will also provide an excellent way to start the second day—by reviewing what occurred on the first.

When they return the next morning, divide the class into four teams. Group 1 (the homework readers) will meet with Group 2 (the recallers of yesterday's learning). These two groups will be responsible for correlating the homework reading assignment with what they remember learning the previous day. (Ideally, neither group will refer to their notes.)

Groups 3 and 4 will do the same, with the recallers integrating their ideas with the readers' ideas. Have spokespeople from groups 1 and 2 make reports. Then ask if the spokespeople from groups 3 and 4 have anything new to add. If not, move on.

Brainteaser: What number is missing?

16	28	58
37	49	?

Answer: 79. Subtract the numerator number from the denominator in each "fraction" and you'll get 21.

---

8. Allow choices based on your designation of what the material covers.

Read the material yourself first. Determine the general theme of each section. Ideally, the number of sections will match the number of table groups. Prepare a transparency to supplement your dialog, which will sound like this: "If you are interested in learning about Shakespeare's life, you'll read Section 1, pages 2–5. If you are more interested in learning about the era in which he lived, you'll read Section 2, pages 6–9. Some of you are distinctly interested in the plays that deal with royalty. You find those summarized in Section 3, pages 10–13 . . ."

(continued)

8. **Allow choices based on your designation of what the material covers.** *(concluded)*

Once they have decided which section they want to read, allow time for individual exploration and note-taking on their reading preferences. The second part of this assignment is to have all those who read Section 1 join together and discuss what they read. The other groups will do the same thing. (Reports are optional.)

Brainteaser: How many non-slang body parts, spelled with three letters only, can you name?

Answer: Here are just a few: arm, leg, toe, eye, and ear.

---

9. Have groups do the dividing and titling.

Ask the class to skim the material and to make gross divisions of the entire passage. Have participants choose which section interests them. Form groups based on designated interests. The groups are tasked not only with reading their self-assigned section, but also with deciding, as a group, what is the proper headline for the section they have read.

Brainteaser: How long will it take you to match these "b" words with their meanings?

1. badger		A.	To give and take; to toss about
2. baleful		B.	Harmful
3. banal		C.	Commonplace
4. bandy		D.	Evil or sinister
5. baneful		E.	Repartee
6. banter		F.	To deceive
7. baroque		G.	To irritate or tease
8. beguile		H.	Ornate, highly ornamental

Answers: 1. G 2. D 3. C 4. A 5. B 6. E 7. H 8. F

Brainteaser: What number belongs in the blank space?

        4   11   32   95   ___

Answer: 284. Each number is tripled and then has 1 subtracted from it.

10. Assign paragraphs in round-robin fashion.

In advance, number each paragraph in your copy of the material to be read. When class begins, move from person to person, telling each what they will read, paragraph by paragraph. If necessary, do a second and even a third round, depending on the length of the passage, until all the material has been assigned. (Be sure to proceed in an order you can remember, in case you need to repeat the assignments. In other words, don't jump around. Do sequential assignments. It may help to write the name of the assignee next to each paragraph as you assign it.) Give each person one (or more) paragraphs to read. Their job is to distill the essence of the paragraph into one sentence.

Allow time for them to read. Tell them if they finish ahead of the others, they should read as much of the passage as they can, to get a sense of the whole and not just their fragment of it.

Then call on each person to read her sentence in the proper sequential order. If possible, tape record the sentences so they can be typed later on (along with the names of their authors). In this way, you'll have a summary to which each person has contributed.

11. Provoke deep thinking.

Read the material yourself in advance of the class, and isolate the two points or sentences you feel are most valuable. Then say, "I've chosen two points." Identify their location, and allow time for participants to read them. Then ask, "Why do you think these were so important to me?"

Call on a few people for their opinions, and then discuss the passages.

Brainteaser: What do you think is the correct interpretation for this Italian proverb?

"He gives twice who gives quickly."

1. We tend to be more generous when our emotions are involved.
2. Stingy people don't give generously, as a rule.
3. Stingy people think long and hard before making a donation.
4. Charity does not depend on the amount of money people have.
5. You'll regret a quick decision regarding money.

Answer: 1.

12. Add variety to the two-point theme.

This exercise, like the preceding one, is easy in that you will have done the reading for them. (You will have isolated the three most important points from the passage.) Again, you will point out the two most significant points made in the reading passage. Then you will admit that there actually were *three* points. It is their task to skim the material and isolate the third significant point.

Form triads and have them share *their* most significant third-points. Encourage them to vote on the one point that is clearly more salient than the other two.

If any group has three members who have all made the same selection, ask them to explain the rationale behind their choice. Otherwise, call on groups at random to share the point that was ranked at the top by the members of that triad.

Brainteaser: Which person does not belong in this list?

Powell   Nelson   Schwarzkopf   Hannibal   Napoleon

Answer: Nelson. He is the only admiral among generals.

---

13. Have them create headlines.

This exercise will develop their ability to synthesize. It asks that they divide the material into four or five sections. (You will have determined that number in advance.) Then, they are to create a heading for each section, a heading that encapsulates the information contained in that section.

Brainteaser: Four students—Alex, Bob, Charlene, and Desiree—had this to say about a number they were shown:

Alex: It has two digits.   *Bob:* It goes into 150 evenly.
Charlene: It can be divided by 25.   *Desiree:* It is not 150.

One of the four students is mistaken about the number. Can you tell which one?

Answer: Desiree has the wrong information. If Alex were mistaken, the number would have three digits. If it did, either Bob or Charlene would have to be mistaken, because 150 would be the only three-digit number that would go evenly into 150. Therefore, Alex must be correct, because there is only one mistaken person.

If Bob had the wrong information, then the number does not go into 150. But then either Alex or Desiree must be mistaken, because the only two-digit numbers that can be divided by 25 all go evenly into 150. So, Bob must be giving accurate information.

If Charlene were wrong, then the number would be 150. But then Alex would also have to be wrong, because 150 has three digits, not two. And we know Alex is correct. So that leaves Desiree.

14. Call for outlines of the reading passage.

In a sense, participants will have to crawl around inside the author's head to learn the logical flow she must have envisioned for the selected passage. In this reverse-engineering exercise, they will wind up with the outline that the author probably *started* with as she planned her presentation of the material. Have them compare outlines.

Brainteaser: What number goes where the question mark now resides in the box?

3	4	5
552	772	?

Answer: 992. The lower numbers always end in 2. The first two digits in the lower number are obtained by adding two to the top number and repeating the result. Three is added to the next top number and the result is repeated. Continuing with the sequence of two and then three, the next number to be added to a top number and then repeated would be 4, giving us 99.

---

15. Do a mix 'n' match.

Review the material in advance, and write one sentence for each paragraph. Assign each one-sentence paragraph summary a letter, but not in sequential order. (In other words, if there were five paragraphs and five summaries for them, your first summary would not be labeled A, and your second would not be B. Assign random letters to the summaries—one out-of-order letter for each paragraph.)

Make copies of the labeled, one-sentence summaries—one for each group. Cut the sentences into strips and place them in envelopes—one summary-filled envelope for every group. Make sure to have your answers ready (the number of the paragraph and the random-letter assigned to it).

(continued)

15. **Do a mix 'n' match.** *(concluded)*

When the class assembles, give them the pages for the reading selection. Then have them sequentially number the paragraphs in the material. Next, distribute to each group one envelope filled with the summary-sentences. Have them decide which lettered summary-sentence goes with which numbered paragraph. The answers will not be 1A, 2B, 3C, but rather 1X, 2T, 3C, and 4R because when you lettered the summaries, you did not go in order.

Note: To lend a little spice to this basic read-the-material recipe, turn the exercise into a competition and award prizes to the first pair to successfully match the paragraphs and sentences.

---

16. **Ask them to develop a test.**

Ask each participant to work with one other person. They will divide the reading selection in half. As each person reads her half, she will write questions based on what she is reading. When each person has five questions (or ten, depending on the length of the passage), she is to stop— even if she has not finished reading her entire half.

These ten or twenty questions from the pairs will then be given to another pair, and that pair will give *their* questions to the first pair. The questions should be answered without the benefit of notes or books. The pairs then go over each other's answers.

Brainteaser: What combination of words best fits the blank spaces in this sentence?

"Despite _____ for her charitable contribution, the dowager still felt _____."

1. praise   weathered
2. desire   ignored
3. acknowledgement slighted

Answer: 3.

17. Have them report only new knowledge.

By now, participants should have learned to skim or even omit information with which they are already familiar. Ideally, they will focus only on new knowledge. Speed-readers do this. Poor readers . . . do . . . not. They . . . read . . . every . . . single . . . word.

Surprising stat: Four hundred small "structure" words constitute about 65% of all we see and hear. Researchers at Brown University examined a passage of 134,000 words. They found 20,172 mentions of the word "the," and 12,427 mentions of the word "of." This suggests that nearly 33,000 words out of about 134,000 (about 25%) can be skipped over. These small structure words don't contribute much to the meaning of the passage.

In this technique, their task is to report—individually or in small groups—only new knowledge that they gleaned from the selection they have read. As they glean, they should skip right over the small structure words like "the" and "of."

Brainteaser: What word best completes the sentence?

"He got the job not because of his outstanding computer skills, but because of his _____ skills."

1. singular
2. electronic
3. diversified
4. desktop

Answer: 3. diversified.

---

18. Have them choose a word or concept from the reading selection and report on it.

As you prepare for the class, write down important words or concepts (one per small sheet of paper) from the reading selection. Place the words in an envelope—you should try to have twice the number of words as participants in the class.

When the class convenes, have each person pull a word from the envelope. Allow about five minutes for them to find information relevant to their word from the reading passage. When they are ready, call on various participants to share their reports.

If time permits, do a second round with new words.

(continued)

18. **Have them choose a word or concept from the reading selection and report on it.** *(concluded)*

Brainteaser: Humorist Bennett Cerf, who died nearly 50 years ago, once wrote a small poem that has in it every letter of the alphabet except one. How quickly can you find the missing letter?

> A jovial swain should not complain
> Of any buxom fair,
> Who mocks his pain and thinks it gain
> To quiz his awkward air.

Answer: You probably didn't expect this: the letter "e" is missing!

---

19. **Request prioritized nuggets of information.**

Ask participants to read the material and to list at least five items of interest to them. After ten or fifteen minutes (more if the passage is extensive), ask them to stop and to prioritize the points they have made.

Then use the flipchart to record the results. Poll participants to learn what their number-one priority-points were. Tally these to learn the most notable of all.

Brainteaser: Here are more analogies. Remember, whatever relationship is evident in the first pair of words will also be evident in the correct answer.

1. numerous : polygon : :
   a) circumference : circle
   b) triangle: sides
   c) hypotenuse : triangle
   d) line: point
   e) four : square

2. log : voyage : :
   a) plan : action
   b) minutes : meeting
   c) route : trip
   d) itinerary : tour
   e) transcript : court

Answers: 1. e   2. b

20. Elicit "fire" analogies.

After participants have read the material, call on several to answer these questions:

> Based on what you read, what "lit your fire" or aroused some passion?
> Based on what you read, what "burned you up" or caused you to disagree?
> Based on what you read, what ignited an ember or gave you a related idea?
> Based on what you read, what preconceived notions were burned down?

Then on a "fire wall" (a wall with flipchart paper pasted to it), list some of the most revealing comments.

Brainteaser: Nearing retirement, an author realized that he had stopped writing after his seventh book was published. But before that, he was putting out one book every two years. He decided to add together all the years in which those books were published. The total was 13,804. How can you determine the years in which each of the seven books was published?

Answer: Think about how you get an average. In this case, the average is the same as the middle year or the year in which the fourth book was published. Thus, dividing the total by 7 gives you the middle year: 1972. Then, you go backwards every two years for the first three books (1970, 1968, 1966), and forward for the next three books (1974, 1976, 1978).

---

21. Have them create questions.

As they look at the reading selection for the first time, ask them to number the paragraphs. Then, assign each person one paragraph until the entire passage has been covered. (Note: If the passage is short and the class size is large, assign paragraphs to pairs.)

After participants have read their selections, ask them to develop a Jeopardy-like question, the answer to which is contained within the paragraph they read. (They should not indicate the number of their paragraph, but they can put their name on the paper that has their question.) Collect and distribute the questions. Participants will then look for the answer as they read the passage, not knowing which exact paragraph contains their answer.

The final step is to have them check back with the question-developer to be sure the right paragraph was selected in answer to the question they were given. They will also check to make sure they have the right answer to that question.

22. Have them express the concept in terms of sports, books, or television.

Once they've completed the passage, ask them to express the primary concept derived from it in terms of a sports team, a book, or a television program. For example, you could ask, "If what you just read were a television program, which channel would it be—Discovery, CNN, Lifetime, or some other? Explain your choice."

Brainteaser: Can you think of a four-letter word that can be combined with each of the following words to make four new words?

```
____TRAP
____PLACE
____BUG
____FLY
```

Answer: Fire.

---

23. Ask them to assign a numerical rating to each paragraph.

Particularly if the passage is short, have them give a numerical rating to each paragraph, based on how relevant or essential they found the information to be. Then have them average the paragraphs to determine the overall rating of the entire passage. Poll the class. If there are extreme differences, have the people who have widely differing ratings meet together to see if they can arrive at a compromise figure.

Brainteaser: These riddles require a kind of silly logic.

1. What two things that you can eat could you never eat for breakfast?
2. If a farmer raises wheat in dry weather, what does he raise in wet weather?
3. What would you call a person who did not have all ten of his fingers on one hand?
4. What is the best way to get down from a camel?
5. Why do Chinese men eat more rice than Japanese men?

Answers: 1. Lunch and supper 2. An umbrella 3. Normal 4. You cannot get down from a camel—you get it from a duck or a goose. 5. Because there are more of them.

24. Take an approach from psychology.

The term "autonomy of object" comes from the world of psychology. Basically, it asks that a problem be viewed as a person. That person is then placed in a specific time and place. The problem of school bullying, for example, could be viewed from the perspective of a sheriff in the Old West in the 1800's. Associations are then made with that era (posse, badges, corrals, and so on) until an idea for solving the problem emerges. The answer to the problem could be a roaming "posse" that reports anyone who is bullying other students.

An extension of this problem-solving approach can be employed by asking the class to choose a person, time, and place to represent the reading selection. A discussion based on associated elements can then be conducted.

Brainteaser: Carlos and Bonita, who are brother and sister, are part of a large family. He has as many brothers as he has sisters, but she has only half as many sisters as she has brothers. How many children are in this family?

Answer: Three girls and four boys are in this family. Carlos cannot count himself as his own brother, so we know that there is one more boy than girl: Carlos plus three boys and three girls. Bonita's sisters are one less than the total number of girls, because she wouldn't count herself as her own sister. So, she has two sisters. Consequently, the number of Bonita's brothers is twice as large as the number of her sisters. Since she has two times more brothers than sisters, she must have four brothers and two sisters, making it a total of seven children in the family.

---

25. Apply Zipf's Law.

This law maintains that individuals naturally tend to use the shortest expression of an idea or concept. "L.A." thus represents Los Angeles. Challenge participants to create an abbreviation or acronym that represents a truncated version of an important class concept. Reminder: An acronym is a pronounceable word in real use (such as "scuba," created from the initial letters of other words: "**s**elf-**c**ontained **u**nderwater **b**reathing **a**pparatus").

Example: "It Ad"

This phrase represents the four major feet in poetry scanning: Iambic, Trochaic, Anapestic, Dactyllic.

Brainteaser: Which will yield you the larger amount: six-dozen dozen, or half-a-dozen dozen?

Answer: Six-dozen dozen—the yield will be 12 times as much as half a dozen dozen.

Bonus:

Create one perfect summary of the material and several not-so-good summaries. Post them around the room. Divide the reading material into five sections. Then form five five-person groups. (Clearly, this exercise will work best in a class of 25 participants, but could be modified to work with four five-person teams, or five five-person teams, and others.) Have each group read one section of the material. (If you have 1, 2, 3, or 4 people left, ask them to read the whole passage on their own.)

Five new groups will then be formed. Each group will have one person who reads section 1, one person who reads section 2, one person who reads section 3, one person who reads section 4, and one person who reads the final section. Group members will discuss what they have learned, in an effort to get a firm grasp on the whole passage.

The new groups will then circulate around the room, reading the summaries you have prepared and selecting the one they think is best in terms of its completeness. The leftover 1, 2, 3, or 4 people will do the same. Reward the team or person who first identifies the best summary.

Brainteaser: The "V" words are next. Again, you will place a check mark next to the words you know. Be ready to defend what you think you know. The group with the largest number of defendable checkmarks will be declared the brainiest.

__ vacillate	__ vacuous	__ vagary	__ vainglorious
__ valor	__ vamp	__ variegated	__ venerate
__ veracious	__ verbatim	__ verbosity	__ verisimilitude
__ vernacular	__ vertiginous	__ vesicle	__ vespers
__ vested	__ vestibule	__ vexation	__ vicarious
__ vicissitude	__ vigilance	__ vilify	__ vintage
__ viperous	__ virago	__ virtuoso	__ virulent
__ viscera	__ viscid	__ vitiate	__ vituperation
__ vivacity	__ volatility	__ volition	__ voluptuous

Chapter 9

25 Ways to Choose Group Leaders

Chapter Overview

The common childhood fear of being the last person chosen to play on a baseball team can cloud an otherwise sunny schoolyard. The fearful and embarrassing memory, unfortunately, comes back whenever teams need to choose leaders. To prevent the most popular personality from being the automatic choice, you can choose among 25 different techniques presented here. They will help you find group leaders without anyone losing face.

To prevent the most vocal or dominant member from selecting himself for leadership, consider establishing guidelines for leader-selection. To escape the inevitable appointment of a woman because hers is the only handwriting that is legible, use one of these techniques to structure the selection.

1. Ask about longevity.

Ask participants to figure out who has been with the organization for the longest period of time. That person becomes the group recorder or team leader. If you teach in a school, have students determine whose family has lived in the area for the longest period of time. That person becomes the group leader. Such determinations also help in the participant-bonding process.

Brainteaser: This time, our proverb comes from Germany. It will require some interpretation on your part.

> "God gives food to the birds, but they must look for it."

1. God delights in playing pranks.
2. The race goes to the swiftest, and the food goes to the early bird.
3. We can survive and even thrive if we are willing to work.
4. Nature is the extension of a divine being.
5. Birds have good eyesight and so will survive.

Answer: 3.

2. Appoint on another "long" basis.

Have groups decide which person among them has the longest hair. That person becomes the group leader.

Brainteaser: Another antonym test. Allow yourself 30 seconds for each answer.

Remember, we are looking for words that mean the *opposite* of the word in capital letters.

1. PERIODIC
   a) temporary   b) beginning   c) future   d) constant   e) unforgiving

2. HACKNEYED
   a) fresh   b) trite   c) familiar   d) hard   e) weighty

3. REPULSION
   a) fear   b) attraction   c) illness   d) retreat   e) illumination

4. TAWDRY
   a) tarnished   b) illicit   c) early   d) victorious   e) elegant

5. EPHEMERAL
   a) powerful   b) religious   c) long-lasting   d) scholarly   e) feverish

Answers: 1. d 2. a 3. b 4. e 5. c

---

3. Alphabetize their names.

Then have the first person on the list serve as team spokesperson or leader. The next time such a position is needed, the second person on the list will serve (and so on).

Brainteaser: What number is missing from the empty pie slice?

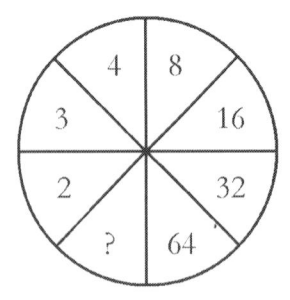

(Pie chart with slices: 4, 8, 3, 16, 2, 32, ?, 64)

Answer: 1. The numbers on the left are decreasing by 1 and the numbers on the right are doubling.

Chapter 9: 25 Ways to Choose Group Leaders

4. Celebrate and appoint a leader at the same time.

Have each table group find out which person in the group will have the next birthday. Ask those individuals, one from each table, to come to the front of the room. Lead a rousing round of "Happy Birthday," and then have those individuals return to their groups and serve as leaders.

Brainteaser: What mixed-up word in each group does not belong?

Group A
1. S N R U E
2. O O R D C T
3. N N H C C I I A E T
4. Y R R R L O D E L
5. T T S R I A

Group B
6. F F D D A I O L
7. L M T O A A E
8. S R I I
9. Y S N A P
10. L P T U I

Answers: 5. ARTIST (The other words are medical terms: NURSE, DOCTOR, TECHNICIAN, ORDERLY.) In the second group, the answer is 7. OATMEAL (The other words pertain to flowers: DAFFODIL, IRIS, PANSY, TULIP.)

---

5. Ask who needs the practice.

Have groups discuss amongst themselves the extent of their leadership experience. After a few moments, ask who has had the least experience. Ask those individuals if they are willing to serve as group leaders to gain the needed experience. If not, ask someone else in the group to serve. (Note: Most people will happily accept the opportunity to gain more leadership experience. However, you don't want to put anyone on the spot, so offer them a chance to decline without embarrassment.)

Brainteaser: Can you figure out the word that belongs inside the parentheses, using only #1 below as a prompt?

1. h a i r   (r a i n)   g r i n
2. f a c e   (_ _ _ _)   w a t c h
3. d a t e   (_ _ _ _)   c a t s

Answers: The inner words are formed by taking two letters from the word on the left: the first is the letter closest to the parenthesis, and the second skips a letter on the left. The last two letters of the missing word are taken from the last two letters of the word on the right. The words are 2. each and 3. eats.

129

6. Rotate the role.

Announce that there will be numerous reports given throughout the class. Then say that in the interest of fairness, everyone will be asked to serve as group leader or group spokesperson at least once. (To lessen the fears of the terminally shy, point out that they can decline the request if they wish.) Then simply have groups keep track of who has served in a leadership capacity.

Brainteaser: The two words that fit in each of the following blank spaces have the same number of letters, and are spelled alike (except for one vowel). For example, in the sentence, "After the ___ ___ me, I needed rabies shots." The answers are "b a t" and "b i t."

1. What was the vote for the uniform color of the basketball _ _ _ _? _ _ _ _.
2. The softball team _ _ _ _ _ _ _ _ year, but they are determined to win this year.
3. Because he was _ _ _ _, _ _ _ _-water exercise was good for him.
4. His favorite _ _ _ _? _ _ _ _!
5. To me, he seemed _ _ _ _: _ _ _ _ will tell, however.

Answers: 1. team, teal 2. lost, last 3. lame, lake 4. meal, meat 5. tame, time

---

7. Ask for a volunteer.

Instead of being straightforward and direct, be a little playful. Simply say, "I need a volunteer." If they ask, "Volunteer for *what?*" just repeat yourself: "I need a volunteer." When you finally get the volunteer (and even if you get *no* volunteers), lead a brief discussion praising those who volunteer when they are not certain of what is required of them. Such actions bespeak:

- Self-confidence

- A willingness to assist when others need help

- An awareness that if the task is to do something the person prefers not to do, he is assertive enough to withdraw his offer.

If you reward the first volunteer with a token prize, you are bound to get a volunteer from each table. If you still cannot find a volunteer, ask for two people to share the role. Then tell them what they have volunteered for: to serve as a group leader.

Brainteaser: S S M T W T ___

What letter goes in the blank?

Answer: "F" for the word "Friday." The letters represent words for the days of the week.

8. Give them a topic related to the course.

Then ask each person to write facts about subject. After two minutes, say "Stop!" Ask them to count the number of discrete facts they had. The person with the longest list at each table will then be asked to serve as group leader.

Brainteaser: There is considerable research that supports the correlation between a good vocabulary and success in life. How quickly can you match these words with their meanings?

1. cacophony
2. cajole
3. calamity
4. callow
5. capacious
6. capitulate
7. capricious
8. captious
9. careen

A. disaster
B. innocent, inexperienced
C. surrender
D. whimsical, flirty
E. critical
F. lack of harmony
G. sway from site to side
H. spacious
I. tease or coax

Answers: 1. F 2. I 3. A 4. B 5. H 6. C 7. D 8. E 9. G

9. Make an acronymic appointment.

Write the word "L-E-A-D" on the board or flipchart with the letters separated by a hyphen. Ask participants to work individually to create an acronymic, four-word sentence, using each letter of the word "l-e-a-d" as the first letter in the four words in their sentence. Ideally, the sentence will relate to the subject matter being studied.

Example for Language Arts: **L**inguists **e**vade **a**cerbic **d**ilettantes.

The first person in each group to create the sentence will serve as the group's leader.

Brainteaser: Attilius was a common soldier in Julius Caesar's army. He was born on the 256th day of 20 B.C. and died on the 24th day of 20 A.D. How old was he when he died?

Answer: 38. Now, you might be tempted to guess 39, with the soldier just a few months away from his 40th birthday, but there is no calendar year known as "0" coming between 1 B.C. and 1 A.D. Consequently, you cannot calculate his age the way you would by counting numbers.

10. Place a star on one set of materials per group.

Each group, then, will have in their set of handouts one packet that has a star on the back cover. Whoever receives the starred handout will serve as group leader.

Brainteaser: This is one of the more difficult I.Q.-test questions. You have to determine which combination of letters is out of place.

   A Z E E T R I U L O S
   O H E E L O R R U M A E L U S
   N I V O E R I N N I U R I S
   R E A L O P P O O S I L I L O O

Answer: Each of these lines contains the name of a god. The letters to the god's name are to be found only when a vowel that is not needed in the name precedes the letter. The third line contains the Roman goddess Venus's name, which does not belong with the other three Greek god names (Zeus, Hermes, Apollo).

---

11. Use a hiring technique.

There are companies that ask job applicants to write a full-page newspaper ad to convince the employer to hire the ad-writer. You can use this technique for selecting a group leader. Ask each person to write an anonymous ad explaining why he should be "hired" to serve as leader of the pack.

Group 1 and Group 2 will exchange their sets of ads. (All of Group 1's ads will go to Group 2, and vice versa.) The other groups will also exchange. Then the groups will decide which one ad reflects a person with a great deal of leadership experience OR a person with a minimal amount of leadership experience or ability. Without telling if they chose on the basis of most or least experience, Group 1 will show Group 2 the ad they chose. The writer of that ad will serve as a leader for Group 1 and will move to that group.

Then Group 2 will show to Group 1 the ad representing the person whom they would like to lead them. That person will move from Group 1 to serve as leader of Group 2. The other groups will select their leaders in the same way.

12. Distribute a list of leadership traits.

First, though, explain that there are a great many traits associated with leadership. No one possesses them all. Point out that several different lists will be distributed during the course of the class. Then ask the members of each group to anonymously determine which person in their group has the best match to the five traits listed in the first distributed list. Tally the decisions, and ask the person who most closely matches the first set of traits if he would be willing to serve as leader.

Later in the day, distribute a second list of five different traits to each group. Again, they will anonymously decide which person in the group seems to have most of *these* traits. No one person will serve more than once. (Note: Only do this two or three times. Otherwise, the last person left will have to serve, whether or not he possesses the traits. This will surely create the "last-person-chosen-for-the-baseball-team" effect, which has a serious and negative impact on morale.)

---

13. Identify those who have not served.

Ask those who have not yet had an opportunity to be a team leader if they'd like the chance to do so. For those who answer in the affirmative, write their names on separate sheets of paper. If you have more names than teams needing leaders, put the names in an envelope and have someone draw out the requisite number of leader-names.

Brainteaser: What do you think this next French proverb means?

"You cannot make the bed and save the sheet."

1) Try not to be greedy in life.
2) If you hold on to things for too long, they will deteriorate.
3) Sometimes in life you have to make a choice.
4) If you want your house to be neat, you have to do your housework.
5) Many people save time by making their bed only when company comes over.
6) You cannot have your cake and let the cook eat it.
7) If the house is too sloppy, hire a maid.
8) Men are as capable as women of doing household chores.

Answer: 3.

14. Do the usual: Appoint.

The old standby, simply having the instructor appoint the leader, is certainly an option. Put a little spin on your appointment: If you teach elementary or middle school students, lend splendor to the job. Have a cape or crown or wand available for the leader. If you work with older students or adults, give them a list of leadership quotes as a token of your appreciation. The quotations will extend their thinking about leadership. (Note: Check the Appendix. You'll find a list of leadership quotes to use as rewards for those you have chosen for the leadership role.)

Brainteaser: Can you think of a scenario that would apply to these identical twins? Kristine celebrates her birthday on one day and her older brother, Tom, celebrates his two days later.

Answer: Think of their mother going into labor as she crossed time zones. Let's say she went from Guam to Hawaii, and Tom was born on March 1. Shortly afterward, the mother crossed the International Date Line and delivered Kristine, the younger twin. In the crossing, the date would be February 28. In leap years, Kristine celebrates her birthday two days before the older twin.

15. Appoint co-leaders.

To reduce any anxiety about having to serve as a team leader, select two people to handle the job. They can do this sharing in any number of ways: They can split the tasks, they can split the time, they can switch back and forth, or each of them can work with their own half of the group.

Brainteaser: If $\frac{1}{2}$ cup of kale contains 80 calories and the same amount of corn contains 300 calories, how many cups of kale will it take to equal the same caloric content as $\frac{2}{3}$ cup of corn?

a) $\frac{2}{3}$ b) 1 and $\frac{1}{2}$
c) $\frac{5}{8}$ d) 2 and $\frac{1}{2}$
e) 3 f) $\frac{3}{4}$
g) 2 and $\frac{1}{3}$

Answer: d.

Brainteaser: Can you figure out the missing number?

3 11 4
2 12 5
4 ___ 6

Answer: 16. The middle number in each row is the sum of the first (left-hand) number in each row plus the right-hand number that has been doubled.

16. Assign roles.

The leadership function, with groups responsible for meeting-like tasks, can be split among five participants. Make the following appointments.

Leader. This person will determine the agenda, write it on the flipchart, and specify the amount of time required for each of the agenda items. It might increase productivity if the leader also writes the objective of the meeting at the top of the flipchart.

Scribe. This person will keep the notes and write on the flipchart as the group generates ideas.

Time monitor. This person, using the agenda time-allocations as a guide, will remind the group when it is time to move on to the next item.

Topic monitor. This person has the task of alerting the group when discussion strays off the topic.

Reporter. This person will make the report to the entire class, once the group has completed its project.

---

17. Enlist judges to help you choose.

Assuming you need a leader for a large-group project, have participants prepare a one-minute "speech" that attempts to sway others to select or *not* select them as leaders. Basically, they will argue that they should or should not serve as a leader. You and/or outside judges can decide who best stated his case. That person then becomes the leader. If he declines, he will appoint someone to serve in his stead.

Brainteaser: Determine which pair of words best fits in the blanks for each sentence.

1. It's true she expressed her _____, but deep down she was _____.
   a) appreciation, thankful
   b) emotion, apathetic
   c) gratitude, resentful
   d) faith, embittered
   e) interest, artistic

2. Whenever _____ is needed, I turn to _____ for ideas.
   a) money, athletes
   b) creativity, children
   c) hope, mysteries
   d) teamwork, music
   e) forgiveness, dictionaries

Answers: 1. c 2. b

18. Experiment: Have a leaderless group.

Try this at least once. Assign the task, and then simply have groups work on it. Circulate around the room to make sure everything is being done collectively and that no one person is making all the decisions or attempting to dominate the group.

Afterwards, lead a discussion regarding this "participative" or perhaps even "laissez-faire" style of management and ask participants how they like it, compared to the more "autocratic" situation in which a leader guides the group on their path toward an end product.

Brainteaser: Alaskan cruise-taker Julie Smith wrote the following haiku after seeing the Hubbard Glacier. Only one thing is wrong with it. Can you tell what that is?

> Inspiring colors
> Ice cracking, falling away
> And then, Arctic silence.

Answer: The last line has six syllables instead of five. (And, for your information, Ms. Smith did have five in the original.)

---

19. Have them make lists.

Form triads and ask them to list as many words as they can that start with the letter "l." The words must all pertain to leading a group. The person with the longest list will choose which person in their threesome serves as leader. (Of course, he can choose himself if he wants to.)

Note: Save the lists of words. They can be used in other assignments. To illustrate: As participants first come in, hand them the list of words. Ask them to select the one word that best describes them and to use it to introduce themselves.

Brainteaser: Here are five words. Find their antonyms in under three minutes.

1.	GILDED	a)	liberated	b)	culinary	c)	prepared	d)	dulled	e)	painted
2.	ITINERANT	a)	wrong	b)	happy	c)	permanent	d)	wise	e)	lost
3.	LEVITATE	a)	anchor	b)	yield	c)	lighten	d)	observe	e)	medicinal
4.	PALLID	a)	colorful	b)	dirty	c)	healthy	d)	politic	e)	weary
5.	DISCERN	a)	learn	b)	doubt	c)	specify	d)	cook	e)	attribute

Answers: 1. d 2. c 3. a 4. e 5. b

20. Divide and compare.

Divide the class in half. One half lists the attributes of leaders on flipchart paper. (Use a breakout room if it's available.) The other half, working individually, will list the leadership attributes they believe they each possess. The whole group then compares individual lists of attributes to the collective lists of leadership traits.

The individual whose personal list of attributes is most aligned with the collective list of traits will serve as the leader of a large-group or whole-class assignment.

Brainteaser: Which pair of words best fits in the blanks?

Ever the "pleaser," she _____ his decision without _____ his motives.

1. accepted, questioning
2. opposed, citing
3. refuted, knowing
4. acknowledged, acknowledging
5. decried, understanding

Answer: 1.

---

21. Have them vote on you as their leader.

If you are not easily wounded by the "I-wasn't-chosen" syndrome, offer the class two choices: They can either have you lead them, or they can vote to work on their own for a large-group or whole-class assignment. No matter what they choose, though, they will be expected to accomplish a specific goal within a specific time frame.

If they opt to work without your direction and then fail to meet their goal, they will be penalized in some way (an extra homework assignment, perhaps). However, if they *do* work without you and they accomplish the task within the allotted time, they will be allowed to leave class ten minutes early. (If this is not possible, offer an equally tempting reward.)

Brainteaser: Can you think of a word that is somehow connected to the other words in each line?

1. piano: door   point   player
2. left: rate   loan   account

Answers: 1. key   2. bank

22. Use world-famous leaders as exemplars.

Take five or ten minutes, as a whole class, to list admired world leaders, living or dead. Lead a discussion about the attributes/accomplishments of these leaders. Then have the groups vote: Who in their group most resembles one or more of these leaders (not in a physical sense, but in terms of attributes or actions)? That person will lead.

If they cannot reach consensus on who the leader will be, group members can look for a resemblance between one of their members and some other famous leader that does not have to do with a physical trait. (Using physical attributes such as big ears might embarrass participants.) Instead, the similarity could be something like this: "Fashion-conscious Queen Elizabeth wears matching hats, purse, and shoes, and so does Terri in our group. She's always perfectly attired.") Do this kind of comparison *only* if the group cannot make their decision on the basis of actual leadership traits.

Brainteaser: Here's a chance to be both a romantic and a detective. Determine what is wrong with the following description:

"The circumstances combined to create an amorous atmosphere: the passion in his eyes, the balmy breezes, the sight of a full moon rising in the midnight sky."

Answer: The full moon rises at sunset, not at midnight.

23. Prevent deep-vein thrombosis, and find a leader in the process.

It's important to take stretch breaks—not only to stimulate participants' mental energy, but also to prevent blood clots from forming when people sit too long. Have the group stand and form a circle. Then begin a beach ball toss as you quietly step out of the group.

After a minute or two, blow a whistle. The person holding the ball when the whistle is blown will be the leader of one group. If the assignment calls for more than one leader, repeat the process.

Brainteaser: Which mixed-up word does not belong with the others in the list?

1. O O L L T F A B
2. C C S R E O
3. N N T S E I
4. G G N N A E I R D

Answer: 4. Gardening. The others are sports: football, soccer, and tennis.

Chapter 9: 25 Ways to Choose Group Leaders

24. Have group members listen and decide.

Within a small group, have group members share their "bio's," focusing on the opportunities they have had to assume a leadership role. The person with the shortest list will be the leader.

Brainteaser: Do you possess pronoun prowess? If so, you should have a perfect score on this brainteaser: Which sentences contain a pronoun error?

1. I can't say with certainty, but the former committee head may have been her.
2. Between you and I, word has it that Nancy is resigning.
3. I predict the next general manager will be she.
4. We'd be behind schedule without Lundy and he.
5. It will no doubt be them who complain about the pay raises.
6. The one who raised all that money was him.
7. Mr. Brizend distributed the reports to we engineers.
8. In the past, the culprits have been them.
9. The boss sent out a memo about you and I and the volunteer work we've done.
10. For Secretary's Day, Mr. Allison bought a gift for Tami, Yolanda, and she.

Answer: The only correct sentence is number 3.

---

25. Develop their ability to "read" other people.

Group members will identify and then list the non-physical (and thus not readily apparent) attributes they believe you possess, the activities they would guess you engage in, the places you like to vacation in, and so on. Of course, because they have no way of knowing about your personal life, they can only employ their powers of best-guesstimating—powers that can be critical in a leader's career. Leaders who cannot pick up on the unspoken thoughts and feelings of their constituents don't usually serve for long.

Collect the lists. Without specifically identifying which items were on target, announce which group had the most accurate list. The members of that group (who seem to have the most finely honed people-radar) will then separate and serve as leaders for all the other groups.

Option: Demonstrate your own "reading" skills. Go up to each person and provide a one-word, non-obvious assessment of them or a best-guesstimate of some aspect of their life. Have them confirm your accuracy.

Brainteaser: When is a cook mean?

Answer: When he "whips" the cream and "beats" the eggs.

Chapter 10

25 Ways to Fill "Odd" Moments

Chapter Overview

They used to be called "sponge" activities: those fillers that can be used when you have a few minutes left before lunch, before breaks, or before dismissal, as well as *after* a large chunk of material has been covered, after a break when you need to transition back to the subject matter, or after a video has been shown. You can also use them when some of the students have finished working and others are sitting there waiting for them to finish. Call the faster workers together and do a sponge activity with them.

The word "sponge" is most appropriate, by the way, because the majority of these exercises can be expanded or contracted, depending on the amount of time you wish to allocate to them.

1. **Do an assessment.**

This assessment will test participants' knowledge of the subject matter at any point during the course: Following the presentation of a discrete concept or learning module, distribute small scraps of paper. Ask each participant to write one word on the paper that reflects their comprehension of the concept presented: "Little"; "Half"; or "Total." Have someone tally the results. If the results show that the majority understood only a little or a half of the material, assign one "Total" teacher to small groups of "Little" and "Half" participants. Have those who wrote "Total" teach the concept to one or two others.

The student assessment of their comprehension is also an assessment of your approach to that particular module. If the tally shows that fewer than one-third of the class have a total understanding of the concept, you should probably re-write the lesson plan.

Brainteaser: Which mixed-up word does not belong with the others?

1. E I A T L N C R
2. T T H G P S E A I
3. B M N T R O O E
4. I I O L N V

Answer: 2. Spaghetti. (The others are musical instruments: Clarinet, Trombone, and Violin.)

2. Have them walk in a curriculum-designer's shoes.

Ask participants this question: "If you were in charge of writing the curriculum for this class, what would your top emphasis be?" Tell them they can select a single concept or module, or provide a prioritized list of items. They can also make suggestions regarding the "flow" of the curriculum: Which concepts would they present first? Second? How much time would they spend on each? What would they omit? What would they include? And so on.

Collect their responses and lead a discussion as you review them.

Brainteaser: What number is missing in the center of the second circle?

```
       17                        24
  26  (35)  38            18   (?)  22
       82                        42
```

Answer: 26. You have to add the number at the top and bottom, and then subtract the numbers on the left and on the right.

---

3. Employ metaphoric assessments.

Ask participants: "How do you see yourself in relation to your understanding of the information presented thus far? Do you see yourself as a sword, a sponge, an eraser on a pencil, a paper clip, a sieve, a feather?" (Any number of objects will serve this assessment purpose.) Write the words on the flipchart as you mention them. Better yet, for visual excitement, have the actual objects available for viewing.

Ask several students to select one and then explain their selection.

Brainteaser: How quickly can you determine which word in each line does not belong there?

1. Mozart	Plato	Verdi	Bach	Souza
2. Bird	Magic	Mailman	Air	Piazza
3. Klimt	Rockwell	Frost	Moses	Modigliani
4. Dylan	Jones	Keyes	McCain	Nelson
5. Schumer	Kennedy	Adams	Truman	Carter

Answers: 1. Plato is the only non-musician. 2. Piazza is the only baseball player among basketball players. 3. Frost is the only poet among artists. 4. McCain is a politician among musicians. 5. Schumer is a senator among presidents.

Chapter 10: 25 Ways to Fill "Odd" Moments

4. **Utilize a musical comparison.**

   Use a flipchart to record the names of popular musicians and musical groups, going as far back as you/they can (include some musicians from the contemporary scene, as well). Then ask pairs or triads to select one name from the list in answer to this question: "How do you rate the course thus far, and why? Is it, for example, a Guy Lombardo big-band sound, or a ballad from Josh Groban? Tell us why you have selected what you did."

   Brainteaser: Consider these statements and then try to discern the pattern among them.

   1. Mariah had her fruit.
   2. Jerry had his apples.
   3. Maxine had her cider.
   4. Linda had her burger.

   Which of the following sentences comes next in the pattern?

   A. Susie had her spinach.
   B. Philip had his grape.
   C. Tonia had her pies.

   Answer: B. The pattern goes like this: When the name has six letters, the food has five. When the name has five letters, the food has six.

---

5. **Elicit ideas for applying knowledge.**

   You've probably heard it said that the man who does not read has no advantage over the man who cannot read. In a similar vein, the student who acquires knowledge and does not use it is no more advanced than the student who did not acquire the knowledge in the first place.

   This activity calls on students to probe and then declare their future intentions as far as the course-knowledge is concerned. Have them work in groups of five or six to share the ways they intend to apply knowledge in the future. Then have a spokesperson from each group share the ideas.

   When you call on the second spokesperson, have him note only those ideas not already mentioned. Tell the third and subsequent spokespeople the same thing. By eliminating duplicate ideas, you are more likely to maintain total-group interest. (Note: If you have a negative or hostile student, call on him last. Otherwise, he is likely to say something like, "I can't see any possible use for this in the future," and his statement might start a trend.)

500 Creative Classroom Techniques for Teachers and Trainers

6. Have them respond to a parent's or boss's question about what they have learned so far.

In an effort to have participants think beyond the confines of the classroom, have them contemplate this situation:

(For elementary/middle school students) "If your mother or father or grandparent asks you what you have learned so far, what will you say?"

(For corporate participants) "If your boss asks you what you have learned, what will you tell her?"

Don't hesitate to point out that education/training is not free. Someone is paying, directly or indirectly, for these participants to be in the classroom. The accountability factor acknowledges that they are responsible for learning and for *using* the learning. Questions like the ones above bring that accountability-awareness into sharper focus.

Brainteaser: What letter comes next in the series?

B E H K N ___

Answer: Q. Each letter is separated by two from the one that precedes it.

---

7. Have them write a "singles ad" to attract others to their school or firm.

A number of Hollywood movies use the singles ad as a pivotal plot point—*Sleepless in Seattle* or *Must Love Dogs*, to name a few. This will be your students' opportunity to write a singles-like ad. The ad is not designed to attract someone for dating purposes, however. Rather, the ad will be written to attract other students to the school or employees to the company.

Example: Serious computer company seeks meaningful relationship with someone who loves to keep busy.

Brainteaser: If four proofreaders can read 400 sheets of a manuscript in 4 hours, how long will it take eight proofreaders to read 800 sheets?

Answer: Four hours.

8. Distribute a sheet of animals from cartoons or a coloring book.

Ask participants to think about the animal with which they most identify, and why. For example, the person who selects a rooster might have done so because she is always concerned about time. Then have them work in pairs to discuss their selections and the rationale behind them.

After five minutes or so, ask for volunteers to relate their insights or ideas to the course being studied.

Brainteaser: How would you interpret this Hungarian proverb?

"If you kick one walnut in the sack, all the rest clatter."

1. It's wrong to take physical action against people, animals, or things.
2. Most people don't realize how noisy their actions are.
3. Actions speak louder than words.
4. It's impossible to do things in isolation.
5. The early bird gets the worm, because the world is quiet in the morning.

Answer: 4.

9. Stretch them to develop a course definition.

Infinity has been defined as one lawyer waiting for another to return her call. *Education* has been defined as a building with four walls and tomorrow inside. Use these and other interesting definitions as examples. Then challenge triads to come up with a one-sentence definition that describes the course or a course concept in a unique fashion.

Brainteaser: Why is "whale" out of place in this list? Select the most accurate response.

     herring   whale   shark   barracuda   cod

1. All the others are fresh-water fish.
2. All the others are fish.
3. All the others can be found in ponds.
4. All the others are edible.
5. All the others exist only in deep seas.
6. All the others are monosyllabic words.
7. All the others can be caught by fly fishermen.

Answer: 2. The whale is a mammal.

10. Have them write sentences with repeated key words.

Ask participants to take one word related to the course and use it as often as they can in one meaningful sentence.

Example: We communicated that communications cannot be communicated if one communicator is not listening to the other communicator.

Brainteaser: Can you find the correct analogy responses in only 30 seconds each?

1. MEN : ANTHROPOLOGY : :
    - a) events : history
    - b) animals : nature
    - c) teachers : school
    - d) operation : surgery

2. HOMONYM : : SOUND
    - a) homogeny : sound
    - b) antonym : person
    - c) synonym : meaning
    - d) eponym : event

Answers: 1. a   2. c

---

11. Teach vocabulary and a course concept at the same time.

Meander through your dictionary and pull out some interesting words. "Quidnunc," for example, is a gossip and "gourmand" is a person who engages in gastronomical excess. Buried in the list will be one word, new to them, that pertains to the course.

Triads will vote on the one word that most intrigues them. If any triad chooses the course-related word, applaud them in some fashion. Define each of the selected words, if time permits, and try to relate the words to the course. Above all else, though, expound upon the one course-related word.

Brainteaser: What letter is missing from the blank "pie-slice"?

Answer: E. The word is "elevator," spelled in a counter-clockwise sequence.

12. Skim the material covered, and give an impromptu vocabulary test.

The test need not be prepared in advance. Instead, when you have a few spare or odd moments that you want to turn into productive instructional time, skim the material that has been covered so far, and circle ten key words. As you slowly give each word to the class, have participants write down the definitions.

Then have them work in pairs to refine their definitions and combine them to come up with one definition both partners agree on. Call on ten pairs to share their definitions. Make calibrations if needed.

Brainteaser: Can you figure out the age of the woman named Jean?

Geraldine and Gerty are sisters. Jean is Geraldine's daughter and she is 12 years younger than her aunt.

Geraldine is twice as old as Jean.

Four years ago, though, Geraldine was the same age as Gerty is now. Also, four years ago Gerty was twice as old as her niece.

How old is Jean?

Answer: Geraldine is 32, Gerty is 28, and Jean is 16.

---

13. Play course-charades.

Write the key course concepts on cards—one per card. Divide the class in half, and have a student select one card. Without using words, she is to convey the word to her team using "Charades." Make note of the time it took for her team to guess the word—up to three minutes.

Then have a person from the other team select a word and attempt to convey that word to her team. Repeat the process, making sure that each team has had the same number of tries. The team with the lower number of minutes wins. (Note: Make sure the words are of equal difficulty. Otherwise, you will face charges of unfairness.)

Brainteaser: Will the fisherman survive, given these facts?

His boat is being pulled toward a waterfall at a speed of 9 miles per hour.

His boat is capable of moving at a speed of 16 mph.

The motor uses 5 gallons of gas each hour.

He has 16 gallons of gas left.

The first safe landing is 21 miles back up the river.

Answer: He'll make it because he's moving at 7 mph (16 minus 9). So, he can reach the landing in 3 hours. He will definitely have time to make it to the landing.

14. Use a continuum.

Draw a line and divide it into increments of one-year or ten-year segments (one-year segments if you are dealing with younger students). Tell participants that the segments represent each year of a grade in school (or decades of their life if the students are corporate employees). Ask them to write down one thing that stands out in their minds from each school year or decade.

Have triads exchange their memories for five to ten minutes. Then give them this assignment: "How might what you are learning now have improved one particular outcome from the outstanding memories you have of the one-year (or ten-year) segments?" Afterwards, lead a discussion that explores their realizations. Emphasize the importance of learning to their particular circumstances.

Brainteaser: Before you jump at the answer to this seemingly simple question, please think it through. At noon exactly, you enter a public building and hear the clock strike twelve times. You wonder aloud, "How many more times will the minute hand pass the hour hand before midnight tonight?"

Answer: 11. Remember that the hour hand is also advancing with each revolution as the minute hand passes it. To illustrate, the sixth revolution will occur when the hour hand is half-way between six and seven, not when it is at six, exactly. The tenth and final revolution occurs when the hour hand is almost touching the eleven. The hands do not pass again before they meet at midnight.

15. Use punch lines, phrases, and anecdotes.

In the 1920's, while discussing her decision to prohibit the teaching of foreign languages, Texas Governor Miriam "Ma" Ferguson picked up a Bible and famously declared, "If English was good enough for Jesus Christ, it's good enough for Texas!"

The foolishness of her comment underscores the importance of diversity training and of cultural awareness. It's embarrassing, and not just for governors, to be unaware of other times and other cultures.

Make a list of questions relevant to the course. For example, in a course on supervision, you might ask "What do subordinates expect from a supervisor?" Before distributing one to each group, elicit from class members punch lines, familiar phrases, and anecdotes of all sorts. (The list should contain about 30.) Then have participants select one item from the list and incorporate it into the response to their question.

Option: Take a significant phrase from the course and ask participants to predict how a famous sports or political figure might respond to the phrase.

16. Have them make their own learning profile.

Working with participants, list opposites in two columns on a flipchart. The opposites will be learning-related words. Then have participants create their own learning profile by selecting the words (from either column) that apply to them.

Examples:

Prefer to read	or	Listen
Work alone	or	Prefer to work with others
Take copious notes	or	File it in my head
Like to be guided to a conclusion	or	Prefer to reach it independently
Like complex problems	or	Like things laid out simply
Like to speak before a group	or	Prefer to remain quiet
Want just an outline	or	Prefer full details
Like to analyze	or	Depend on intuition
Enjoy being the leader	or	Prefer being a follower
Like competition and tests	or	Prefer not to be compared or assessed
Like take-home assignments	or	Prefer to finish in class
Enjoy seeing PowerPoint slides	or	Prefer a more spontaneous approach

---

17. Give them phobias.

Not real phobias, but phobia-related words. Distribute the list that follows. Then have them create a new word—a phobia that is related to some aspect of the course. For example, students without a firm grasp on how a verb can serve as a noun or adjective might suffer from "gerundophobia."

List of phobia words:

Aichmophobia = Fear of sharp instruments
Ailurophobia = Fear of cats
Anthrophobia = Fear of other people
Arachnephobia = Fear of spiders
Astraphobia = Fear of thunderstorms
Batrachophobia = Fear of frogs
Cynophobia = Fear of dogs
Erythrophobia = Fear of blushing

Helminthrophobia = Fear of worms
Ichthyophoibia = Fear of fish
Melisophobia = Fear of bees
Microphobia = Fear of germs
Nyctophobia = Fear of the dark
Ornithophobia = Fear of birds
Phobophobia = Fear of fear
Zoophobia = Fear of animals

(continued)

17. **Give them phobias.** *(concluded)*

   Option: Have token prizes available for the winners of two competitions:

   - Those who can master recall of the meaning of each word
   - Those who can master recall of the spelling of each word.

   Brainteaser: Can you figure out the phrase, word, name, or expression written in the box below?

   ```
   ┌─────────────────────────────────┐
   │                                 │
   │                                 │
   │         F A R E D C E           │
   │                                 │
   │                                 │
   └─────────────────────────────────┘
   ```

   Answer: Red in the face.

---

18. Use letters of the alphabet.

This is a fun exercise bound to push their creativity to the limit. On the flipchart, write the letters of the alphabet to help stimulate their thinking. Then elicit words or phrases related to those letters. Next, form pairs or triads to take one word or phrase from the list and relate it to the course.

Examples:

"A" list or playing your "A" game	L-shaped room	Generation X
Type A personality	The nth degree	X-ray
ABC's	S-curve	Theory Y
"B" schools	T-shirt	Y axis
D-Day	U-turn	Generation Y
E-mail	Theory X	Zero G's
I-beam	X axis	Z's (as in getting enough
"J" card	X factor	so you are not sleepy)

(continued)

18. **Use letters of the alphabet.** *(concluded)*

Brainteaser: Which letter of the alphabet belongs in the blank space?

A D A E A C A E A M A B A E A ___

Answer: R. In between the A's is the spelling for the month of December.

---

19. # Ask for famous-in-the-field bios.

Divide the class into groups of five or six. Then elicit from the whole class the names of people prominent in the field. Next, assign one name to each table group, and have them write down everything they know about that person.

Management examples: Peter Drucker, Fred Fieldler, Warren Bennis, W. Edwards Deming, Ken Blanchard, John Maxwell

Option: Hold a town forum. One person in the group will impersonate the famous person her group wrote about, and the other groups will address questions to the famous-person impersonator.

Brainteaser: What number is missing from the last sequence?

4	9	5	8
2	11	8	5
9	2	8	___

Answer: Three. Add the first two numbers in each line, subtract the third, and get the fourth.

---

20. # Elicit improvement ideas.

Some firms, as part of the hiring process, put applicants into groups, give them a time limit, and ask them to come up with as many ways as they can think of to improve a bathtub. Explore with the class what interviewers and potential employers can learn about applicants by using this technique.

Then give the same assignment to groups of five or six.

(continued)

20. Elicit improvement ideas. *(concluded)*

In the second stage of the assignment, give them the same amount of time, but ask for ways to improve the school or organization or class.

Brainteaser: Think about all the words you know that have a "ph" in them, such as "phone." The sound is almost always an "f" sound. Can you think of any words for which this is not true?

Answer: Those words that have one syllable ending in a "p" sound and the next beginning with an "h" sound, such as the words "upheaval" or "upholstery."

---

21. Ask them to create ground rules.

This exercise can be used at the beginning, middle, or end of the class. If used at the beginning, tell the class they will be expected to abide by the rules, such as "One person at a time speaks." "No side conversations while someone else is speaking." "No ridiculing of ideas."

If you give them this assignment in the middle of the program, say something akin to this: "We are halfway through the course. You've had opportunities to interact and have watched others interact. Based on what has transpired so far, what do you think we could do to make our learning experience even more productive?"

If you seek the ground rules at the end of the course, say that you would like participants, as "graduates," to prepare a list of ground rules that will assist future learners.

Brainteaser: What ordinary word in the English language contains all the vowels, including "y"?

Answer: Not only do the words "unquestionably," "facetiously," and "abstemiously" contain all the vowels, but the last one contains them all in their proper alphabetical order!

Brainteaser: How quickly can you unscramble these mixed-up words? (Clue: The first word is the category and the next three words are things that belong in the category.)

 R W L S O F E
 Y D S I A
 D R V A L N E E
 S T I U P L

Answer: flowers, daisy, lavender, tulips

22. Relate action verbs to the course.

Divide the class into groups of five or six. Give each group a key word (an action verb) related to the course. If you are teaching poetry, such a word might be "scan"; biology: "dissect"; supervision: "direct." Give one word to the leader of the group and ask her to tell her group what the word is.

Then instruct the entire class to close their eyes. Ask, "What do you see in your mind's eye when you hear your word? If your first thought is not course-related, choose a second thought or vision." Have them record their visions.

Ask the group leader to call on each person in her group and find out what thoughts or images came to mind as group members heard the word. Then call on the group leader to tell you the range of visions.

If there are wide gaps or discrepancies in people's comprehension of this word, you may need to re-teach it so that everyone is reading from the same metaphorical sheet of music.

Example for a Literature class: If someone in the "scan" group saw a pair of feet stepping on a sidewalk, that vision suggests comprehension or relevance, because scanning is the process of determining how many "feet" are in a line of poetry. But if all they "saw" was a grocery checkout line with a clerk scanning bar codes on products, that student probably did not grasp the meaning of the word in its poetic sense.

Brainteaser: This true story appeared recently in many newspapers. The incident took place in Connecticut. Can you figure out the circumstances?

> A man was watching television when he saw an advertisement offering a shirt to the first 100 viewers who phoned in. He called the number given, stated his size, and provided such relevant information as his name, address, and so on. He was assured that he would receive the shirt in a few days. He did. He also received notification that he had committed a federal crime and that there was a $2,000 penalty—even though his action was perfectly legal and the call was perfectly legal.

Answer: The ad could be seen only by those who were illegally tapping into cable circuits without paying for them. The whole thing was a trap.

23. Use an old standby from IQ tests.

This exercise will take some thinking on your part, but once you have your list, it can be used over and over. And, it's bound to sharpen your participants' wits in a fun way.

You'll often see a question on IQ tests that asks respondents to come up with one word that is related to three others. For example: Find the word that is related to these three words or phrases: "flower," "to the people," and "walk." The answer that relates to all three is the word "power": flower power, power to the people, and power walk. Compile a list of at least ten course-relevant items.

Shakespeare example:

        "Lear"   "of the road"   "fit for a . . ."

The answer is "king."

Brainteaser: The word "noon" means the same when spelled in reverse as it does when spelled the regular way. But a word like "time" becomes a *new* word when it is reversed: "emit." Can you think of any six-letter words that become different words when reversed?

Answers: Repaid/diaper, drawer/reward, spools/sloops

---

24. Develop one-minute teachers.

Ask for volunteers (or have every participant participate) to teach some aspect of the course in a one-minute lesson. Allow them time to develop their lesson plans and then to instruct the others on the topic.

If you use multiple volunteers, survey them before they start working to ensure that no two people are doing the same topic.

Brainteaser: From India, a proverb. What does it mean to you?

"A man who misses his chance and a monkey who misses his branch cannot be helped."

    a) Time waits for no man (or woman).
    b) There are numerous similarities between men and jungle creatures.
    c) Always have a back-up plan ready.
    d) Take advantage of opportunity.
    e) The sure things in life are often not so sure.

Answer: d.

Chapter 10: 25 Ways to Fill "Odd" Moments

25. Develop course-related brainteasers.

Take ten words that are related to the course, but not the ten that are obviously most important. Instead, use names of individuals who have contributed to the field or the name of a theory or a book. Write that word, clockwise or counter-clockwise, inside a circle of pie wedges. Then go back and remove one letter.

Award a token prize to the first person who figures out the word, but add a stipulation: she has to tell something about the word in order to claim her prize. Be sure not to start the word at the twelve-o'clock point, because this makes it too easy to figure out the answer. Go clockwise as often as you go counter-clockwise.

Example for History or Social Studies:

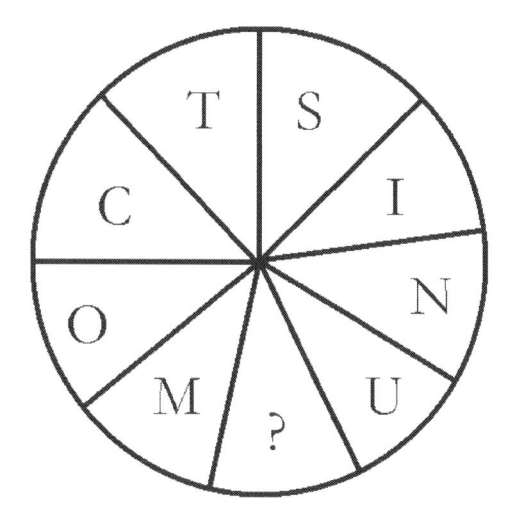

Answer: The missing "M" yields the word "communist."

Chapter 11

25 Ways to Deal with Reluctant Learners

Chapter Overview

If you haven't met a reluctant learner yet in your career, you will before you retire. He's the person who really doesn't want to be sitting before you, for any number of possible reasons. There are people who are bored by learning. There are people who would rather be at their jobs than be in a classroom. There are people who have problems with authority figures such as yourself. There are people who have personality problems in general. There are people who are having "bad hair days." The list could go on *ad nauseam,* but we'll stop here.

It's time for you to learn some new ways of dealing with such people.

1. Take him aside.

You don't want to antagonize or embarrass him, but you do want to make it clear what you will and will not tolerate. This private conversation should emphasize that you hope he will be involved in the class in a positive way. Explain that everyone benefits when participants are learning-receptive.

Brainteaser: So you think teachers are among the rare few who are good spellers? It ain't necessarily so! A test of 60 common words was given to 800 people with college degrees. Among them were a large number of teachers, editors, journalists, proofreaders, and people in the advertising industry. Not a single one of these verbally sophisticated individuals had a perfect score. Among the words most often misspelled are the ten that follow, written as they sound. Can you spell all ten words correctly?

1. brag-uh-doe'-C-O
2. rare'-uff-I
3. lick'-wuff-I
4. puh-vill'-yun
5. ver-mill'-yun
6. im-pah'-stir
7. mock'-uh-sun
8. roe-ko'-ko
9. soo'-per-seed
10. may'-uh-naze

Answers: 1. braggadocio 2. rarefy 3. liquefy 4. pavilion 5. vermilion 6. impostor 7. moccasin 8. rococo 9. supersede 10. mayonnaise

2. Pair him with an enthusiastic learner.

Our classroom decisions may appear to be guileless, but they are often deliberate. Under the guise of wanting to form partner-pairs for a given assignment, pair the reluctant learner with a truly enthusiastic learner, and hope that the osmosis process goes into effect.

Brainteaser: How fast can you match these "c" words on the left with their meanings on the right?

1. castigate
2. cataclysm
3. cathartic
4. catholic
5. caveat
6. celerity
7. celestial
8. celibacy
9. cerebral
10. chaff

A. heavenly
B. cleansing
C. to criticize
D. a vow made by priests
E. to tease; (as a noun) a worthless thing
F. having to do with the brain
G. sudden, often violent, change
H. warning
I. speed
J. universal

Answers: 1. C 2. G 3. B 4. J 5. H 6. I 7. A 8. D 9. F 10. E

---

3. Give a mini-lecture on the importance of learning.

Pretend to address the whole class, even though your lecture is being delivered for the benefit of one person—that reluctant learner. Talk about the importance of learning, the cost of such learning, the expectations others have for the application of the learning, and so on. Usually, some of this wisdom will sink in and cause at least a slight shift in the person's attitude.

Brainteaser: More analogies coming your way. Time yourself. Can you do this in a minute or less?

1. CHAR : SINGE : :
   a) smashed : crack
   b) ebb : flow
   c) dance : sway
   d) move : twirl
   e) emerge : project

2. TAUNT : TEMPER : :
   a) gasoline : fire
   b) gunpowder : shot
   c) crime : victim
   d) catalyst : revolution
   e) gamble : loss

Answers: 1. a   2. a

4. Give him the choice to leave.

If the person is truly disruptive, offer him (privately) the opportunity to leave. In a school setting, the departure will be for the principal's or the dean's office. In the corporate setting, the employee will have to explain to his boss why he walked out of class.

If he refuses the offer, explain that he will have to conform to your standards of acceptable classroom behavior. If he refuses to leave *and* refuses to conform, use your cell phone and call for outside assistance.

Brainteaser: Even your mathematically inclined friends may miss this. Ask them to write the largest number they can. They are allowed to use only two digits. They will probably write 99. What two numbers exceed this by far?

Answer: 9^9. Taking 9 to the 9th power brings you to nearly four hundred million: 387,420,489.

---

5. Ask him, and four others, what aspect of the course would be most appealing.

To avoid making it seem as if you are singling him out, ask the reluctant learner to sit with four or five positive-attitude students. Divide the remaining class members into groups of five or six. Then have the groups list the aspects of the course they would most like to study.

Circulate around the room, stopping for the longest time at or near the table at which the reluctant learner is seated. Gain information on what interests him and try to, whenever possible, emphasize that element.

Brainteaser: Imagine that you are seated at a table. Five others, Charlie, Sabina, Ervina, Frank, and Ida, are wondering where they should sit. You remember having seen a sheet that had the placements for each table. You recall that Charlie is not next to Sabina. Ervina is not next to Frank or Kristina. Kristina is not next to Ida. Neither is Ervina. Fred should sit on Ida's left. Can you seat them correctly?

Answer: The correct order for them is Ervina, Charlie, Ida, Frank, and Sabina.

6. Make your expectations clear from the outset.

If you sense that you have a reluctant learner in the class, begin the class in the usual way. Describe the course and explain the course objectives. Then segue into the ways participants can optimize the learning experience. Reveal your experience with reluctant learners in a non-obvious fashion. For example, "I know some of you would rather be at work than in class. Such a preference is a tribute to your conscientious nature. You care about your job and you want to keep current with your work responsibilities. I applaud that. However . . ."

You could then point out that an authority higher than either you or them has decided they should be present today. Explain that they are bound to learn at least one thing that will make their jobs and/or their lives easier. If you are a corporate trainer, suggest that they deserve time away from the job to think and to explore new ideas.

Brainteaser: Can you imagine a scenario in which a person could be seriously injured by tomatoes?

Answer: If the tomatoes are in cans, the injury could be severe.

7. Point out that your job is to teach.

And their job is to learn. It's as simple as that. Questions of personality, preferences, usefulness, relevance, and so on all fall by the wayside in light of these two roles: teacher and learner. Explain that you will do your best to teach, and you hope that they, in turn, will do their best to learn.

Brainteaser: Ready for more vocabulary matches? Can you finish the following in five minutes?

1. condole
2. condone
3. conducive
4. confidant
5. congeal
6. congenital
7. conglomerate
8. congruent
9. conjecture
10. conjure

A. to become solid from a liquid state
B. to employ magic
C. a trusted person
D. guess
E. to pardon
F. matched, in accord
G. born with
H. to offer sympathy
I. mixture, combination
J. leading to, receptive to

Answers: 1. H 2. E 3. J 4. C 5. A 6. G 7. I 8. F 9. D 10. B

8. Ask a direct question.

"What can I do to make this a better experience for you?" If you have a truly antagonistic individual in your class, you'd best *not* call on him, for you may not like the answer he is likely to give. Some participants you call on are bound to say that they like what they have seen so far. Some may offer positive ideas for alterations as well. When such comments are provided, they help you build group support.

When the difficult person realizes he is in the minority and that he is the only one who considers the class a waste of time, he often realizes that the problem is not you or the class, but rather himself. When you have extensive positive feedback presented by other participants and respond positively to suggestions for improvement, you are likely to have created an atmosphere in which the reluctant learner is less likely to express his reluctance.

Brainteaser: If it takes 30 minutes to plant six rows of flowers, how many hours will it take to plant 126 rows of flowers at the same rate?

a) 6.3 hours   b) $10\frac{1}{2}$ hours   c) 15 hours   d) 25 hours   e) 630 hours

Answer: b.

---

9. Try to determine what his problem is.

If you're an experienced instructor, you've probably encountered this type of participant before and have evolved some strategies for dealing with the problem of the problem student.

If, however, you are not experienced or if the student's behavior is well beyond anything you have ever encountered, get thee to a library. Or to the Internet. Read some books on psychology. You are certainly not the first person in the world to have faced a situation like the one that is confounding you now. Profit from the experiences of others.

Once you have a better understanding of the cause of the problem, you stand a better chance of solving it.

Brainteaser: Assume that there is a 45-minute period of free time at a playground. Thirty children want to participate in the game being played, but only ten can play at once. To be fair, how many minutes should each player play?

Answer: 15. Figure it out with fractions: $\frac{30}{45} = \frac{10}{x}$; $30x = 450$; $x = 15$.

10. Use the "Crawford Technique."

Professor C.C. Crawford of the University of Southern California originated a technique that has wide application for business and problem-solving situations. It can be modified to use with the reluctant learner as well.

Decide if you want to make the situation hypothetical ("What would you do if you had a colleague who was not as keen as you are to learn a new procedure?") or specific ("I've noticed that a few of you are not participating in this learning experience as fully as most others are.") Even though you have only noticed one reluctant learner, you don't want to identify him or make him stand out. It will only increase his sense of isolation and thus defiance. So, use the words "a few of you."

Whichever approach you take, the process will be the same. Ask the question. Then, distribute ten small sheets of paper to each person. Tell them they have ten minutes to come up with ten ideas—one per sheet of paper. Push them after they seem to have run out of ideas—often the best, truly innovative ideas come after all the obvious and easy responses have been recorded.

You can either collect and analyze the papers then or assess them when you have a quiet moment. Then make a report to the class about some of the things you are considering.

Option: It may be easier to ask a few people to leave the room and prepare a summary of the responses.

Brainteaser: This Scottish proverb endorses which value?

1. "Who heeds not a penny shall never have any."
   a) Love
   b) Family
   c) Thrift
   d) Religion

This Kenyan (Kikuyu tribe) proverb emphasizes which concept?

2. "Nobody cries who has not been pinched."
   a) Revenge
   b) Justice
   c) Pranks
   d) Cause-and-effect

Answers: 1. c   2. d

11. Give an imaginative assignment.

Sometimes we create a problem by acknowledging that we *have* a problem—even though the "problem" may only be in the initial stage of development. ("Reification" is the word that describes this process of making something concrete from something that is still abstract or amorphous.) Instead of acknowledging that there is a problem with a reluctant learner, deviate from the situation by giving an imaginative assignment.

Example: What would you ask the words that follow if you could meet them?
Knowledge. Learning. Study. Future. Survival. Standards. Employer expectations.

It doesn't always work, but *nothing* works all of the time. Use this take-his-mind-off-the-potential-conflict technique to try engaging the reluctant learner before he becomes too set in his negative ways.

Brainteaser: You have only a four-minute hourglass and a three-minute hourglass, yet you need to cook something for five minutes. How can you do this?

Answer: Start both timers together. When the three-minute timer ends, turn it over immediately until the four-minute timer ends. Then turn the three-minute timer over again to add the one minute needed to make five minutes.

---

12. Share a personal anecdote.

It's easier to win someone over when you acknowledge that you are not perfect. Acknowledge that you may have had feelings at one time similar to what he is feeling. Of course, you will be subtle in your selection of a story to share, one that shows the consequence of your having defied or been rude to an authority figure.

Option: Choose an anecdote related to what they probably are interested in (from the fields of sports or music or politics or the military, for example). Do your research and have ready a quote or a story about someone who was difficult or reluctant (who later regretted his behavior).

Brainteaser: An inexperienced chef needs to make a large quantity of soup. Unfortunately, his kitchen is not well stocked, and he can only find an eight-cup and a five-cup measuring container. He needs two cups of water. How can he use the two containers he has to get what he needs?

Answer: He begins by filling the five-cup container and pours it into the eight-cup container. Then he fills it again and pours the water into the eight-cup container. When it is full, he will have two cups left in the five-cup container.

13. Appoint him as leader.

Sometimes pretending that a reluctant learner is not a challenge for you makes this individual feel that his efforts to repel your teaching attempts are futile. I've often had success by complimenting the individual (sincerely) on a special talent or by appointing him leader—just to show there is no animosity on the instructor's part.

The reluctant-learner-turned-leader will usually become so engrossed in the task he is heading that he will forget about his defiant act. This is just one more tool to add to your kit.

Brainteaser: Can you arrange the numbers from 1 to 9 in the squares below (one per square) so that you will get 15 when you add the numbers horizontally, vertically, and diagonally?

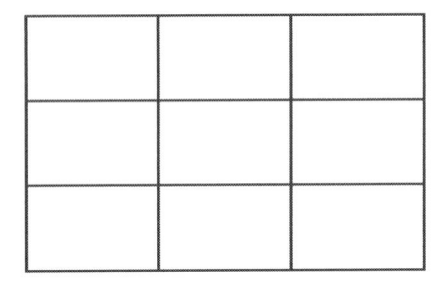

Answer: Top row: 4, 9, 2; middle row: 3, 5, 7; bottom row: 8, 1, 6. Note: Other configurations are possible, but not other numbers.

---

14. Share some research.

More than a decade ago, an article in the June, 1994 issue of *Management Review* reported the opinions of 350 executives regarding the success factors associated with organizational change. Chief among the responses were:

- a clear vision
- demonstration of senior support
- a measurable target
- a do-able program
- belief that the improvement is worthwhile, and
- empowered employees.

It doesn't matter if your reluctant learner is a high school senior or a senior manager, you can still share this research. Then ask (preferably in a one-on-one meeting with the reluctant learner), "Which one of these success-factors would be most likely to change your attitude to a more receptive one?" Explore with him ways you can use that factor to create a more beneficial experience for both of you.

Chapter 11: 25 Ways to Deal with Reluctant Learners

15. Have him hold up signs.

In advance of the class, cut out a six-inch red circle, a six-inch green circle, and a six-inch yellow circle for each member of the class. Glue each circle on to a Popsicle stick and distribute the three different circles to each participant.

Then explain that you like a classroom in which control is shared. Therefore, you are giving them the silent opportunity to tell you when you should stop (red) because they are lost; when you should proceed slowly because you are beginning to lose some of them (yellow); and when you should keep going (green).

Sometimes, the reluctant learner is merely ensnared in a self-created power struggle with you. This simple strategy may help him realize that he has some power, too, and thus need not struggle quite so much with you.

Brainteaser: What fraction of 4 equals $\frac{1}{2}$?

a) $\frac{1}{10}$ b. $\frac{1}{8}$ c) $\frac{1}{4}$ d) $\frac{1}{2}$ e) $\frac{2}{3}$

Answer: b.

Brainteaser: Can you use the numbers 1, 2, 3, 4, 5, 6, 7, 8, 9 in such a way that the numbers on each of the three sides of this triangle add up to 20?

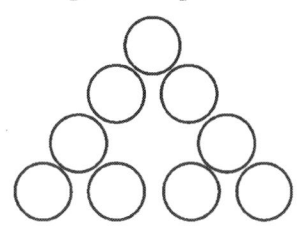

Answer:
```
        1
      8   3
     6     7
    5 2   4 9
```

---

16. Use the K-I-N-D approach.

On occasion, you'll find (or create) an acronymic tool to help you overcome resistance. Rather than rely on spontaneous and perhaps intuitive reactions to a difficult situation, you can use a tool such as the K-I-N-D approach.

While the rest of the class is busily engaged in an assignment (preferably a group assignment so that the noise level will help cover your one-on-one talk), ask the reluctant learner if you can talk to him for a minute or so.

(continued)

16. Use the K-I-N-D approach. *(concluded)*

K (Kindness)

Begin by stating something positive you know about him. For example, "Your fourth-grade teacher (or your supervisor) tells me you have a real talent for numbers."

I (Intuition)

Try to learn what is bothering him. Make a statement such as "It seems you are not enjoying this class as much as the others are. I don't think it's because of something I said or did, but if so, please tell me. If I have done something wrong or offensive, I will apologize. What I think is really going on, though, is that you're dissatisfied because you'd rather be working with numbers than learning grammar rules. Am I correct?"

N (Negotiation)

Acknowledge that there is some strain between you, and then express your wish/intent to have it eliminated. Make a proposal: "I certainly cannot teach math, but I will try to show why command of the English language is important to mathematicians and economists and computer operators. I'll do this whenever I can. In return, would you be willing to refrain from making snide remarks under your breath about the usefulness of this course? Yes, I've heard them and they create an awkward atmosphere in the room. Can we agree we'll both make an effort?" (If he does agree, be sure to shake hands. This symbolic gesture helps ensure he will keep his word.)

D (Deal)

Keep your end of the deal by doing what you said you would. In the preceding example, you could point out that mathematicians frequently present white papers to their colleagues. Look directly at the reluctant learner each time you demonstrate that you are keeping your promise. On occasion, thank him as well for keeping up his end of the bargain.

---

17. Confer with colleagues.

Even if you are near retirement with forty years of experience behind you, you can increase that experience 500 percent, just by asking four other near-retirees for their help. They may already be familiar with the individual who is causing some difficulty in your class and know some methods that work, or have had similar students in the past and would be willing to share with you the strategies that worked for them.

(continued)

17. **Confer with colleagues.** *(concluded)*

Brainteaser: At first glance, the pair of words in each line seem to have nothing in common. However, if you take one letter from one of the words and put it into the other word, you will get two new words that are synonyms for each other.

Example: For tar and ripe: Take the "e" from "ripe," leaving you with "rip." Put that "e" into "tar" and you get "tear," a synonym for "rip."

1. d i e d   a n t e
2. w h i l e d   s p u r n

Answers: 1. The "n" from "ante" leaves "ate" and turns "died" into "dined." 2. The "p" from "spurn" leaves "spun" and turns "whiled" into "whirled." "Ate" and "dined" are synonyms and "spun" and "whirled" are synonyms.

---

18. **Invite someone important to the class.**

An individual who exhibits less-than-gracious behavior in one situation can suddenly be transformed when that situation has a new arrival placed in it. Consider inviting someone for whom the individual probably has respect to observe the class—if only for a half-hour. That person could be a coach or the principal or a parent. In a corporate setting, the person could be the head of Human Resources or even the reluctant learner's boss.

When the reluctant learner sees the person you've invited, he will probably begin to act less reluctant. It's altogether possible that he will be on a behavioral roll and will continue in the new role even after the outsider leaves. Remember Shakespeare's exhortation to "laugh me out of myself"? Just as we can talk or laugh ourselves into a better mood, so can the reluctant learner change his attitude.

Brainteaser: More "move-one-letter-into-the-other-word" exercises like the one in the preceding Brainteaser.

1. g r o v e   r o u t
2. c u r t   c a v e
3. p e s t   c a r e s

Answers: 1. The "o" from "rout," added to "grove," gives you "groove." 2. The "r" from "curt" turns "cave" into "carve." 3. The "s" from "pest" turns "cares" into "caress."

19. Leave a funny card or note.

Scour your local Hallmark store. Try to find an amusing card that asks for cooperation without seeming obsequious. You can leave it, unsigned, at the person's seat or put it in the middle of materials you hand to him. He will no doubt get the message. If he doesn't, consider writing your name on a second card.

Option: Consider buying one card for each group. Choose a special card for the group of which the reluctant learner is part. The card will really be given with him in mind.

Brainteaser: Here's our final set of "move-one-letter" words.

1. salve   savage
2. shred   ban
3. our   start
4. flat   pump
5. lopes   shills

Answers: 1. The "l" from "salve" turns "savage" into "salvage." 2. The "r" from "shred" turns "ban" into "barn." 3. The "s" from "start" turns "our" into "sour." 4. The "l" from "flat" turns "pump" into "plump." 5. The "s" from "shills" turns "lopes" into "slopes."

Brainteaser: Susan is 15 years old. She is 3 times as old as her sister Linda. How many years must pass before Susan is twice as old as Linda?

Answer: 5. In five years, Susan will be 20 and Linda will be 10. Susan will be twice as old as her sister at that point.

---

20. Place relevant quotes around the room.

They need not pertain to the subject matter itself, but rather to education in general (or receptivity to learning or cooperation, et cetera). Call on various people to interpret the quotes. Call on the reluctant learner to interpret at least one dealing with or alluding to negativity, such as this by General Colin Powell: "Optimism is a force-multiplier."

There's no guarantee the quotation will alter his behavior, but you will at least be giving him something to think about.

(continued)

Chapter 11: 25 Ways to Deal with Reluctant Learners

20. **Place relevant quotes around the room.** *(concluded)*

Brainteaser: Given the example in the first line, what configuration completes the second line?

Answer: ○○

---

21. # Ask about his easiest learning modality.

Again, in a private conversation, ask the difficult learner how he learns best or most easily—orally, tactically, or visually. Ask what kinds of learning experiences he most enjoys. Then briefly explain your teaching philosophy: to make the learning experience as positive as possible for every single student. Acknowledge that his feedback will help you structure the delivery of the material. And it will help him to learn more easily. Incorporate his answers in your subsequent presentations. Often, the mere expression of genuine concern is sufficient to overcome attitudinal barriers. So that he does not feel singled out, ask a few others the same question.

Brainteaser: LONG   BLOOD   GUARD

Which of the following words goes with these three words? (All four will share a common word.)

        bird   time   fox   leaf   house

Answer: "Time." All four words form a new term when the word "life" is added to them.

169

500 Creative Classroom Techniques for Teachers and Trainers

22. Observe him carefully.

From the moment you first realize you have a reluctant learner on your hands, you'll have to engage in detecting. Notice to whom and to what he responds best. Then structure subsequent assignments to employ those individuals and activities.

If you can get out of his way, so to speak, he may forget to give you a hard time. Often, the difficult behavior is simply an act or a plea for attention. Involvement eliminates the need for game-playing on both sides.

Brainteaser: Which of the following words does not belong in the list?

A. I I E A A H H L L P P D
B. T T S E E L A
C. T T O A A W
D. F F B O A L U
E. Q Q B E E U U U R L A
F. O E A T K P

Answer: C. Ottawa. The only city not in the United States (Philadelphia, Seattle, Albuquerque, and Topeka are the other words).

---

23. Hand out classroom dollars.

Many learners are stimulated by the prospect of getting something free. If you are willing to spend a few dollars on pieces of fruit, candy bars, books, or dollar-store goodies, you may be able to get the reluctant learner to join your academic plans.

Have him work in a group, as he is probably not prone to volunteering answers on his own. Every time a group gets a correct answer or finishes first, award computer-generated dollars to the members of that group. At the end of the class, the group that has earned the most can spend their dollars on the appropriately priced gifts you will array in the front of the room. Such an incentive doesn't work with everyone, but it seems to work with *almost* everyone.

Brainteaser: AMERICA'S   BOARD   CAKE

Which of the following words goes with these three words?

clock   tea   hour   book   life

Answer: "tea." All four words form a new term when the word "cup" is added to them.

Chapter 11: 25 Ways to Deal with Reluctant Learners

24. Switch activities every 15 minutes.

As you'll no doubt remember from your own college days, the worst professors were those who droned on . . . for hours. Usually, they were the most degree'd, and yet they were also the most boring.

If you switch activities every 15 minutes, you are more likely to capture the interest of the reluctant learner. Straight lecture, non-stop, is an invitation to mental fatigue. Give *mini*-lectures followed by hands-on activities all day long.

Brainteaser: How quickly can you find the meanings of these words?

1.	Consecrate	A.	To tighten
2.	Consign	B.	Next to
3.	Constrain	C.	To complete
4.	Constrict	D.	Quarrelsome
5.	Consummate	E.	To dedicate
6.	Contentious	F.	To hand over
7.	Contiguous	G.	To hold back

Answers: 1. E   2. F   3. G   4. A   5. C   6. D   7. B

---

25. Give him a chance to prove himself.

There's a .001% chance that this suggestion may not be worth the risk, but the chances are in your favor—clearly in your favor. Privately tell the reluctant learner that if he can prove he already knows what you are going to teach, you will get official permission for him to leave the room. Of course, it will be very difficult for him to prove that he knows everything you have in store for the class. When and if he fails to answer your questions regarding the curricular agenda, then *you* will have proof that you can teach him something new.

On that basis, he is expected to remain and to absorb as much as he can.

Brainteaser: Which of the four lower-case words on the second line goes with the three upper-case words in the first line?

1. TREE   ARREST   GREEN
   recreation   plant   pool   silk

2. BIG   MARK   STREET
   law   money   fidelity   personality

Answers: 1. "Plant." All four words form a new term when the word "house" is added to them. House plant in line 2 leads to tree house, house arrest, and greenhouse in line 1.   2. "Money." All four words form a new term when the word "easy" is added to them. Easy money in line 2 leads to Big Easy, easy mark, and Easy Street in line 1.

Chapter 12

25 Ways to Make the Subject Matter Relevant

Chapter Overview

You know the relevance of your subject matter to the real world. Chances are, participants don't. To optimize the learning experience—i.e., to help ensure that they will actually *use* what they have learned—it's your job to show how the subject matter can be applied.

There are any number of ways you can do this. Twenty-five of them are listed in this chapter. The more reinforcement you can provide, via these relevancies, the greater the likelihood that students will fully participate in the exchange of ideas.

1. Find newspaper articles.

Grammar is not an especially popular subject, yet I'd rather teach it than any of the other 33 topics listed on my course-description list. To make it relevant, I've collected a number of newspaper articles that show what can happen as a result of grammatical errors, such as these examples:

- One U.S. insurance company had to pay $7 million because of a typo.
- A couple received a refund check from the IRS that was 100 times greater than it should have been— and they got to keep it!
- A woman was released from prison because of a misplaced comma.

Sometimes the articles reveal horrifying mistakes. At Ground Zero in New York City, for example, a new Freedom Tower will be built to honor the lives of the 3,000 people who died there. Its completion date is the end of 2008. The cornerstone has already been laid; this 20-ton slab of granite has only one sentence—a sentence that contains TWO grammatical errors.

No matter what subject you teach, if you are willing to scour the newspapers, you will find comparable examples. Keep files on the articles you find that will lend another voice to your one-person chorus—a voice that also insists, "Pay attention. This is important."

Note: The text engraved on the cornerstone mentioned above: "To honor and remember those who lost their lives on September 11, 2001 and as a tribute to the enduring spirit of freedom."

2. Have table groups do "brain dumps."

Divide the class into groups of five or six. Ask them to prepare a collective list. It might be a list of all the facts they know about the subject, but it could also be a list of ways they have used the subject matter in the past, or their projections on how the material might be used in the future.

Sometimes these peer-generated ideas carry greater weight than instructor-generated emphases.

Brainteaser: Which of the following words goes with these three?

1. DAYS   MAD   BIRD
   recreation   plant   hot   silk

2. STATION   WALL   FIGHTER
   fence   hoax   radio   under

3. INCH   GLOW   EARTH
   hole   cluster   vegetable   cast

Answers: 1. "hot." All four words form a new term when the word "dog" is added to them.   2. "under." All four words form a new term when the word "fire" is added to them.   3. "hole." All four words form a new term when the word "worm" is added to them.

---

3. Lead a discussion.

Based on your experience, your research, and your thinking about the subject matter, record some of your most salient points before the class convenes. Then convert the points into questions. Use them to lead a fact-laden discussion that stresses the importance of the material you are presenting.

Example for a session on listening:

1) When you talk with people, do you watch their facial expressions?
2) Do your expressions show sincere interest?
3) Do you maintain eye contact throughout an exchange?
   (A significant other and I were once discussing the future of our relationship at halftime during a Rams game. Yes, that's right. At halftime. Alas, the Ram-ettes were out there, doing their eye-popping thing. Few men, I suspect, are able to maintain eye contact with the person they're speaking with when cheerleaders are on the field.)
4) Do you give feedback to show you're interested? (How?)
5) Do you deliberately avoid interrupting others as they speak?

(continued)

3. **Lead a discussion.** *(concluded)*

   6) Do you maintain a comfortable distance from the other person?
   7) Do you paraphrase to check your understanding?
      (A building manager once called the police about a bum in the lobby of her building. They sent the bomb squad.)
   8) Do you inquire about the feeling behind the words? Do you listen empathically?
      (My sister was once hit by a car. When I tell the story to students, I never mention the word "guilt"—guilt that I feel to this day because I was the one who encouraged her to cross the street. Empathetic listeners "hear" it, nonetheless. Just as it's possible to read between the lines, it's also possible to "listen" between the lines.)
   9) Do you try not to finish sentences for other people?
   10) Do you show respect for the opinions of others who disagree with your viewpoints?

   Brainteaser: Examine this sequence:

   A ☐   Z ◯   E ☐   V ◯

   Which of these will come next?

   1. W ◯   2. I ☐
   3. K ☐   4. L ◯

   Answer: 2. The sequence alternates shapes and goes from the front to the back of the alphabet, skipping three letters in between each time.

---

4. **Invite a guest speaker.**

   No matter the age of your participants, they'll enjoy seeing a new face, hearing a new voice, and listening to some new viewpoints regarding the relevance of the subject matter they are studying. When I teach career development, interviewing, and think-on-your-feet classes, I invite the head of an employment agency or the head of Human Resources in to discuss what employers are looking for.

   Caution: It's a good idea, if the guest doesn't mind, to review what she will be saying, just to be sure it doesn't conflict with what you have already told your students.

   (continued)

4. **Invite a guest speaker.** *(concluded)*

Brainteaser: Complete this sentence by choosing one word for the four blanks in the saying that follows. You'll find the correct words scattered among the words in lines 1–4 below. _____ "a root is a flower that disdains fame," then a _____ must be a celebrity _____, to use the _____.

1. When	There's	If	Admitting
2. bud	blossom	stem	leaf
3. disguise	star	wannabe	entertainer
4. comparison	metaphor	parallel	vernacular

Answers: 1. If 2. bud 3. wannabe 4. vernacular

---

5. Find fascinating factoids.

I have a whole box labeled "Miscellaneous." In it are files and files of intriguing facts. When I need to spice up a lecture or a book chapter, I paw through the box and find those that are relevant. Because they are, they will lend sparkle to the subject matter at hand.

Example from a recent book for salespeople:

Robert Montgomery, author of *Get High on Yourself*, maintains that every product has a story, and if it doesn't, it has no right to exist. "Salesmanship," he says, "is telling that story." If you're not intimately familiar with *your* product's story, learn as much as you can, as soon as you can.

Brainteaser: Surgery to remove a lump is called a "lumpectomy." To remove your tonsils, a "tonsillectomy." To take out your appendix, an "appendectomy." What is the word for the removal of growths from your head?

Answer: A haircut.

Brainteaser: Not synonyms but antonyms are what you need for each of the five words below. Note: Each answer must begin with the letter "s"

A. sharp
B. silly
C. surplus
D. scary
E. seated

Answers: A. smooth B. serious C. scarcity D. soothing E. standing

Chapter 12: 25 Ways to Make the Subject Matter Relevant

6. Reflect on your own student-experiences.

You've probably had at least sixteen years of schooling. Some of your instructors from some of those years no doubt stand out in your mind. It's altogether possible they stand out because they were able to share their fascination with the subject—even if you weren't especially interested in it to begin with.

Try to recall exactly what those instructors *did* to bring relevance to their course. (It will help to keep an ongoing list of your recollections.) Then consciously work to adopt and adapt their practices to your own instructional situation.

Brainteaser: Tell which two words in each group are the most alike.

1. dapper	vulgar	fortress	convex	neat
2. chivalrous	gallant	historical	whimsical	trim
3. ill	feisty	decrepit	chide	rebuke
4. poor	covetous	hidden	greedy	strong
5. artificial	corpulent	attractive	fat	irregular
6. poised	original	social	convivial	criminal

Answers: 1. dapper, neat 2. chivalrous, gallant 3. chide, rebuke 4. covetous, greedy 5. corpulent, fat 6. convivial, social

---

7. Have them make a five-year projection.

Pass out paper and have each person write where she sees herself five years from now. This can be done anonymously, but she should place an assigned number on the page for later identification. Then collect the papers. Distribute them so no one has the paper she originally wrote. (Have the second person, the one who has received the paper, write her number on the paper.) In this second stage, participants will comment on the five-year projection by telling how the current course can facilitate that future experience.

Collect the papers once again and distribute them. (Say to the third recipient, "You're not number 1 or 13, are you?" If not, you will know they have not seen the paper before.) Then have small groups share what's on the papers they have received. Have them discuss the comments.

Brainteaser: The maid in a resort hotel has taken four pillows from four different rooms and placed a handwritten a note for each guest on each pillow. If she attaches the notes at random, each to a different pillow, what is the probability that exactly three of the notes will wind up on the pillows of the people from whose rooms the pillows were taken?

Answer: Zero. If exactly three were matched, then the fourth would be matched as well.

8. Have them imagine themselves as award recipients.

Ask participants to imagine that they have won an award, such as "Outstanding Corporate Citizen" or "School Scholar." Their task now is to write an acceptance speech. In it, they must tell how the knowledge they are acquiring in this class helped them become what they are.

Brainteaser: Complete this sentence by choosing one word from each of the five sets that follow it, in consecutive order, so that the sentence makes sense.

_____ an amusing _____ of his own often _____ behavior, artist Salvatore Dali once declared, "The only _____ between me and a _____ is that I'm not mad!"

1. between	without	in	during	with
2. agreement	acknowledgement	confession	whisper	mystery
3. bizarre	gentle	funny	secretive	sour
4. parallel	similarity	difference	separation	match
5. painter	musician	madman	sculptor	author

Answers: 1. in 2. acknowledgment 3. bizarre 4. difference 5. madman

---

9. Have them list ten negatives often heard in relation to training or schooling.

It may be that they have expressed some of those negatives themselves. Not to worry. Their job now, working with one or two others, is to take those negatives and convert them to positives.

Examples:

From: "This course is taking time away from my job."
To: "This *is* my job."

From: "I'd rather be playing baseball."
To: "Unless I'm as good as Alex Rodriguez, baseball will not help me earn a living. This course might."

Brainteaser: How many times in your lifetime have you looked at a phone and dialed or punched in the necessary numbers? There's no way of knowing, but the number is probably well into the thousands. So you should know this one: Which letters of the alphabet are missing from the dial pad?

Answer: Q and Z.

10. Challenge them: What is the most important word (or sentence) in the world of education?

The first step in this assignment is to have triads decide what single word or single sentence, in their opinion, is the most important thing that can be said about education.

Step Two is to have the triads exchange their education-based decision. When each triad receives the statement from another triad, their task is to correlate that statement to the subject matter being studied.

Example: If a given team lists the word "discover" as the most important word, the triad receiving that word might respond in this way: "In this Time Management course, we've *discovered* that a log will help regulate our time; that we have (or don't have) procrastinating tendencies; and finally, that there are tools to help us stay on track."

Brainteaser: What comes next in the series?

$$5 \quad 7 \quad 11 \quad 19 \quad 35 \quad \underline{}$$

Answer: 67. Subtract the first number from the second, multiply it by 2, and add it to the second number. So 7 minus 5 = 2; 2 is multiplied by 2 to yield 4; 4 is added to 7 to get 11.

The difference between 7 and 11 is 4, multiplied by 2 = 8; 8 added to 11 is 19. Next, 19 minus 11 is 8; 8 × 2 is 16; 19 + 16 = 35. Finally, 35 – 19 is 16; 16 × 2 = 32; 32 + 35 = 67.

---

11. Appoint a designated listener.

In the 1980s when "total quality management" (TQM) was king in American business, one of its chief gurus, Philip Crosby, said that quality should be spoken throughout the organization. Determine what one word you believe captures the essence of the program you are presenting. What one word is the foundation on which all other learning is based? Write that word on the board and then appoint one class member to stand and clap her hands once every time she hears the word spoken by you or any class member from that point on.

This action will lend a dynamic quality to the class and will continuously remind participants of what the course is all about.

Example for Memory Improvement: The most critical word is "association."

Brainteaser: If a man says, "Lew's son is my son's father," what relationship is that man to Lew?

Answer: Lew is the speaker's father.

12. Distribute skewers or chopsticks.

Given the uncanny ability of younger students to harm themselves and others, I'd only do this activity with responsible adults. Have small groups decide what, for each of them, is an important word or name or theory or concept. (In an art class, for example, "Renoir" might be an important name.) Distribute the chopsticks.

Allowing no more than ten minutes, have the groups compose a rhythmic beat and an accompanying chant for the word or phrase they have selected. Throughout the day, whenever you or another group mentions the word/phrase of a given group, have that group perform their music. This exercise is not only fun, it's an excellent way to remind the class of significant points.

Brainteaser: Which of the following mixed-up words does not belong in the set?

1. E B A D R V
2. P P I I E E O O N T R
3. G L V R E I U
4. N N T T E E I I N O J C

Answer: 3. Virgule (better known as the "slash") is a mark of punctuation, and not a part of speech (as are the others).

---

13. Make a game of relevant words.

Take ten important words related to the curriculum and mix up the letters in each word. Then omit one letter. Make copies and distribute the list when the class assembles. Not only will the game remind students of the key words or concepts associated with the course, it will also provide hints about what is likely to appear on an exam.

Award a non-material prize to the first person or group to figure out all the words. Such a prize might be the right to choose the first discussion question following a curriculum section, or the right to eliminate one question from the final exam.

Example for a class on stress management: The word "exercise" (minus one letter) could be written as "r-e-e-e-s-x-c."

Brainteaser: What is meant by this German proverb?

"The morning hour has gold in its mouth."

1. Even the early birds get hungry.
2. Wealthy people get up early.
3. Sunrise is as beautiful as sunset.
4. Get an early start each day.

Answer: 4.

14. Make journalists out of them.

Upon completion of a module or following your presentation of a discrete concept, divide the class into groups of four or five. Have them write headlines to describe what they have just learned. Then, have them write a short collective article that elaborates on the headline's content. Submit the articles to the school newspaper or the company newsletter. Do this several times throughout the course.

Brainteaser: Can you match these words with their meanings in under four minutes?

1. dale
2. dalliance
3. dank
4. dappled
5. dastard
6. dawdle
7. dearth
8. debauch
9. debilitate

A. scarcity
B. to reduce in dignity
C. damp
D. to weaken
E. a time-wasting activity
F. coward
G. to tarry or fail to move quickly with a purpose
H. marked with small dots or spots
I. valley

Answers: 1. I 2. E 3. C 4. H 5. F 6. G 7. A 8. B 9. D

---

15. Turn them into subject-matter-experts (SME's).

After the halfway point of the course, divide the class into small groups. Ask each group to determine the one area covered so far that they feel they understand best. They will then be named the gurus of that subject and will teach the rest of the class the core knowledge affiliated with that area.

As the groups make their presentations, jot down questions and answers based on their reports. After all groups have "taught," have them put away all notes and materials. Tell them to take out a clean sheet of paper and a pencil. Proceed to give an oral test based on the notes you took from the guru presentations.

Brainteaser: What possible reason can you think of to explain the following situation?

An entrepreneur started his own small car-repair business, open seven days a week. He hired seven people to work with him. Soon, he noticed that only six were ever at work on any given day. Further, he noticed that on each day, a different one failed to show up for work. Each employee was a dedicated, honest, and hardworking individual.

Answer: All his employees were religious. Each had a different day of worship. The Christian did not work on Sunday, the Greek on Monday, the Persian on Tuesday, the Assyrian on Wednesday, the Egyptian on Thursday, the Muslim on Friday, and the Jew on Saturday.

500 Creative Classroom Techniques for Teachers and Trainers

16. Capitalize on the scrapbooking craze.

If you don't mind bringing in a supply of paper and page embellishments, as well as magic markers, you can have groups put together a scrapbook page to reflect their collective assessment of the most relevant points in the course.

Then invite an independent panel of judges from the school or organization to vote on the page that is most aesthetically appealing. The prize? An actual scrapbook into which this and all other pages will be entered in order to maintain a class record of the participants' progress down the course-path.

Brainteaser: Find one word in each grouping that best fits in each blank.

_____ is not merely a _____ of following the _____. If it were, Navy Captain Samuel Ginder maintains, we could just program a _____ to be moral.

1. Morality	Legality	Trust	Truth
2. policy	process	procedure	question
3. Bible	rules	standards	inner voice
4. dog	machine	person	computer

Answers: 1. Morality 2. question 3. rules 4. computer.

---

17. Prepare a time capsule for the next class.

Decorate a tube of some sort—even a paper towel core can be made to look very attractive. On the outside, write the name and date of the class and the names of participants. Then hold it up and explain that they will have an opportunity to communicate with a future class, working in whatever configuration they wish.

They are to write their reflections, reminiscences, predictions, or summaries of the learning experience they are about to complete. Allow ten to fifteen minutes for this—more if they opt to work in large groups. Then collect the papers, roll them into the tube, and share with the next class.

Brainteaser: Can you add three lines to the following number in order to turn it into a traveling man?

1030

Answer: H O B O. Two lines—a vertical and a horizontal one—are need to complete the letter "H." The third line, placed in front of the 3, will change it to the letter "B."

18. Have them determine an "oops" moment.

Tell participants they can work alone or in pairs, triads, or groups. Whichever they choose, however, they will be asked to give a brief report. Then write these words on the flipchart:

Oops   Whoops   Droops   Coups   Scoops   Troups

Explain the significance of each word.

"Oops" If they choose to tell about an "oops" moment, they will discuss their realization that they made a mistake or that they changed their thinking about the course.

"Whoops" If they choose to tell about a "whoops" moment, they will discuss a time when they felt like whooping it up, so to speak—a time when they felt like shouting "whoopee" because of an insight they had related to the course.

"Droops" If they choose to tell about a "droops" moment, they will describe a time when their energy level flagged or they started to feel discouraged or disappointed in some aspect of the course.

"Coups" If they choose to tell about a "coups" moment, they will explore a time when they felt victorious about something they accomplished in class—perhaps when they were first to complete something, or when they finally "got" a concept they'd been struggling to understand.

"Scoops" If they choose to tell about a "scoops" moment, they will share a learning experience that was so exciting or interesting, they couldn't wait to rush out and tell someone else about it—an experience that made them feel like telling the world about it before anyone else could.

"Troups" If they choose to tell about a "troups" or "troops" moment, they will describe their feelings of *esprit de corps*, telling about a goal that their group accomplished or the pride they felt in working as part of a particular team.

Conclude the activity by calling on each person or group to share her/their "oops" moment.

Brainteaser: What do these two words have in common?   boiling   tipping

Answer: Each word is part of a phrase that has a second word in common: "point."

500 Creative Classroom Techniques for Teachers and Trainers

19. Call on each person to repeat the objectives.

You no doubt begin your classes by specifying the course objectives, and you probably have them in the course materials or on the flipchart—perhaps even on the tent cards that participants write their names on.

Keep a list of participants in front of you. Throughout the day, call on someone to tell you the course objectives with their eyes closed or their back turned to the flipchart. Cross off the person's name on the list so that by the end of the day, ideally, everyone has been able to state the course objectives.

Brainteaser: You know that pronouns take the place of nouns. Can you name ten pronouns in ten seconds? The catch is that the first one you name must have only one letter; the second, only two letters; the third, only three letters; and so on until you get to the tenth pronoun, which must have ten letters.

Answers: I, he, she, they, itself, herself, yourself, ourselves, and themselves (for example).

---

20. Distribute an evaluation form halfway through.

This action requires some courage on your part, but if you are truly interested in continuous instructional improvement, you'll do it. Pass out the course/instructor evaluations at the halfway point, rather than at the end of the course. (If your organization does not require these, make up some of your own.)

Collect and study participant comments. Then report back to them, assuring participants that you will incorporate their suggestions as fully as possible. Mention, too, that those aspects of the course that won universal approval will be continued, and those aspects that seemed to be universally disliked will be altered or eliminated. Then keep your (courageous) word.

Brainteaser: What three-word set bests fit the blanks in the quotation?

"We can do no _____ things," said Mother Teresa, "only _____ things with _____ love."

1.	charitable	selfless	giving
2.	great	small	great
3.	ordinary	miraculous	ordinary
4.	childlike	adult	adult

Answer: 2.

21. Explore two types of structure.

Divide the class into four groups. Have two of the groups explore "deep" structures—the course concepts that were complex or that required deep thinking or that caused shifts in their cognitive terrains, for example.

The other two groups will consider "surface" structures—those concepts that were easy to understand or concepts with which they were already familiar, for example. Surface structures might also include some of the more lighthearted aspects of the course.

If a dispute arises as to the proper designation for a concept—deep or surface—you will serve as arbiter.

After approximately 20 minutes, ask one representative from each group to meet in a breakout room (or the corridor) to prepare one report that brings together or unifies the deep and the surface structures. As they do this, you will move on to the next module in your lesson plan, which you will interrupt when the outside group returns to give its report.

22. View the course from the eyes of a famous figure.

Divide the class into teams of four or five. Then, using the flipchart to capture their ideas, ask for the names of some of the more interesting characters of our times. Ideally, they'll lean toward the likes of Donald Trump and Donald Rumsfeld than toward the likes of Paris Hilton and Jessica Simpson, but write whatever they suggest, including a few of your own favorites—Oprah or Russell Crowe or Luciano Pavarotti or Condoleeza Rice, for example. Aim for a minimum of twenty individuals.

Then have groups prepare a report that discusses a given course concept from the perspective of the chosen man or woman. Explain that concept, incorporating her views from her unique place in the world.

Brainteaser: How good is your knowledge of geography?

Which state in the United States is the most northern? The most eastern? The most western?

Answer: This may surprise you, but Alaska is the answer to all three questions. Because the Aleutian Islands extend across the 180th meridian into the eastern hemisphere, Alaska is both the most eastern and the most western. And, clearly, the most northern as well.

23. Orchestrate a chorus.

A chorus of readers, that is. A choral reading requires relatively little time to prepare, but yields interesting and effective outcomes. Divide the class into large groups of six to eight participants. Ask each group to choose their favorite aspect of the course thus far and to prepare a one-paragraph summary. When they rehearse their reading of the summary, they may choose to have a refrain, dramatically delivered by the same two or three people at particular points in the report presentation.

They can make their own decisions regarding who and how many will read which lines, in what way.

Brainteaser: What familiar word, name, place, or expression can be found in the box?

```
R O W H E N M E
```

Answer: "When in Rome..."

---

24. Have them personify a course concept.

Working alone or in groups, participants will take a course concept and personify it, using the first person. To illustrate: If the concept is the syntactical structure known as the "expletive," the personified concept might sound like this:

> "I am an alternative to the boredom of sentences that all start the same way. Although some of you will associate me with the phrases Rosemary Woods removed from President Nixon's tapes, those of you who know your grammar will associate me with a phrase that is not really needed, yet serves as a filler—especially at the beginning of a sentence. The phrase *There is* tells you what I'm about."

Then have participants read their personified concepts without revealing what they are describing. Have the class decide who or what is being represented.

Brainteaser: The English language contains over a million words but just a few cannot be rhymed. Can you name some of these words that cannot be rhymed?

Answers: month, oblige, orange

25. "Columnize" their persona and the way the course impacts it.

Prepare a worksheet that has four columns:

> The "you" you are today
> The "you" you used to be
> The "you" you'd like to become
> The "you" this course can help you become

Distribute copies and allow 5–10 minutes for participants to fill in all four columns. Collect the sheets and respond to each person with written comments on his or her worksheet. (For a one-day course, you may need to collect the sheets before lunch and then sacrifice your lunch hour to comment on them.)

Brainteaser: Which word in each of the lines numbered 1–3 fits with the capitalized words above each line and shares a common word with them?

	GUN	WET	GREASE	CAN
1.	subject	veil	brush	triangle
	BERRY	MAN	DRINKING	LAST
2.	beret	hat	fedora	tie
	SAINT	DOWN	TIME	PUNCTUATION
3.	Anthony	Albert	Alicia	Aretha

Answers: 1. brush (they all relate to "paint") 2. hat (they all relate to "straw") 3. Anthony (they all relate to the word "Mark")

Chapter 13

25 Ways to Review

Chapter Overview

To use a culinary analogy, if you don't stop to sip water while you are dining, you might choke on your meal. The water helps the food go down, but it also makes it easier to digest.

Similarly, reviewing material throughout the course helps break the information down into digestible chunks. Review prevents learners from being overwhelmed. In this section, you'll learn some new and clever ways to help students consume their food-for-thought without choking.

1. Have them determine MSF's (most significant facts).

Give participants a few minutes to make note of the two most significant facts they have learned so far. Then ask them to find a partner and tell him what they've written.

The next step requires the partners to find two other people who have written four facts, at least three of which must differ from what the original partners wrote. Once the four have formed their own team, give them some time to discuss what they wrote and why.

Brainteaser: If you're somewhat of a grammatical guru, you should be able to deal with the five choices here. Which is the grammatically correct sentence?

1. If the choice were between you and me, they would have no problem making it.
2. If the choice was between you and me, they would have no problem making it.
3. If the choice were between you and I, they would have no problem making it.
4. If the choice was between you and I, they would have no problem making it.
5. If the choice were down to you and I, they would have no problem making it.

Answer: 1.

Brainteaser: Can you decipher the following four-word sentence?

C4MP5T2RS1R2V1L51BL2T44LS

Answer: Computers are valuable tools. The letter "A" is equal to 1; "E" to 2; "O" to 4; and "U" to 5.

2. Use an outline.

A *big* outline. Attach it to the wall, and then have a representative from each team come up and write a total of five facts related to one or several of the points on the outline from memory (no notes). If the writer gets stuck, he can call for help from his group members.

Option: This activity can be done in the form of a relay race. Each person on a team will write one fact, and pass the baton (the magic marker) to the next person. The challenge will be after the first person on each team has written one fact: The subsequent writers are not allowed to repeat anything that has already been written. Make sure each team has the same number of players.

Brainteaser: The synonyms for each capitalized word can be found in the line of words beneath each capitalized word. You're good if you can find the synonym for both in fewer than two minutes.

1. WONT
   desire   need   custom   privilege   nativity

2. WIZENED
   withered   caring   noteworthy   mean   knowledgeable

Answers: 1. custom   2. withered

---

3. Assemble and moderate a panel.

You can ask for volunteers. You can make appointments. You can require every group to participate. No matter how you get the people on the panel, though, the "rules of review" will be the same:

1. You will pose a question.
2. The panelists will respond.
3. You will intervene if the debate becomes too heated or if any one person is long-winded.
4. You will call on those who are not contributing and ask for their opinion. (Tell them you are not doing this to force them to share their ideas, but because you know that the best ideas are often contained within the quietest people, and you are inviting their input.)
5. You will involve the audience at appropriate times.
6. You will summarize the work of the panel at the end.

(continued)

3. **Assemble and moderate a panel.** *(concluded)*

   Hint: Master the art of the segue so you can make the discussion flow seamlessly and easily from one person to another, from one topic to another. It won't be as easy as you think. Practice by asking a friend to carry on a conversation with you. At the end of his first sentence, you still step in. You'll take the last word he spoke and use it as the first word in your response. Or take two totally unrelated words and find a common link between them.

   Practice example: "December" and "memory"

   How to segue between them: "T. S. Eliot said that April is the cruelest month of all. But those of you who live in Buffalo, New York, have winter memories, I suspect, that show December has its own kind of cruelty."

   Brainteaser: Let's say that you have a friend who never shows up when she is supposed to. You've decided to track her arrivals for the next five Saturdays, since you two have planned to have lunch together at noon. On the first Saturday, she showed up at 12:30—just a half-hour late. The next Saturday, she appeared at 1:20 p.m. The next week, she arrived at 2:30, and on the fourth Saturday she arrived four hours after noon, at 4 p.m. Using the pattern she has established, when is your friend likely to show up for the fifth (and final, you've decided) Saturday lunch?

   Answer: 5:50. She was 30 minutes late the first time. 30 + 50 the second time. 30+ 50 + 70 the third time. 30 + 50 + 70 + 90 the fourth time. And, because the combinations increase each time by adding 20 minutes to the last number in the combination, the final combination will be 30 + 50 + 70 + 90 + 110.

---

4. **Pop-quiz them.**

   Quizzes can be used for more than just finding out how much learners have learned. They can also be used to remind learners of what they *should* have learned. And you don't have to take time to write the quiz out in advance: the "pop" should apply to both your and their willingness to *carpe* the *diem*.

   Tip: As we cover the material in the book, handout, or curriculum, I pencil in a number in the Instructor's Guide, next to a point I want them to remember. When I hit ten or twenty, I tell them it's time for a pop quiz. Then, I just go back to the first penciled number and pop the question. Do all ten and you have an easy 100-point quiz, with each question worth ten points (five each if you have twenty questions).

   (continued)

4. Pop-quiz them. *(concluded)*

Brainteaser: What is the word below that is formed going clockwise or counter-clockwise, starting anywhere on the circle? (One letter is missing.)

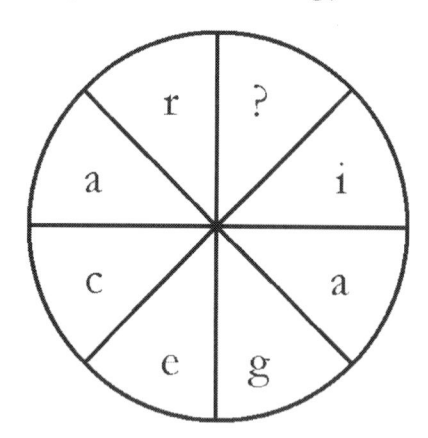

Answer: The word "carriage" is missing an "r."

---

5. Draw a body on flipchart paper . . .

. . . and post it on a wall. Depending on the size of the class, have large groups go up, with magic markers in hand, and write one course-fact somewhere on the body. First, though, explain the body parts.

Head: Here they will record something that increased their knowledge of the subject.

Heart: Here they will record something about which they feel strongly, perhaps even passionately.

Hands: Here they will record a hands-on activity and what they learned from it.

Legs: Here they will record something that "has legs." In other words, something that they will continue to use or will share with others.

Feet: Here they will record something that they will take immediate action on.

Brainteaser: What's next in this sequence?

2   10   4   14   6   18   8   22   10   ___

Answer: 26. The sequence is +8, −6; +10, −8; +12, −10; +14, −12. The + numbers go up by 2 over the previous + number and the − numbers go down by two over the preceding − number.

6. Have each one teach one.

In advance of the class, determine which concepts are most relevant. After you have covered approximately half of the course material, write the concepts relative to the first half on flipchart paper. Divide the class in half. While you teach a "special activity" to one-half the class, have each person in the other half choose the one concept he understood best. Ideally, you'll be able to align each concept with one person, but certainly, you can allow two people to do one concept if need be.

Do the special activity for a few minutes while the teaching-half of the class prepares their remarks. When you and they are ready, have the teach-one-concept participants find a partner in the half of the class you worked with. They will each teach their one concept to one person.

Then, near the end of the class, write the remaining course concepts on the flipchart. Assign one per person to those who have not already served as teachers. Then, you will do the same special activity with the half that has already completed their teaching stint, while the other half prepares a short lesson. In time, call upon the second round of teachers to do their pedagogical thing.

7. Use forced fits.

You can creatively force the issue of review by giving a structure and then having groups of three or four prepare a statement that adheres to the confines of the structure. The structure in this case is a series of letters—A B C D E, for example. The groups have five minutes to create a sentence that reflects their learning thus far—a sentence containing only five words. The first word in the sentence must start with the letter "A"; the second word must start with the letter "B"; the third word must start with the letter "C," and so on.

Example for a class on Problem-Solving: **A**ll **b**afflements **c**ontain **d**iverse **e**lements. (This relates to the tendency of problem-solvers to rush to judgment without considering the many and diverse complexities of a situation.)

Caution: Any combination of letters can serve as the structure, but try to avoid using "Q," "X," and "Z."

Brainteaser: Why is this number unique? 8,549,176,320

Answer: All the numbers spelled out one by one are in alphabetical order.

8. Obtain permission to create a rock garden.

First, obtain permission from the head of the organization to create a small rock garden (two feet by two feet is really all you need) in one corner of the grounds. (If this is not possible, build the rock garden in one corner of the classroom by simply placing the rocks on a large tray.)

If the class is a one-day thing, you'll have to give the assignment before lunch so the rock-gatherers can find their stones at lunch. If it's a multi-day course, you could do it group by group over an extended period, with the second group's rocks replacing those of the first. After a few days, the rocks from the third group will replace those of the second, and so on.

Divide the class into groups of four or five. Have each group think of a word they believe is most critical to the course. Poll the groups to make sure there are no duplicate words. Then have them find their rocks and, somehow, write or paint that word on their rocks. They can decorate the rocks in any way they wish and add their names if they wish to. Assemble the rocks in the garden, take pictures, invite others to appreciate, and dodge the inevitable comments about people who have rocks in their heads.

9. Create a fill-in-the-blanks letter.

The letter will be addressed to participants' managers. If you teach school, address the letters to parents or guardians. Essentially, the letter will tell this person what the student has learned today. Each participant receives a letter that has at least five bullets in front of long blank lines. It's the participant's job to write one thing he has learned on each line.

They will sign their names and you will co-sign.

Brainteaser: What set of words fits best in the following blanks?

Known for his hyperbole, Joe claimed that _____ he _____ Jocelyn, his heart _____.

1. whenever   saw   stopped
2. because   loved   beat
3. while   adored   wandered

Answer: 1.

10. Have them take an analogy test.

This may not be an easy assignment for you to create, and it may not be an easy assignment for participants to accurately complete. But it will be an easy way for you to determine if they truly grasped the ideas/information you've presented. The review requires you to create an analogies test.

Then go over the answers and lead a discussion, answering any questions people have about the reasons for the correct answers.

Grammar example: Semicolon : complete thoughts : :

- a) Fabric : dress
- b) Step : dance
- c) Weightlifter : ten-pound weights
- d) Voice : recording
- e) Money : bank.

If the semicolon is regarded as something that separates two equal parts of a sentence, giving weight to each and helping each maintain the syntactical balance of the sentence, then c) is the only possible answer. The weightlifter stands in the middle of two equally weighted objects. The semicolon, by comparison, stands in the middle of two complete thoughts.

Brainteaser: More analogies. Beneath each capitalized word is a set of other pairs, one of which contains the same relationship as the capitalized pair. As usual, aim to finish this in under three minutes.

1. DISHEVELED : NEAT : :
   - a) unorganized : organized
   - b) rich : poor
   - c) hero : villain
   - d) neat : messy

2. SPECTACLE : VISIBLE : :
   - a) taste : feel
   - b) glasses : nearsighted
   - c) maid : cleaning
   - d) sound : audible

3. ROOF : PITCH : :
   - a) television : remote
   - b) computer : mouse
   - c) mountain : grade
   - d) school : students

4. ENTHUSIASTIC : ZEALOUS : :
   - a) work : income
   - b) scare : terrify
   - c) native : bilingual
   - d) roar : lion

5. HEMI : DEMI : :
   - a) whole : half
   - b) quad : tetra
   - c) fraction : integer
   - d) angle : square

Answers: 1. a   2. d   3. c   4. b   5. b

11. Twist popular phrases into course-related ideas.

If you have an especially bright or creative group of participants, this is the review tool for them. Challenge them to take a popular phrase and twist it into a play on words. From there, they will take the twisted phrase and make it meaningful in relation to the course.

Example: Jurassic Park

Twisted phrases for use in science or medical transcription class:
Potassic Park, Jurassic Perk, Jurassic Bark, Jurassic Port, Sebacic Park, Boracic Park, Thoracic Park

Example: Karl Rove (very much in the news at the time of this writing)

Twisted phrases for Political Science, Leadership, Ethics class:
Karl Rave, Snarl Rove, Karl Wove, Karl Trove, Karl Dove

Brainteaser: What bird can run faster than a horse and roar like a lion, but is not capable of flying?

Answer: Ostrich.

12. Use the "been-there/done-that" phrase to review.

Draw a line down the middle of a flipchart paper. Elicit from class members the names of places they have been (for the left-hand column) and things they have done (for the right-hand column). Post that two-column list. (The longer the list, the better.) Then start a new list for the course objectives or the course outline.

Have participants explain one item on the second list by correlating it to one item on the first list.

Example for a Psychology class: Light deprivation, a key ingredient in SAD (Seasonal Affective Disorder), can be discussed in relation to a trip to Seattle or Alaska or Iceland.

Brainteaser: Two mothers and two daughters went to the mall, where each bought a shirt. Yet they only brought three shirts home with them. Why is this?

Answer: The shoppers were a grandmother, a mother, and a daughter. True, there were two mothers, but one of them was also a daughter—three people and three shirts.

13. Draw inspiration from the Great Communicator.

President Ronald Reagan once commented: "Government's view of the economy could be summed up in a few short phrases: If it moves, tax it. If it keeps moving, regulate it. And if it stops moving, subsidize it."

Have triads use this same structure to synthesize their thoughts about what they have learned so far.

Example for Conflict Management:
Experts' advice for dealing with difficult people can be summed up in a few short phrases: If they shout, lower your own voice. If they keep shouting, tell them you'll talk to them at another time, and walk away. If they move toward you, run!

Brainteaser: A popular fictional character has "gone Hollywood," so to speak. (In other words, the book about him has been turned into a movie.) His name has had the vowels removed and all the letters mixed up. Who is he? T T R P Y R H R

Answer: Harry Potter.

---

14. Ask them to connect national issues to the subject at hand.

You've no doubt seen them—the surveys that ask ordinary Americans to identify the most-important issues facing America and the world. No doubt terrorism would top the list. That aside, present participants with this list of issues and have then work in groups to determine how what they are learning might ameliorate one of these issues.

Economy	Drug abuse
Shared values	Corporate ethics
Polarization	Medicare reform
Global leadership	Care of the elderly
Population control	Growing number of autistic children
Education	Teen violence
Child care	Crime
Health care	The environment
Crumbling infrastructures	Others:

15. Make the review an emotional experience.

Ask participants to work in small groups. Give each group a list of emotions. Then ask them to choose at least three and explain how their choices relate to the course as a whole or to specific modules.

Possible items for the list:

compassion	awe	wonder	goodwill	love
passion	empathy	excitement	ecstasy	joy
appreciation	enthusiasm	gratitude	acceptance	eagerness
respect	happiness	respect	commitment	self-respect
fear	terror	loneliness	depression	shame
exhaustion	rejection	hysteria	desperation	resignation
guilt	sadness	regret	bitterness	powerlessness
rage	stubbornness	hostility	frustration	annoyance
self-acceptance	desire	relief	honesty	self-awareness
self-confidence	hope	calmness	affection	peace
self-esteem	certainty	devotion	amusement	solitude
curiosity	withdrawal	shock	paranoia	apathy

16. Do list compilations.

There are numerous variations on this basic theme: Working alone or in any combination they wish (and without the benefit of books or notes), participants will try to recall and write down everything that has been covered up to that point. Find out who has the longest list. Ask that person to slowly read what is on his list as others cross off the duplicates on their lists. Then call on each person to add something that has not been mentioned.

As they do this, you will write the list-additions on the flipchart. When you've heard from everyone, ask the owner of the longest original list to add the rest of his items to what is on the flipchart. While he does this, call on a few people to take an item on the list and explain, define, or discuss it. (Cross the item off once it's been explained.)

Note: Keep the list posted. You can refer to it throughout the day, crossing off the explained items until the entire list has been covered.

Brainteaser: What famous American landmark is continuously moving backwards?

Answer: Niagara Falls—its brink is actually receding two and a half feet a year.

17. Be the fact-finder and ask them to be the fact-embellishers.

A fun alternative to traditional review sessions involves you acting as the fact provider. Call on different people, give them a fact, and ask that they embellish that fact.

Example:

FACT: Peter Drucker is the author of *The Effective Executive*.
EMBELLISHED FACT: He is known as the "Father of Modern Management Science."

Option: Divide the class into two teams. Allow them to select their own team names. Appoint a scorekeeper to track how many embellished facts were provided by the members of each team for each fact provided. Start with the first team. Give a fact. They, in return, will provide as many (correct) embellishments as possible. Then go to the second team and repeat the process, alternating back and forth between the two teams. Offer a token reward to the winners.

Brainteaser: What does the distress signal "Mayday" actually stand for?

Answer: "M'aidez!" is French for "Save me" or "Help me," and is pronounced *"Mayday."*

---

18. Use birth order to bring order to the review.

Divide participants into four groups: Those who are only children; those who are the oldest; those who are the youngest; and those who fall somewhere in the middle. After a few getting-to-know-you minutes, ask them what traits they believe are associated with their particular birth order. Have them record those traits in their groups. Then ask them to discuss how those traits may have served as either barriers or boosters to the course content/course activities. (In other words, could these traits have anything to do with those things that were easy for them to learn? What was hard for them?)

Ask one spokesperson from each group to summarize the group's observations and make a report.

Brainteaser: Which of the following numbered choices most closely resembles the meaning of this Italian proverb?

"Flies don't enter a closed mouth"

1. "There is no shame in keeping silent if you have nothing to say." (Russian)
2. "Don't count your chickens before they are hatched." (American)
3. "No use crying over spilt milk." (British)

Answer: 1.

19. Ask them to make anonymous admissions.

List the course outline or the names of the modules or the curriculum headings on the flipchart. Say, "Look these over. Is there any one you still don't understand? Which would you *least* like me to call on you to explain?" They will write their answers on 3 × 5 cards.

Collect the cards and conduct the review session by addressing each of the concerns listed on the cards.

Note: You may wish to tally the responses and structure your review session based on the most-cited items.

Brainteaser: Which answer contains the correct spelling for the appetizer?

- a) orderves
- b) horsedeorves
- c) hors de ervres
- d) hors d'oeuvres
- e) hor derves

Answer: d.

---

20. Ask them to be lie-detectors.

Prepare a ten-item list (twenty for a longer course) of statements related to the course. All items should have the ring of truth. For example, Dr. Joseph Juran is associated with the Quality (TQM) movement. He made many brilliant statements regarding management. This is *not* one of them: "Drive out fear." This statement actually belongs to Dr. W. Edwards Deming. But if you had presented information about both gurus and had quoted each of them, only those who had truly paid attention to your lectures would know the statement "Drive out fear."

Then read the statements aloud and have participants write down whether they are true or false. Discuss the answers afterwards.

Option: You could throw out one question at a time—say once an hour, all day long.

Brainteaser: When could a pitcher make four or more strike-outs in one inning?

Answer: If the catcher drops the ball after the third strike and fails to throw the batter out at first, the man is safe.

21. Let reporters report review-news.

Divide the class into five groups, assigning each group one reporting role: the news anchor, the entertainment reporter, the world affairs reporter, the sports reporter, and the medical news reporter. (Depending on the course you are teaching, other reporting roles might be used instead of any of these.)

Have each group prepare a review-report, emphasizing the slant that their reporter-role calls for in relation to what they have learned.

Example for a class on Supervision: The news anchor group would report on contemporary books or articles that have been mentioned or studied in class. The entertainment reporters might address ways supervisors can improve morale or report on the parts of the class that were most fun for them—approaches, again, that have been studied as part of the program or that are tangential to it. The world affairs review-report could talk about the need for supervisors to be aware of world events and their potential impact on the workplace. The sports reporters could review some of the games or competitions held during the course. The medical reporters could address ways supervisors can relieve stress or discuss techniques for dealing with conflict at work.

22. Produce a class video.

Depending on your access to video equipment, create a short video that details the main elements of the course. Involve participants in the design of the script. Various "stars" can dramatize or simply report on the concepts that most appealed to them (the video could cover course chronology, introductions, group reports, the closing comments, and everything in between).

Brainteaser: Which choice will complete the sequence?

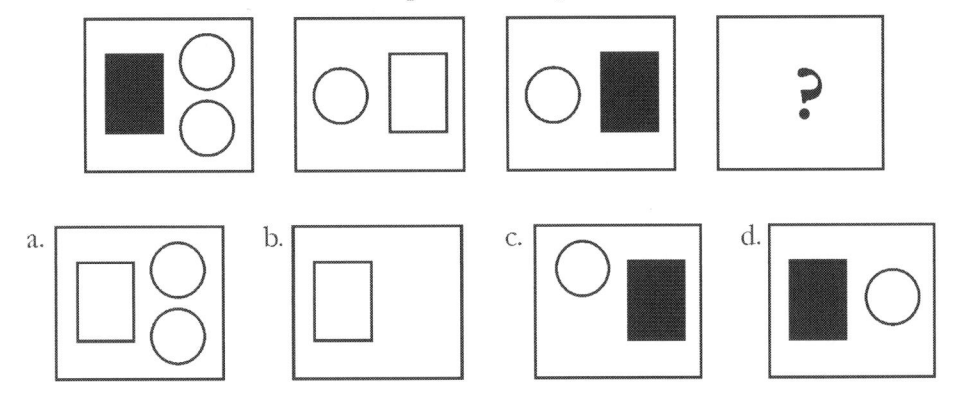

Answer: b. The pattern seen in the first two boxes shows that the second box has a rectangle that is not filled in and is on the opposite side from the rectangle in the first box. It also has one less circle. The only answer that fits these criteria is b.

23. Make masks and use them to liven up a review.

You can find these masks in any dollar store, but if you prefer to make your own, follow these directions for making simple but artful masks. Once the masks are hung, label each with one of the key themes of the course content. Then assign each group one theme. They are to summarize what they know about that topic into statements. Paste the statements beside the masks hanging on the wall.

Directions:

1. Use a mask or a doll's face. You don't want it too detailed or too sharply-edged, as the points will puncture the paper. (If this happens, just tear a small sheet of paper and place it over the rip.)

2. Place an ordinary sheet of copy-machine paper over the figure. While running the paper-layered face under warm tap water, press down so the features of the figure will show through.

3. Allow the paper to dry overnight.

4. While the dried paper is still on the figure, paint it. Nail polish works beautifully, as does polyurethane, paint, gesso, or ordinary watercolor. (An alternative: Depending on the figure, if you outline the figure with an ordinary Flair pen and then brush water over the outline, you will create an interesting blend of blue colors.)

5. After the paint has dried, lift the paper off the figure.

6. Now the fun part begins. Decorate the object any way you wish If you have the face of a woman, glue on feathers or beads or flowers. Give your imagination full rein here.

Brainteaser: Match the words with their meanings. Try to finish in two minutes.

1. De facto   A. Actual
2. Defame   B. Act of respect
3. Defection   C. Disgrace
4. Deference   D. Dead
5. Defunct   E. Desertion

Answers: 1. A   2. C   3. E   4. B   5. D

24. Seek partial if not total recall.

Distribute paper and pencils and ask participants to write down everything they remember learning so far. Collect their papers and ask for a volunteer to leave the room (with a magic marker and piece of flipchart paper) to analyze and tally the results. Once he returns, thank him and post the results next to the flipchart (on which you have already listed the major points for review). Read aloud the results of the tally. Then, wherever you spot an omission or a gap between what they recall and what you believe you taught, use that opportunity to review the concept that was recalled by only a few (or perhaps none) of the participants.

Brainteaser: How do you interpret this American proverb?

"A stitch in time saves nine."

1. Seamstresses have a hard life, but their work is valuable in an industrialized society.
2. People who attend to things that need attention before they become serious can avoid a great deal of expense, time, and trouble.
3. There are numerous kinds of stitches, from the simple to the complicated.
4. Those who do not waste time will always come out ahead.

Answer: 2.

---

25. Have them itemize benefits.

Ideally, participants will realize the benefits that will accrue to various individuals as a result of their participation in the class. Have them work as partners or in triads to record at least one benefit in at least three of these categories.

- Benefits to the participant
- Benefits to their team
- Benefits to the organization or school
- Benefits to their supervisor or manager
- Benefits to their families
- Benefits to a larger community (neighborhood, Scouts, place of worship, places where they volunteer, et cetera)

Brainteaser: Can you tell which of the following words does not belong with the others?

friend   advocate   smart   restaurant   value

Answer: Smart. It's the only adjective. The others are all nouns.

Chapter 14

25 Ways to Encourage Participant-Learning After the Course Has Ended

Chapter Overview

It occurred to me one day, as I was cleaning the room and pulling flipcharts off the wall, how wrong it was for knowledge that is created in a classroom to subsequently *die* in the classroom. I had an educational epiphany then and realized that it doesn't *have* to die. There were so many things I could do to make sure the learning lived on long after the course had ended. I've collected those ideas for you here in this section.

1. Write a letter.

Depending on who your "customers" are, you can write a letter to help others help the participants make the learning continuous. The participants are the ones who receive the benefit of your services, of course, but they are in front of you because of the efforts and cooperation of others. So, the letter can be sent to parents if you teach in a school. It can also be sent to the principal. To the school board. To the teacher who is likely to have this group of students next year.

If your training is done in a business setting, you can send a letter to the training department, to the managers of the attenders, even to the editor of the company newsletter. The letter will recap what has been taught and will suggest ways that the letter-recipient can keep the learning alive.

Example for a class in Business Writing: Accompanying the letter I send to their managers is a list of 24 ways managers can encourage future improvement in the realm of communication.

1. COMPILE a list of the most-frequent errors made by the members of your department. Ask staff members to be especially careful to avoid them in the future.
2. LEARN who the grammar czars/czarinas are in your department. Ask them to serve as resources for the department.
3. START staff meetings with a newspaper sentence containing a grammatical demon. Read it aloud, have staff write it down, and then show them the correct, original sentence.

(continued)

1. **Write a letter.** *(concluded)*

    4. COLLECT and share examples of grammatical errors. At the very least, they are embarrassing because they are unprofessional, but they can also be costly.
    5. HAVE grammar reference books in a small, easily accessible library.
    6. INSTITUTE a friendly competition. Award token prizes to the team that made the fewest errors in a given month.
    7. ASSIGN each person a brief report to be presented at staff meetings. The report can be a survey of the staff's awareness of good writing, it can consist of interesting facts about syntax, or it can consist of examples of poor writing from your own or other departments.
    8. RENT a video that explores the importance of good writing. Show it at lunchtime.
    9. INVITE a local college professor in to give a brief lecture about communication.
    10. WRITE letters of commendation for those staff members who have had (grammatical) error-free months.
    11. ENCOURAGE staff members to relate this emphasis on good writing to what their children are learning in school.
    12. ESTABLISH an ongoing program of excellence, comparable to "Six Weeks to Wellness."
    13. CALCULATE the cost of errors, and share your report with the staff.
    14. MAKE your expectations for good writing part of the performance appraisal process.
    15. FIND online resources for your staff (www.grammarlady.com, for example).
    16. ESTABLISH and visibly record goals and their attainment—e.g., three weeks without a typographical error.
    17. WRITE an article for an internal or external newsletter commending your staff's efforts.
    18. POST sayings around the office relative to good writing.
    19. BEGIN staff meetings by asking, "What have you done since our last meeting to promote good writing?"
    20. BENCHMARK to learn what other departments are doing to achieve high-quality writing.
    21. APPOINT a rotating spot-checker to periodically scan reports.
    22. INVITE top management to a meeting so they can affirm the importance of effective business communication.
    23. BE an exemplar. Demonstrate both your commitment to writing excellence and your willingness to be a continuous learner.
    24. KEEP an office notebook of interesting articles and news reports relevant to written communication.

2. Appoint a scribe to send updates.

I usually ask for a volunteer to do this, but I try to make it worth her while. (See letter in Appendix to be sent to volunteer's boss, commending her willingness to go beyond what is asked.) Instead of taking classroom-created knowledge or group reports off the flipchart or off the walls and throwing them away, I hand them to the volunteer and ask that she type up all the information and e-mail it (a one-time mailing) to the class participants within the next two weeks. (Be sure to circulate a list asking for the e-mail addresses.)

Sometimes, an oral report is given with information that is really valuable. I will ask the volunteer to make notes on this as well, and to add it to the flipchart information to be sent out.

Brainteaser: Which of the following does not belong on this list?

      Washington   California   Alaska   Utah   Arizona

Answer: Utah. It is the only word with two syllables. The others all have three or more.

---

3. Seek a ten-minute commitment.

Throughout the day, remind participants that you will not be able to "haunt" them in the future. So, the best you can do is get a commitment from them to continue practicing their skills for a mere ten minutes a week.

Suggest that they read for that amount of time, go online, buy a course-related audio tape for their drive in to work, or form a group committed to having lunch together once a week to further their learning. If possible, have them make their commitment aloud, and remind them of it several times during the course.

Brainteaser: What conclusion can you draw from these two conditions?

    L is above K and O
    K is above O and below R

    a. L is not over O and R
    b. O is above K
    c. R is above O
    d. O is above R

Answer: c.

4. Ask partners to exchange e-mail addresses at the end of the course.

Suggest that partners contact each other every other week with a comment on what they learned or how they are using it or what they have come across recently that pertains to the course material. Advise participants that if you do something 30 times in a row, you have created a habitual action (according to America's first psychologist, William James). Once partners get into the habit of sending updates to each other, they can continue the learning for the rest of their lives.

Brainteaser: Complete this sentence by choosing one word from each of the five sets of words that follow it.

_____ from the Iroquois Nation _____ us that in our every deliberation, we must consider the _____ of our _____ on the next seven _____.

1. Truth   Leaders   Tribes   Sayings
2. remind   compels   orders   shows
3. wealth   power   future   impact
4. problems   decisions environment   people
5. generations   years   tribes   children

Answers: 1. Leaders 2. remind 3. impact 4. decisions 5. generations

---

5. Call on them to become one-person teachers.

A little drama goes a long way when it comes to eliciting promises that will be kept beyond the classroom door. Near the end of the class, I will call on one person at a time. I'll ask each to stand (in order to heighten the histrionics) and will then ask, "Who is one person who could benefit from something you have learned?"

If they hesitate, I'll prompt—"Perhaps a child. A family member. A co-worker. Your boss. Someone in your neighborhood. Someone with whom you used to work. Someone with whom you used to go to school. Someone in your congregation. Someone in a chat room you visit."

(continued)

Chapter 14: 25 Ways to Encourage Participant Learning After the Course Has Ended

5. **Call on them to become one-person teachers.** *(concluded)*

Once they have identified the person, ask the participant what exactly he could tell that person in relation to the course. Then go over and shake his hand. Such actions deepen the commitment to future learning and increase the likelihood that he will talk about the course once it's over.

Brainteaser: What word should be removed from this list?

file   turn   set   murder   bracelet

Answer: Bracelet. All the other words can be both nouns and verbs. "Bracelet" is only a noun.

---

6. **Have them do an action plan.**

Pass out 3 × 5 cards. Tell participants to write their home or work address on one side. Then have them write their action plan on the other: What will they do differently as a result of having taken this course?

Collect these plans. A few weeks after the course is over, stamp them and mail them to remind participants of their stated intentions. Invite participants to contact you by e-mail if they'd like to discuss their plans further.

Brainteaser: What number belongs in the second circle?

```
        24                          80
12    (80)    36          14    ( ? )    48
        88                          40
```

Answer: 91. Take half of the outside numbers and add them. They yield the number in the center.

209

7. Build a library.

Or plan a field trip to one. If you build it, do it in a convenient place, so they will come. Assuming you work in a school, work with the librarian to find a corner that can be used for the materials pertinent to your course. In that corner, you could have a scrapbook that was compiled by the class, you could include relevant articles you have found, you could assemble library books, you could loan some of your own articles.

If the library-logistics don't work for you, plan a field trip to the local public library. Call in advance to give the librarian time to assemble materials. If you can't take students to the library, invite the librarian to come to your classroom. In short, there are numerous ways to broaden the exposure of participants to the subject matter under review.

Brainteaser: Can you explain the circumstances in this true story? A man decided to add on to his house, so he took his plans to a builder. Although they had never met before, the builder agreed to do the work at no charge at all to the man. Can you figure out why?

Answer: The man was Picasso. The builder correctly realized that the plans would be worth a great deal more than any fee he could charge.

---

8. Set up a schedule for pairs or triads to reconnect with class members.

Have the next twelve months listed on a sheet of paper. Then ask pairs or triads to choose a month when they would like to either send out a relevant article or essay to the other members of the class (or post an essay on an intranet), or call other members about a tool that is working for them. By having two or three people involved, you are reducing the amount of work any one person has to do.

You'll have some work to do as well: a few days before the new month begins, call the scheduled members of the pair or triad to remind them of the commitment that must be executed within the next several weeks.

Brainteaser: How do you interpret this American proverb?

"You can't unscramble eggs."

1. Lawyers sometimes attempt deceitful actions, knowing they can't un-ring the bell.
2. Good cooks are always willing to experiment.
3. What's done is done.

Answer: 3.

Chapter 14: 25 Ways to Encourage Participant Learning After the Course Has Ended

9. Conduct a post-class survey.

Divide the class into teams of four. Ask one person if he would be willing to poll the other members of his team, just once. Then, a few weeks after the class, call or e-mail the team leaders. Give them the questions you'd like to have answered. (Questions will pertain to their use of the knowledge, skills, or abilities they acquired during class.) Assure them that you do not want their names—just their responses.

The leader will contact his teammates, ask the questions, respond to the questions himself, and then summarize the responses. Based on what you learn from the team leaders, make adjustments accordingly before the next class. (It may prove valuable to share the results with the head of the Human Resources department.)

Brainteaser: What meteorological phrase can be derived from the following?

$$\frac{0}{\text{Ph.D.} \quad \text{M.D.} \quad \text{Ed.D.}}$$

Answer: Three degrees below zero.

10. Encourage participants to ask themselves questions.

These two questions should be asked every single morning for the rest of their lives, and every single evening as well. (Again, have them get into the *habit* of self-assessment.)

THE MORNING QUESTION: What am I going to learn today? (To be sure, they cannot predict the future, but they can state their intentions: "I'll learn one thing about nutrition from the magazine on my desk.") The answers could be shared or recorded in any number of ways, including in a log.)

THE EVENING QUESTION: What *did* I learn today? (Those who are truly introspective will explore the gaps that exist between intent and actuality.)

Brainteaser: Add some vowels to the following string of letters and you'll have the title of a movie classic. It has four words, but all the letters from all the words are mixed together.

S S N M C D T F H

Answer: *The Sound of Music.*

11. Optimize e-feedback.

Depending on your skills or your access to those who possess the requisite e-tools, set up a chat room, a blogging site, or a Web site. Encourage participants to submit new course-related material as often as they can, or have them tell how what they learned in the course helped them once the course was over. Have a monthly raffle, using the names of those who contributed.

Brainteaser: You may have heard a different version of this puzzle, but you may not remember the answer. If you do, share the puzzle with someone who has not seen it.

> You have a wolf, a goat, and a canary on your camping trip. The wolf, of course, wants to eat the goat, and the goat is looking hungrily at the canary. You are determined that neither temptation will be realized. You reach a river, and realize that the boat that's there is so small, you can only carry with you the wolf or the goat or the canary. You can't leave the wolf with the goat nor the goat with the canary. So, how can you get everyone safely to the other side?

Answer: Begin by taking the goat across. Return and get the wolf. Deliver it to the other side and bring the goat back. Leave it there and take the canary across. Return for the goat. This way, the goat is never alone with either the wolf or the canary.

---

12. Invite them to come up with their own ways to continue the learning after the class is over.

Start a flipchart list of ways you've thought of to continue the learning when class is over. Ask each group to come up with two additional ways before the class is over. Remind them when there are spare moments that they will be asked to add to the list. Then, near the end of the day, call on the first group to share their continuous-learning ideas and record them as the spokesperson gives his report. Continue with the other teams, asking them to give their reports as well.

Implement a few ideas right away if you can. If not, ask for a team of volunteers to assist you in implementing the others' ideas for the other class members in the future.

Brainteaser: Can you figure out the common expression below?

> CRIPARTNERSME

Answer: Partners in crime.

13. Encourage journal-keeping.

While a diary contains outpourings of the heart and is personal in nature, the journal is both personal and professional. Scientists use journals to jot down their ideas. So do writers and actors. People undergoing therapy are encouraged to use journals, as are people on diets or other special programs. Essentially, journals allow us to specify our goals and our progress toward them.

They also promote the capture of the details of lessons learned, and thus help us avoid making the same mistakes over and over again. Journals help us determine in advance the best way of asking for what we want or need. They clarify our thoughts and help us deal with difficult issues privately, before we have to do so publicly. They offer assurances that our esteem has been properly placed in our *self*.

If you can afford it, pick up enough journals for class members at the dollar store. If you have access to a binding machine, you can easily make the journals yourself. Another option is to ask participants to bring a journal of their own. However the journals are obtained, structure at least the first two segments you'd like them to address in those journals.

Two ideas for structured assignments follow.

Example of journal segments for History students:

Foreign Governments

What did you read in the newspaper this week (or see on television) that relates to the various kinds of governments we have discussed?

Foreign Leaders

What world leader recently made a surprising and perhaps even shocking statement? What was that statement? What repercussions could it have?

Brainteaser: Can you connect the words with their meanings in three minutes?

1. derogatory   A. aimless
2. despoil   B. skill
3. desultory   C. division
4. dexterity   D. pedagogical
5. dichotomy   E. hesitancy
6. didactic   F. disparaging
7. diffidence   G. plunder

Answers: 1. F 2. G 3. A 4. B 5. C 6. D 7. E

14. Invite participants to visit your Web site or the organization's Web site.

Every two weeks, have a new assignment or puzzle posted on the Web site. The three people who have the most correct answers for the next six months will receive a prize of some sort, and their picture, their name, and their answers will be posted on the site.

Brainteaser: How quickly can you find the antonym of each capitalized word?

1. INTRODUCTORY
   a) inventive   b) substantial   c) preliminary   d) investigative

2. IRASCIBLE
   a) pleasant   b) tragic   c) authoritative   d) quick-tempered

3. RAMPANT
   a) military   b) skeptical   c) total   d) meek

4. PROFOUND
   a) purposeful   b) fugitive   c) shallow   d) primary

Answers: 1. b 2. a 3. d 4. c

---

15. Extend an invitation to group leaders to make a presentation in the next course.

Allow them time in class to plan what they will say and how they will deliver the message. Have them exchange e-mail addresses so they can continue planning during the interval between the end of this class and their appearance in the next one. Their presentation should provide highlights from the course, and should reveal how they plan to use their newly acquired knowledge.

Suggestion: If they do an outstanding job, encourage them to make an annual presentation. Yes, it can be in your class, but it can also be beyond the walls of your building. All kinds of organizations are looking for speakers. Students might consider presenting at PTA meetings or school board meetings or principals' meetings, or at educational conferences—with parental approval and chaperonage, of course.

Presenters in a corporate setting should consider making a presentation for the Chamber of Commerce or for a local business association.

16. Distribute a reading list.

Teachers have been doing this in June for decades—distributing a reading list so that, come September, students will be primed. While your students may not have the breaks to which schoolchildren are subjected, you can nonetheless keep them in prime learning-receptivity mode by preparing and distributing a list of course-relevant books. You might even help establish a book club!

Brainteaser: If you study the first figure-8, you should be able to figure out what number is missing from the bottom half of the second figure-8.

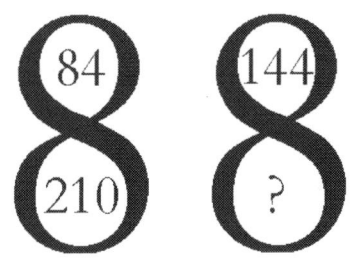

Answer: 360. The bottom number equals twice the top number, plus one-half the top number.

---

17. Use the walls for hanging.

No matter where you do your instructing, there are corridors in the building—corridors that typically reflect nothing but the fluorescent lights above. Begin to view all that space as a way to keep learning alive. Have groups write their end-of-class learning summaries, along with their names, on a sheet of flipchart paper. Post the summaries around the building and don't take them down until the next class has its own set ready for posting.

Brainteaser: Which line below the passage contains the best missing words?

"According to artist Hans Hofmann, the _____ of simplification _____ you to _____ the _____ so that what *is* necessary can speak to you."

1. act	invites	include	beautiful
2. process	exhorts	embellish	necessary
3. process	requires	eliminate	unnecessary
4. creation	pushes	analyze	background

Answer: 3.

18. Arrange informational interviews.

Even if you don't personally know the power-players who could help convince participants that the course can impact their futures, you can still make phone calls. (You'd be surprised how many business people and college professors are flattered and willing to speak to students as part of the informational-interview process.) When you make your calls, explain that you'll need only 15–30 minutes of the individual's time, and that the student's interview can be done by phone or e-mail. Set these up and invite participants to take advantage of them.

Note: The more experts you have, the less likely that any one of them will be over-burdened. In fact, you can assign five students to each of the experts, and then leave it up to them to decide when and if they wish to follow through with the informational interview. More experts will mean that each will have only one or two commitments.

Brainteaser: Find the pair of words with the same analogy pattern as that shown in these two words: SCULPTURE : CHISEL : : :

a) building : lumber   b) book : computer   c) painting : artist   d) quilt : design

Answer: b.

---

19. Develop connections with former students.

At the end of each class, ask participants if they would be willing to serve as mentors for future class members. Obtain the e-mail addresses and/or phone numbers for those generous enough to help others. Then, when you meet your next class, distribute the list. Encourage students to ask questions, explore ideas, and seek mini-tutorials or short professional-coaching time with their mentors. (Be certain that mentors are evenly assigned to participants. One way to avoid over-burdening any one person is to tell new class participants to choose a surname on the list that is alphabetically closest to their own name.)

Brainteaser: What's your interpretation of this Portuguese proverb?

"There's no catching trout with dry breeches."

1. Fishermen and women usually wade in deep waters.
2. People who don't like water should not fish.
3. Be prepared to make some sacrifices to reach your goal.
4. The best fish are found in the deepest waters.

Answer: 3.

20. Use completion certificates as bribes.

Many organizations have done away with certificates of completion in an effort to save money. It's easy enough, though, to prepare your own with the aid of a computer and printer. (The nicer the paper, the more eager participants will be to receive the certificates. Also, you may want to affix a gold seal to make the certificate really special.) As an enticement, I tell participants that I know of people who go in for job interviews with copies of all their course-completion certificates and leave those with the prospective employer, stapled to their résumé.

To encourage post-course postulation, tell participants that the certificates will only be delivered or mailed to them if they have communicated with you three times in the next three months. The "communication" should be a brief report of how they are using the information they acquired in class.

Brainteaser: Your Friday was an especially full day, and you decide to retire early, knowing that you can sleep until nine the next morning. You wind and set your alarm clock accordingly, and decide to make it an early night by going to bed at eight. How many hours of sleep will you get?

Answer: 1. If you go to bed at 8 and the alarm is set for 9, it will ring one hour after you have set it.

---

21. Have them create a game board.

If you offer choices for homework assignments, make one of them the creation of a game board that uses dice and cards pertinent to the course content. Have a few of the other students try the game out in class, and ask for their honest opinion (in private). If it's positive, make copies of the game board on 8½ × 11-inch paper. Make copies as well of the instructions and the cards. Be sure the names of the game creators are prominently displayed.

Give the game as a "graduation gift" at the end of the class. Encourage participants to play it at least once a month (preferably with non-class members) so the knowledge can move in ever-widening circles.

Brainteaser: Can you conceive of the circumstances that explain this true story from Buckinghamshire, England? It happened in the 1800's. An inefficient employee ruined a whole batch of the factory's product. Instead of being fired, though, he was actually thanked by his employer! Can you imagine why?

Answer: If necessity is the mother of invention, then mistake can be called the father: The employee left out an important ingredient in the production of paper. He wound up with a new product: blotting paper.

22. Find a course-related competition.

If you watched Donald Trump's television reality show "The Apprentice" in its third season, you might remember that Staples holds an annual competition (with very handsome rewards) for new office products. A class geared to office managers or administrative assistants could be advised to enter such a competition. So could a class that has entrepreneurship or creativity as its core.

Such competitions abound on the internet. If you are willing to take the time to locate them, you can promote further learning and further wallet-fattening.

Brainteaser: Here's a conundrum that requires you to think, quite literally, outside the box: Harry loves to ski on the world's greatest slopes. Since there are none in his home state of Florida, he flew to Switzerland for a ski vacation. Unfortunately, he had an accident and wound up in the Intensive Care Unit of a hospital in Geneva. On his return trip home to the United States, he was not required to show his passport when the plane landed in New York. Can you figure out why?

Answer: Harry did not survive the accident, and his body was shipped home in a box in the cargo section of the plane.

---

23. Create a hook to entice them to keep on learning.

Salespeople are fully aware of the kinds of "hooks" that pull buyers in. Among them are:

- THE FEAR FACTOR. While you don't want to deliberately scare participants in your efforts to get them to continue their learning, you should have no compunction in reminding them that the future belongs to those who are prepared for it. And the only way to prepare for that future is to continuously update their knowledge and skills.

- THE VANITY FACTOR. Well-read people are usually admired, attended to, and listened to. And we all want to experience those reactions from other people. You can use quotations as the vanity hook that will reel students in. (Quotations suggest that the person using them is well-read and thus admired.) Choose quotations that specifically relate to the importance of ongoing education. Here are three for your consideration:

    "Where there is not vision, the people perish."
    —Proverbs 29:18

    "We never do anything well 'til we cease to think about the manner of doing it."
    —William Hazlitt

    "Change your thoughts and you change the world."
    —Norman Vincent Peale

(continued)

23. Create a hook to entice them to keep on learning. *(concluded)*

- THE USP FACTOR (unique selling proposition). Think long and hard about what separates a continuous learner from an ordinary student. Once you've ascertained the advantages that accrue to people who keep on learning, use this as your hook.

Do not let students leave your class unless you've used one or more hooks to encourage ongoing knowledge-acquisition (i.e., quantity, fear, professional advancement).

Brainteaser: Just think of how word-wealthy you are becoming with all these vocabulary quizzes. Can you complete the following in five minutes?

1. Disdain	A. Lacking harmony
2. Disparage	B. Distribute or spread
3. Disparity	C. To lose or squander
4. Disputation	D. Lacking morality
5. Disseminate	E. Difference, lack of equality
6. Dissertation	F. To show a lack of respect for, to reject
7. Dissipate	G. To stretch
8. Dissolute	H. To separate, to move in another direction
9. Dissonant	I. To belittle
10. Distend	J. Extremely upset
11. Distraught	K. Formal essay or research paper
12. Diverge	L. Disagreement

Answers: 1. F 2. I 3. E 4. L 5. B 6. K 7. C 8. D 9. A 10. G 11. J 12. H

---

24. Poll the class regarding pedagogical proclivities.

Ask for a show of hands in response to your question regarding who is interested in teaching either as a future or a second career. Point out that teaching doesn't necessarily require a teaching certificate; Little League coaches and aerobics instructors and Bible school teachers have no such certificate.

Once you've identified those individuals interested in teaching, meet with them briefly and ask if they would be willing to help you make changes to the curriculum. Elicit their opinions on how the course could be improved. If they'd like to teach or co-teach a segment of a future class, invite them to do so.

(continued)

500 Creative Classroom Techniques for Teachers and Trainers

24. **Poll the class regarding pedagogical proclivities.** *(concluded)*

Brainteaser: Can you figure out what Richard liked?

Joe enjoyed reading books; Germaine preferred to read poetry. Paul enjoyed making things from wood; Sara was inclined to make things from metal. Don liked working with materials that were smooth; Betsy liked the irregularities of rocks. Tony liked to cook; Anne would rather bake. What did Richard enjoy?

    1. archery   2. fishing   3. swimming   4. movies

Answer: 3. The first person [male] in each pair liked something with a double vowel or consonant, such as "books."

---

25. **Collaborate with another instructor.**

Exchange course outlines and reinforce one another's course emphases, whenever possible. Such reinforcement helps create the impression that knowledge truly is inter-connected. As an anonymous sage once wrote, "At the most basic level, it all coheres."

Brainteaser: Study the row of boxes on the first line. Then figure out which box in the second line should complete the empty box on the first.

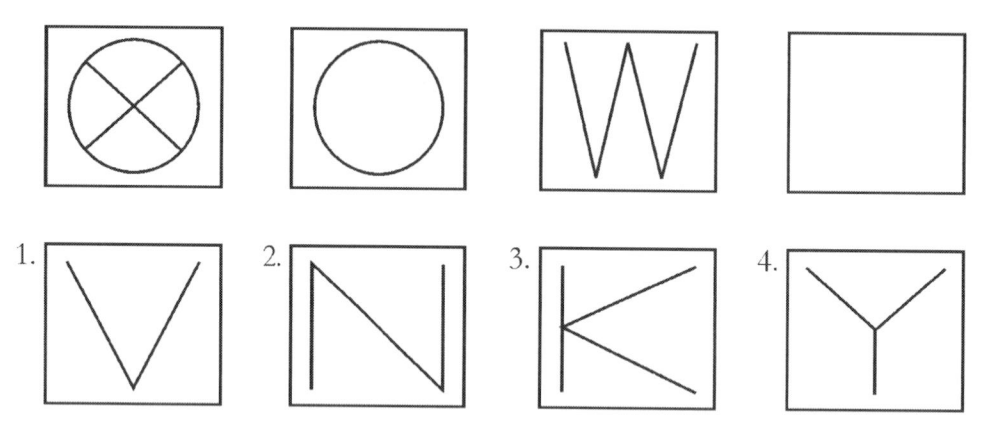

Answer: 1. The second box in the top row has two fewer lines than the number of lines in the first box. So, the fourth box would also have two fewer lines, changing the "W" to a "V."

Chapter 15

25 Ways to Encourage Managers, Principals, and Parents to Continue the Learning

Chapter Overview

It will not surprise you to hear that learning and retention are two separate things. Unfortunately, what separates them is the intrusion of daily living upon the acquired knowledge. As a result, the knowledge fades and in time is forgotten. Unless, that is, deliberate efforts are undertaken to keep the learning alive.

If there is no follow-up on the part of the participant, the organization, or the community in which he lives or works, the knowledge disappears. In fact, a study by the Xerox Corporation found that 87 percent of the information acquired from training sessions is lost unless subsequent attention is paid to it.

This section provides you with 25 ways to help participants choose to use what they've learned via gentle pressure exerted by those who matter in their lives.

1. Extend an invitation to the most senior person in the organization.

Retired three-star general Vito Morgano of the New Jersey National Guard always stopped by at the beginning of the sessions I presented for his employees. He talked to the participants about the importance of what they were about to learn, and pointed out that it was his decision for them to be in that room, learning that material (teambuilding and facilitation skills, in this case). He stopped by unexpectedly during the program, and always asked for my feedback in relation to his employees. Needless to say, he also made an appearance at the end of the class.

Invite someone who is significant in the lives of your participants to address them at the beginning of the class. But don't stop there: As various topics are covered, invite those who have some relationship to the specific knowledge presented to stop by at different times in the course.

And don't overlook the value of inviting these significant individuals to say a few words at the completion of the course as participants prepare to move on. The last word heard is often the first word remembered.

2. Seek funds for an annual consortium.

This need not be as formidable a task as it first appears. The "funding" can be minimal (such as coffee and doughnuts for the initial meeting) and can increase as the success of the conference grows. Invite local experts to participate; trainers and university professors will often make *pro bono* presentations, especially short ones.

Again, start small. Perhaps the first consortium could be just a half-day. If it's difficult to take time away from the school- or work-day, consider a Saturday morning meeting. Invite numerous organizational officials. Invite those from other schools or companies. Perhaps even invite the press.

But do all you can to launch an annual meeting at which the subject matter is strengthened and reinforced.

Brainteaser: Complete this analogy with a four-letter word that ends in "L."

Future is to the present as ideal is to _ _ _ _.

Answer: Real.

---

3. Help them find advocates.

As an outsider, I'm often in the position of being able to praise my students after the class is over and to make recommendations regarding issues that were brought up in class. Outsider or insider, though, you carry some clout. Instructor-types always do. Tell participants upon the conclusion of the class that you will champion them, and that you will seek others (instructors, managers, school officials, parents) to serve as champions. Specify the ways the championing can be done.

Possibilities: If you are a corporate trainer, meet with the person who arranged for the class to be held and offer suggestions for extending the learning.

If you work within a school system, give periodic updates, even if they are not solicited, to your administrators. Or speak at a conference at least once, and bring along students to speak as well.

Tell participants you will be happy to write a reference for them if they ever need one. Include a comment from a manager or administrator in the reference letter, if possible.

If you do some writing, include participants' work and names in your articles or books, along with commentary from their principals, managers, or parents.

4. Send a monthly e-newsletter.

Not only to participants, but to their significant academic/professional others as well. Keep it short, but make it useful. Reinforce the learning and include suggestions for applying the information they have learned.

Brainteaser: How about a few more antonyms? The completion-goal is five minutes or less.

1. Despotism		A.	Dabble
2. Detail		B.	Lack of ability
3. Deterrent		C	Song of jubilation
4. Deviate		D.	Democracy
5. Dexterity		E.	To make convenient
6. Diaphanous		F.	An aid or boost
7. Diffidence		G.	Thick
8. Diligent		H.	Arrogance
9. Dirge		I.	Lazy
10. Discommode		J.	Conform

Answers: 1. D 2. A 3. F 4. J 5. B 6. G 7. H 8. I 9. C 10. E

---

5. Organize a competition.

If you have had the good fortune of seeing the movie *Mad Hot Ballroom* in the theatre or on DVD, you'll remember teachers advising students that there can only be one trophy-winner, but that even those who don't win it have won many other things. They've won self-respect, admiration, and new skills. In addition, they won an early chance to deal with disappointment. The bounce-back motivation that often ensues from not coming in first can lead, as it did for the Indigo Team in the movie, to winning-status later in their lives.

Before, during, and after the competition, try to emphasize some learning points, especially with those who you suspect will not deal well with disappointment. The competition could be a simple Jeopardy-like meeting of the minds, or a competition in the form of the increasingly popular spelling bee. Or it could also be structured as a team effort, such as "Family Feud," or something much more elaborate. You'll find that local merchants are often willing to contribute merchandise to the winners.

Include family members, managers, administrators, and community leaders among the people you invite to watch the competition.

6. Create a Hall of Fame.

Literally. Ask permission first to decorate the walls of the building with photographs (or at least names) of those who have completed a post-class assignment. The photos can be placed in frames to be found at garage sales. The non-uniform nature of these frames could create a really interesting effect. Be sure to walk visitors down the corridor whenever you can.

Brainteaser: Which set of words best completes the sentence with blanks in it?

Did Henry David Thoreau _____ the _____ when he encouraged being ". . . a _____ to whole new _____ and worlds within you, opening new channels, not of trade, but of thought"?

1. predict, future, traveler, areas
2. find, answer, explorer, terrains
3. know, mystery, seeker, discoveries
4. foresee, Internet, Columbus, continents
5. describe, future, wanderer, arenas

Answer: 4.

7. Start a "concept club."

There are half a million book clubs in existence today. They're an integral part of our history, and have been for a century and a half. Many of us too busy to read books in their entirety would nonetheless benefit from gatherings at which *ideas* can be discussed.

For participants who are idea-hungry but can't afford more than fast-food for thought, start a concept club. Limit it to about 15 members per club, and encourage them to meet at least once a month. Invite an outsider (manager, principal, parent) to each meeting. Appoint a discussion leader and set time limits for discussion. Each person will share one course-related concept or talk about one individual he has come across in the last month—something or someone who has had a profound effect on the participant. Those ideas are shared and briefly recorded.

At the end of the year, donate the recorded ideas to the organizational library or to an incomeing class.

Brainteaser: Complete this analogy with a four-letter word that ends in "e."

Reticent : Glib : : Ice :

Answer: Fire.

8. Collect loose change and subscribe to a trade journal.

If you work in a school setting, you may want to take the money out of petty cash, but in a corporate setting, one dollar per person will probably cover the cost of the journal for a year. Type up the names of class members and one manager or school official as well. Leave space beneath each name for a comment or two. When the first issue of the journal arrives, read it, make a comment beneath your name, and pass the magazine and roster to the first person on the list. Request that he read it, comment, and pass it along within a week's time. Ask the others to do the same.

Brainteaser: Samantha believes in the health benefits of onions. On her weekly shopping trip on Monday, she bought a bag of onions. That very day, she used a third of them in her stir-fry vegetable dish. On Tuesday, she used half the remaining onions to make onion soup. On Wednesday, she looked in the onion bag and found that she only had two left.

How many did she start with?

Answer: Samantha started the week with six onions. She used two the first day and two the second day.

---

9. Make eponyms part of the organizational culture.

They have the Tonys for Broadway, the Emmys for television, and the Oscars for Hollywood productions. Take this idea and extend it to your classes. Think up an award for those class members who are truly exemplary in terms of various course concepts.

Ask yourself, *Who really understood the concept of Contingency Theory? Who grasped Lewin's Change Model easily? Who was able to breeze through the Paramedic Method exercises?* The answers to such questions will yield the names of people whose first names will be used as the award recognizing the particular skills they mastered. The "Yvonne," for example, would be named for the woman who really understood the Contingency Theory (or whatever other educational element pertains to the material *you* teach).

Once the awards have been established, hold a small ceremony to recognize the individuals. Invite parents, co-workers, and managers to the event. Then, regularly identify subsequent recipients and present the awards to them each year. (Small trophies can be found in the dollar store.) Ideally, before the course if over, one eponym-award will be associated with each .

Option: For each class, you could have reigning figureheads who will keep their titles until the next class begins.

Examples for Language Arts: The Prince of Pronouns; the Comma Czarina; the Syntax Scion; the Duke of Dangling Participles.

(continued)

9. **Make eponyms part of the organizational culture.** *(concluded)*

Brainteaser: If you write the numbers 1 through 6 in the circles in the right way, you will always get a total of 9 by adding the numbers along each side. (You can only use each number one time.)

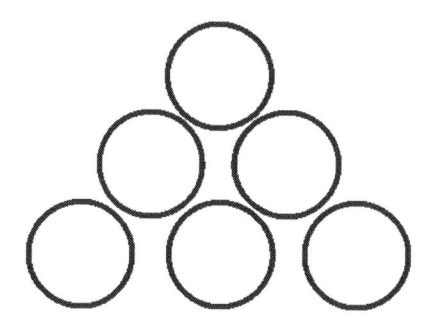

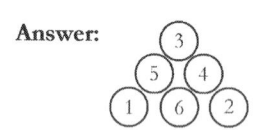

Answer:
```
    3
  5   4
 1  6  2
```

---

10. Enlist the aid of others significant in participants' lives.

No matter who those significant people are, they can be called upon and *usually counted on* to help you extend the learning. All they have to do is ask a question. Managers, for example, could start every staff meeting with this question, "What did you learn in your training that will help you do your job better?" Parents could ask, "Can you teach me what you learned in school today?"

We know that it takes a village to raise a child. It also takes more people than the classroom instructor to reinforce the learning. Count on those people and collaborate with them.

Brainteaser: Each of the answers required to complete the analogies is a four-letter word ending in the letter "e" or "g."

1. Antipathy : hate : : passion : ___ ___ ___ ___
2. Syllables : haiku : : beat : ___ ___ ___ ___

Answer: 1. Love 2. Song

11. Initiate an organizational Kwanza.

Dr. Maulana Karenga initiated the tribute to ancient African virtues the same year Dr. Martin Luther King was assassinated. Nearly 40 years later, 28 million people worldwide spend seven days in December affirming unity, self-determination, collective work, cooperative economics, purpose, creativity, and faith in Kwanza celebrations.

Assemble a team of class participants, organizational administrators, and community members to identify common values associated with learning. Decide how those values can be recognized. Give the celebration a name, pick a time for its observance, and begin spreading the word.

Brainteaser: A little more challenging this time. The answers to these analogy questions will all be four-letter *or* five-letter words ending in either "e" or "g."

1. Sophistication : refinement : : elegance is to _____
2. Beds : make : : papers : _____
3. Idaho : potato : : key : _____
4. Roman numeral : outline : : ladder : _____

Answers: 1. Grace 2. File 3. Lime 4. rung

---

12. Move into other realms.

Dr. Jonas Salk, when asked how he came up with the cure for polio, told a reporter, "I learned to think the way Mother Nature thinks." Transfer this perspective to post-class learning. Ask each participant to contact someone associated with the animal kingdom: a zookeeper, a pet store owner, an ornithologist, a beekeeper, and so on. Have them learn about the habits and habitat of the particular animal or insect. Then, have them transfer their insights about the animal kingdom to the learning they are acquiring in your class.

Suggestion: If possible, prepare a one- or two-page newsletter containing their insights. Share it with those who were interviewed, as well as organizational leaders. If you suspect that corporate executives will question the relevance, simply remind them of what Warren Bennis had to say: "If I were asked to give off-the-cuff advice to anyone seeking to institute change, the first thing I would ask is, 'How clear is your metaphor?'"

Or refer them to his books (and those of Kouzes and Nanus). These management experts hold that our nation's best corporate leaders employ metaphorical language. Your participants' animal-related insights are simply metaphorical connections between two worlds.

13. Create a boon box.

Every participant will experience, has experienced, or is experiencing a setback or disappointment—perhaps in his learning-journey, perhaps with some other aspect of his life. Not surprisingly, our satisfaction with life is directly proportional to the mechanisms we have discovered for coping with the trials, tribulations, and sometimes even the tragedies that befall us.

To facilitate the transition from setback to steady course, decorate a good-sized box. Ask other class members, organizational leaders, politicians, community members, religious leaders, parents, and so on to add a quotation, a story, or even an object that can be shared with the person who is temporarily "down." (Ask that the addition be related to education or careers, if possible.)

Then, after the class is over, as you learn about unfortunate circumstances that have befallen a class member, present him with the box. Ask that he keep it as long as he needs to derive strength from it, and to pass it along, when he is ready, to someone else in the school or firm who is going through a difficult time. Ask that he add a written message about how he overcame his particular adversity (anonymously, if he wishes).

14. Invite participants and stakeholders to a Serendipi-Tea party.

"Stakeholders" are those individuals or groups who have some vested interest in the participants' future. Depending on your teaching situation, those individuals might be colleagues, team members, supervisors, customers, vendors, parents, other teachers whom the students will encounter, classmates, administrators, and so on.

Just before class disbands, give them a date (one month hence, during the lunch hour, for example) when you will be holding a tea party, to which their significant stakeholders will be invited. Advise that you will be calling upon class members to talk about serendipitous discoveries, such as a shortcut they stumbled upon, an interesting course-related fact, a way to work smarter, faster, or less expensively, and so on.

At the tea, make every effort to tie participant discoveries to learning. In the general sense, you could make a tie-in regarding receptivity to new ideas or heightened awareness of their circumstances. And, of course, if you can make specific tie-ins to the subject matter they studied, that's even better.

15. Send course-related birthday cards signed by their supervisor or leader.

At the beginning of class, ask each person to list his birthday. With adults, it's best to avoid the years—just get the month and day. Then, throughout the year, send a birthday card or postcard that contains a quote from a course-related figure and the signature of someone who is significant in the participant's life (a manager, a principal, a department head, and so on).

Examples of course-related figures to quote:

Shakespeare: "There was a star that danced and under it was I born." Add: "May the stars keep on dancing on your birthday and always." (for an English or literature class)

John Muir: "I never saw a discontented tree. They grip the ground as though they liked it, and though-fast rooted, they travel about as far as we do." Add: "Here's wishing you a birthday of contentment." (for an environmental studies or science class)

16. Hold a benchmarking meeting.

From the Total Quality Management (TQM) movement that started in the 1980s, we learned about the value of benchmarking—the process of comparing one organization's methods to those methods employed by best-in-class organizations. Here are the official steps in that process:

1. Identify potential benchmarking requirements.
2. Prioritize and select one process.
3. Prepare the benchmarking project plan.
4. Gather data on existing practices.
5. Identify possible benchmarking partners.
6. Contact the potential partner and negotiate mutually beneficial terms for the partnership agreement.
7. Arrange a visit to the partner's site.
8. Analyze the partner's operation.
9. Synthesize results of the visit, delineating gaps between your existing operation and the ideal operation.
10. Develop an action plan, incorporating findings from the benchmarking visit.
11. Implement the plan and monitor it.
12. Make adjustments as needed.

(continued)

16. Hold a benchmarking meeting. *(concluded)*

Now, you may not want to do a full-blown benchmarking study. And you certainly don't have to. But it will no doubt behoove you and the organization if you do some research about what's happening in other learning centers/situations and attempt to replicate those successes in your own organization. If you can't actually visit the site, at least visit the Web site of the best-in-class organization. Find one new thing that you think will work in your own organization.

Ask class members if they are interested in participating in your improvement project. Then, when you hold the meeting at which you will make your proposal for undertaking this new learning project, have decision-makers present, as well the class participants who have agreed to assist.

If you gain approval for your proposal, launch the improvement project. If you don't gain approval, scale it down or propose a smaller project. Remember, administrators are more likely to say yes to a new possibility if they can be assured that it is already being done elsewhere and is working.

---

17. Award a prediction prize.

Before class is over, pass out uniform-size paper and ask each participant to make a specific course-related prediction or a prediction about the organization, and then sign it. Collect the papers and put them in a nicely decorated box. Write an appropriate label on it and store it for one year.

Then hold a ceremony to which participants and organizational leaders are invited. (Invite parents of the participants, too, if you teach in a school setting.) Read the predictions aloud and award a prize to the person whose prediction was most on-target.

Examples for organizations: Predictions might concern new appointments at the executive level, merger news, test scores, who the valedictorian will be, how the sports teams will do, or what budget cuts employees will have to live with.

Course-related examples:

Finance class: What the Dow-Jones number will be on a specific day. *Science class:* What new drug will be on the market. *Journalism class:* What will be the hottest story in the news in the next twelve months. *Political science class:* Who will be appointed to a high judicial or legislative position. *Science class:* What medical breakthrough will be announced.

18. Make a verbal necklace with pearls of wisdom; get leaders to use or display it.

I have a file labeled "Satchelisms." It contains those wonderfully pithy statements made by people like baseball great Leroy Satchel Paige, who had his own way with words:

"Avoid fried meats which angry up the blood."

"If your stomach disputes you, lie down and pacify it with cool thoughts."

"Keep the juices flowing by jangling around gently as you move."

"Avoid running at all times."

"Don't look back. Something might be gaining on you."

Every class has its own Satchel or two—the people who offer up clever or insightful or startlingly intelligent comments. Ask someone to write them down each time they are expressed, along with the originator's name.

Type the comments and distribute them to organizational leaders. Just as the President will cite the words of an ordinary citizen in a State of the Union address, the principal of your school or the president of your company could easily quote one of the wry observers of contemporary reality who reside in your class for a while. The quote could be used at the start of a staff or faculty meeting; it could be placed on the intranet; it could be used as part of the P.A. announcements, and so on.

Brainteaser: What word in the second line of each question fits with the capitalized words in the first line?

1. FIRE   BOY   POP   OFF
   husband   fishing   doll   garden

2. BOWL   CARD   RABBIT   OUT
   drunk   finished   celery   oven

3. PETER   GRASS   SHAKER   CAKE
   argument   velvet   church   box

4. SPORTS   MOVIE   DANCE   MAIL
   twilight   enchant   light   shadow

5. PLAY   BALL   LINE   RUN
   tree   out   between   hill

Answers: 1. Fishing (All words relate to "fly.") 2. Drunk (All words relate to "punch.") 3. Box (All words relate to "salt.") 4. Light (All words relate to "fan.") 5. Out (All words relate to "foul.")

19. Publish a collective poem.

Poet William Carlos Williams once observed, "It is difficult to get the news from poems, yet men die miserably every day for lack of what is found there." Poems have power. And companies like AT&T, Boeing, and Kodak are hiring poets to help employees find that power.

Collective poems can be written in several ways. One of the simplest requires each person to draw an image of the workplace or school and then to add words to describe that image.

Another technique is to have one person start the learning-related poem and to pass his line to another participant, who adds one more line before turning the versatile verse to yet another participant.

A third possibility is to take the first word or two from each line of a given poem and have would-be poets add their own words to complete each line. Some very interesting results can be produced in this way.

Example (words taken from Calvin C. Hernton's "Madhouse")

Here is _____
And here is _____
A _____
And beyond _____
Bring _____
Yet _____
And _____
In _____
From _____
And those _____

Once the poem is complete, use the Internet to find the places and people seeking poems to publish. When the poem appears in cyberspace or in print, be sure to notify the training administrators and others interested in the progress participants are making.

Brainteaser: What four-letter word, ending in "t," completes the analogy?

"Penultimate" is to "ultimate" as "next-to-the-last" is to _____.

Answer: Last.

20. Get rid of mental and physical white elephants.

During the last hour of class, tell participants about an upcoming "white elephant" event that they are expected to attend. What's more, they'll be expected to participate by sharing one perspective (or old or erroneous belief) they have discarded as a result of the class they attended.

In the next few weeks, make arrangements to hold the auction of "white elephants" during the lunch hour. (You may have to restrict the number of attendees to 50. That number will include the members of your class.) Be sure that at least some of those who directly or indirectly paid for the class members to receive their training/tutelage are present. Collect things people no longer want—those things will be auctioned off. The proceeds can be used for either a charitable cause or to purchase supplies, such as scrapbooks, for the next class.

Begin the event by calling on each class member present to tell what *mental* white elephant he has recently discarded as a result of the training. Then let the bidding begin. Keep the action moving; if something is stalled at 50 cents, sell it and move on.

21. Pave two-way streets via personification.

The former CEO of Ford Motor Company, Don Petersen, was fond of saying that results depend on relationships. And relationships depend on knowing one another. One of the best ways to forge the ties that bond is to have each person select some simple object and then tell how it embodies his particular essence. Encourage them to share this "essential" insight with those outside the classroom.

Examples: Someone might choose an ordinary sponge to represent his desire to absorb as much knowledge about this subject as he possibly can. Someone else might choose a pencil and explain that he took a lot of notes in the class and made an occasional error on a quiz, but that he knows how to erase the mistakes and profit from them. They are then expected to share their insights with someone whose life impacts the participant's in a meaningful way. Invite that person to think about and decide upon a personified object of his own. Use that information with future classes and in future newsletters. Invite the inside student and the outside mentor to make a joint presentation regarding their insights.

Note: Participants can employ either similes ("I am like a sponge") or true personification ("I am a sponge").

500 Creative Classroom Techniques for Teachers and Trainers

22. Take a hint from secretaries.

Secretaries deserve all the accolades they can get. The national day established in their honor is a fitting tribute to the excellence on which they pride themselves. Secretaries, though, have learned a secret—one that your learners might benefit from: *Ask and you shall receive*. They've asked to be recognized every April, and they are!

You may not want to make a nationally recognized day out of it, but you could establish one day each week or each month to recognize the subject matter and those working to become experts in it. Work with the stakeholders we've talked about so often in this section to organize special events for that one particular day. Put banners around the building. Dedicate a special cafeteria meal. Write a song or theme to be sung or shouted at rallies.

Suggestions: Time-Management Thursday
Stress-Reduction September
Geographers Day
Mathematical Mondays
Foreign Language February

---

23. Invite collaboration on M-Proves.

To paraphrase a popular refrain, "I like you just the way you are . . . almost." This activity asks participants to see themselves as others see them, and then to make the good even better and the excellent, exemplary. Collaboration between participants and their supervisors or leaders is what's called for.

Ask each student to think of someone he believes is genuinely concerned about his well-being and to then ask that person to rank-order ten adjectives that best describe the participant and his attitude/approach/way of working or learning. (To really challenge the stakeholder, suggest that all the words start with the letter "M.") The participant will also compile his own list of M words and then rank-order those he feels best represent his personality, work ethic, et cetera.

Then have the two meet to compare their lists. Ask participants to make a commitment: To improve in one area and to set a date by which he will *prove* that he has improved.

Note: These list-comparing sessions between employee and supervisor or student and parent could be held once a month.

24. Use class products as part of new-employee orientation.

Make Human Resources aware of the fact that you'd be happy to have new hires sit in on one of your training programs for 15 minutes. If the scheduling proves to be difficult, take some of the products from your training program (a scrapbook, a video, group essays, for example) and leave them with the HR department to show job applicants the kinds of training available to them as employees of your firm.

If you teach in a school setting, you can do the same. Make the front desk aware of the fact that you'd be very happy to have new students and their parents stop by your classroom to get a sense of what the school is like. Leave the class-notebook (or other products) at the front desk so that students who come to register in the middle of the year can be welcomed via a project your class has done.

Brainteaser: From Haiti, a wise proverb: "Once you have said 'Here I am,' don't try to say that you are not there." Does it relate to lying, commitment, or fear?

Answer: Commitment.

25. Celebrate Janus, organization-wide.

The ancient Romans honored the god Janus by showing his two profiles on coins: with one he looked back over the year just ending. With the other, he looked forward to the year about to begin. (The month of January is named for him.)

Use the Janusian example to revamp some of the same ol', same ol' practices your organization or school has been using for years. Form a committee of participants and stakeholders to consider doing things differently, to look at things from the inside-out or in an upside-down fashion. Try combining two opposites and see what improvements can be made as a result.

Example of Janusian thinking: In mystery stories, the murderer is typically not revealed until the very end. Two gifted Hollywood writers, though, decided to do just the opposite: to reveal the "perp" within the first few minutes of the story. And lo, Colombo was born!

Chapter 16

25 Ways to Develop Study Habits

Chapter Overview

It's not just students who seek efficiencies for storing and recalling information. It's everyone who needs to retain information for short-term or long-term purposes. There's an inescapable deluge of information that threatens to drown all of us unless we can cling to mental life jackets that will help us tread water and keep our heads above it.

In this section, you'll find techniques for helping your students take the data they need and store them for easier retrieval when needed. And, if you'll forgive a metaphor mix, you'll all discover techniques to improve listening, concentrating, attending, and remembering—all peas in the same cognitive pod of data-retrieval.

Note: This entire book is addressed to you. Written in the second person, it speaks to your instructional persona. This section, however is really addressed to the student (although it's still written in the second person). It consists of tips that show her how to optimize her time in learning and committing to memory the knowledge she'll need for a variety of purposes. I've addressed the students directly so you can easily replicate the pages.

1. Skim the material.

Before setting out on a journey of any distance, you no doubt consult a map to get a sense of where you are headed. In a similar fashion, consider the skimming process as a means of obtaining an overview of the intellectual direction in which you are heading. If you are alone, it won't embarrass you at all to talk to yourself as you skim. Don't hesitate to vocalize your reaction to the material. The process of doing so will definitely help you remember.

Statements like the following will help you internalize the new knowledge you are attempting to acquire.

Sample statements:

"Now, *that's* interesting." "I never knew that."
"*That* can't be right." "That reminds me of something we learned last year."
"I already *knew* that." "Won't Joe be surprised to hear this!"
"Oh, I need to learn more about *that*." "I wonder why that is."

2. Make use of typographical aids.

Look at a page you are required to study. Select one that is easy to read because of the way it is laid out. Whoever did that layout designed it to make it easy for you, the reader. She deliberately chose typographical devices in order to emphasize certain points, to organize the material, and to facilitate the reading and understanding of all those words.

Study that page carefully. Pay attention to the way typographical aids were used to direct your attention to the main points. Consider the different-sized fonts, the use of white space, the bullets, indentations, print sizes. Also note the use of boldface, the use of headings, and so on.

Accept the author's help—she will have already sorted through the verbiage and will have selected various typographical aids to communicate to you what is most important. Use those aids to help you remember information you will need in the future.

Brainteaser: You may already know that the word "oxymoron" comes from two Greek words: "oxy," meaning "wise" and "moron," meaning "fool." How fast can you match the words on the left with their opposites on the right to create oxymorons?

1. pretty   a. dirt
2. rap   b. landfill
3. clean   c. music
4. sanitary   d. ugly

Answers: 1. d 2. c 3. a 4. b

---

3. Interact with the material.

You've probably heard this bit of Confucian wisdom: "I hear and I forget. I see and I remember. But I *do* and I learn." The more physical you get with the information you need to learn, the more likely you are to retain it.

So, underline or highlight passages as you usually do. But also use your pencil to write questions in the margins and draw a star beside an especially important passage. Write exclamation points or reactive words. Use parentheses or brackets within a passage. Use brackets for entire paragraphs and add your own comments, such as "Skip. Already know this."

Do all you can to build a mental and/or emotional relationship with the material.

Brainteaser: More oxymorons. Can you match them in 5 seconds?

1. alone   A. aggressive
2. sweet   B. together
3. passive   C. sorrow

Answers: 1. B 2. C 3. A

4. Use advance organizers.

If your instructor has not provided an overview of the course before beginning to teach it, ask for one. It's your right to have some sense of how the content will flow from one topic to another. Psychologist Hilda Taba called these outline points "advance organizers." In other words, they help you mentally organize the material before you are exposed to it.

You could also view the outline or advance organizer as a skeleton, to which you will add "flesh." You'll put meat on those bones as your mind takes in new knowledge. In time, you'll have your own "body" of knowledge!

If the material you need to ingest is provided in written fashion (as opposed to an instructor's oral outline), you can do the same thing. Most authors will provide an overview of the chapter you are reading. But if they did not, just take the boldface headlines and write them on a separate sheet of paper, in the order in which they appear. These notes will help your mind organize the material, even before you read it. Then, as you do your reading, glance from time to time at your handwritten outline to remind you of the topics you've already read, are reading, or are about to read.

5. Get some sleep.

Don't try to do all your studying at once. You'll get tired and the data will eventually run together like strands of spaghetti on a plate. Time management experts recommend using schedules for work that has to be done in the future. They tell working people to divide their work day according to these deadlines:

- Three hours for work due today.
- Three hours for work due next week.
- One hour for work due next month.
- One-half hour for work due in six months.
- Leftover minutes for work due within the next year.

Make a similar study schedule (perhaps even a separate schedule for term papers). Take into account the amount of studying you have to do. Also consider the time frame involved. How much time do you have before you have to apply what you've learned? How much time do you have before the examination that will test your knowledge? Don't try pulling an all-nighter to remember information you should have been studying all along.

6. Take breaks.

If you have a great deal of information to cover, divide it into good-sized chunks. Every time you finish a chunk, reward yourself. Walk away from your desk and do something physical. Take a quick power walk. Wash your face. Get a glass of ice water. Do aerobic exercises. Spend a few minutes on a hobby. Watch a few minutes of television.

Do this to clear your mind and refresh your body before tackling the next chunk of knowledge.

Brainteaser: If you're not familiar with tautologies, here's your chance to learn a new word and tease your brain at the same time. A tautology is a phrase or expression with two words (usually)—one of which is totally unnecessary. How quickly can you make tautological matches among the following?

1. qualified
2. past
3. thinking
4. raining

A. history
B. in my head
C. outside
D. expert

Answers: 1. D 2. A 3. B 4. C

---

7. Snack healthfully and helpfully.

When you're studying, try to avoid caffeine or colas. Instead, take bites of foods rich in beta carotene, such as apricots and carrot sticks. They'll help keep you mentally alert but not over-stimulated.

Brainteaser: More tautologies. Time yourself before you begin to look for the redundancies as you match words in the first column with their partners in the second.

1. winding
2. true
3. unsold
4. salty
5. hot water
6. Jewish
7. saw it
8. monogrammed
9. rubber
10. real

A. brine
B. people
C. with my own eyes
D. inventory
E. tire
F. initials
G. curve
H. synagogue
I. fact
J. heater

Answers: 1. G 2. I 3. D 4. A 5. J 6. H 7. C 8. F 9. E 10. B

8. Visualize.

Most of us are visual learners. It's easier for us to remember things if we have a mental picture of them. Try to "see" in your mind's eye the situation you are reading about. You can also use your powers of visualization in this way: Imagine your mind as a huge filing cabinet, waiting to be filled with valuable information. Visualize the drawers of that cabinet labeled with the topics that you are learning about. Also imagine folders inside those drawers. "See" huge labels on each folder.

Brainteaser: How good are you at spotting typographical errors? These error-containing statements actually appeared in print. Find the mistakes as fast as you can.

1. Help Wanted: Sadistical secretary
2. Do in yourself. We have all the supplies you will need to make it.
3. He visited West Point and the United States Nasal Academy.
4. In Chicago, six men have been arrested for bride-taking.
5. He suffered a head injury caused by coming in contact with a live wife.
6. He studied unclear physics at the prestigious Massachusetts Institute of Technology.

Answers: 1. Statistical 2. it instead of *in* 3. Naval 4. bribe 5. wire 6. nuclear

9. Create an environment conducive to learning.

You've heard it said that different strokes are used by different folks. Your learning environment will not look or sound like anyone else's, but it should be suitable for *you*. Soft music in the background works well for some people, but it would never be used by others. A comfortable chair would only put some students to sleep; others, though, can sit in no other seat but a comfortable one. Be sure you have good lighting and all the supplies you need nearby. Food and beverage are up to you. Just make sure that you are set up so you won't succumb to the temptation of getting up to find things (and then losing your way back to your study spot).

Brainteaser: For your error-finding eyes only: more true-life errors. Can you find them all in the first reading of each sentence?

1. Richard Green is playing his old position of right tickle.
2. The popular community leader undressed the D. A. R. Tuesday afternoon.
3. He had his girl fried with him on his trip south.
4. The television advertisement offered a free demonstration of RCA's living colon.

Answers: 1. tackle 2. addressed 3. friend 4. color

10. Record those stray thoughts.

Have paper and pencil nearby to capture the thoughts that come into your head unbidden. Some, of course, will pertain to the material you are studying. Other thoughts, however, will have nothing to do with that material. If you don't write these thoughts down, you may be tempted to act on them. And acting on them will probably mean that you will get distracted from your study-goals.

So if your mind wanders to a report you must write or a call you must make, don't get up to do it then. When you are in the middle of studying, you should stay there. All you have to do is jot down the irrelevant thought and attend to it at a later time.

Brainteaser: You've encountered kangaroo words before this. They are, as you will recall, small words contained within bigger words. (Both the small word and its larger counterpart share a similar meaning.) Can you spot the trickier verbal kangaroos in the following?

1. supervisor
2. separate
3. fabrication ("Fabric" is *not* the answer.)

Answers: 1. superior   2. part   3. fiction

---

11. Make good use of your alarm clock.

Before starting to study, determine how much time you can allocate to the activity. Determine, too, when you will take a break and how much you intend to cover before that break. Stick to your schedule, even if you have to set an alarm clock to keep you on track. Congratulate yourself whenever you meet your study goal.

Brainteaser: The following sentences are what the writers actually meant to say, but their fingers betrayed them and they typed one wrong letter in just one word in each sentence, resulting in a funny statement. What's the word you would change or omit (again, by only one letter) to make the statement a humorous one?

1. "I am a rapid typist," the job applicant wrote in her cover letter.
2. He is a veteran detective in the Burbank police force.
3. He is a veteran detective in the Burlington police force.
4. I was responsible for running an entire store operation.

Answer: 1. "rabid"   2. "farce"   3. "defective" (Note: #2 and #3 have interchangeable answers.)   4. "ruining"

Chapter 16: 25 Ways to Develop Study Habits

12. Add variety-spice to your study recipe.

Periodically change the type of material you are studying. If you have math homework to do and a social studies test to study for, switch after a half-hour and spend thirty minutes on the other subject. Other switches you might make: change the chair you are sitting in or the direction in which you are facing or the temperature in the room or the clothes you are wearing.

Studying can lead to boredom, and boredom can lead to sleepiness. Making changes as you absorb ideas is a good way to retain those ideas.

Brainteaser: While less amusing than the errors you encountered earlier, the following passage is also embedded with typographical errors. Can you find all four errors?

1. Each of us in the Accounting Department look forward to meeting you and welcome you to our organization.
2. To maximize the time spent on evaluating employee's suggestions, the conference room will be reserved for the entire day.

Answers: 1. "look" should be "looks" and "welcome" should be "welcoming." 2. "employee's" should be "employees" and the second half of the sentence should read: ". . . we have reserved the conference room for the entire day." Otherwise, we wind up with a misplaced modifier.

---

13. Schedule a review every 20 minutes.

If you have set aside a whole hour to study, you should stop at 20-minute intervals and review what you have learned. You can summarize the main ideas out loud or write them down. You could even call a friend and tell her what you have learned in the last 20-minute interval. The review process is integral to the learning process, so be sure to build in time for it.

Brainteaser: The English language has over 6,000 "lookalike" words. Knowing the part of speech can help you choose the correct word or spelling. So, how quickly can you identify the part of speech of each word below?

1. accept
2. except
3. adapt
4. adept
5. confidant
6. confident
7. discomfit
8. discomfiture
9. envelop
10. envelope
11. foreword
12. forward

Answers: 1. verb 2. preposition 3. verb 4. adjective 5. noun 6. adjective 7. verb 8. noun 9. verb 10. noun 11. noun 12. verb, adverb, or adjective

14. Expect discomfort.

John Dewey noted that the first step in learning in confusion. Expect some discomfort when you encounter new knowledge. Convince yourself that you can plow through it. Encourage yourself with the reminder that new knowledge is hard for everyone to acquire. But once it becomes "old knowledge," you will be able to tame it much more easily. Remind yourself, too, that all the old knowledge you currently possess was *new* knowledge at one time—new knowledge that no doubt caused some confusion.

Brainteaser: Circle the word in each pair that is correctly spelled.

1. pronunciation   pronounciation
2. occasion   ocassion
3. assisstant   assistant
4. repitition   repetition
5. privilege   priviledge
6. definitely   definately
7. seperate   separate
8. desireable   desirable

Answers: 1. pronunciation 2. occasion 3. assistant 4. repetition 5. privilege 6. definitely 7. separate 8. desirable

---

15. Pep-talk; self-talk.

If you've ever watched athletes before their all-important move or jump or shot or serve, you'll often see them talking to themselves. That form of self-talk is a great enhancer of performance. What *doesn't* enhance performance is reminding yourself of your hatred of studying or your fear of tests.

Don't hurt your chances of successful studying. Help yourself instead by maintaining a positive attitude toward your learning and the reason for it. Make yourself receptive to new material by considering its importance in your life or in your career.

Brainteaser: Which of the following is *not* a legitimate spelling rule?

1. The letter "y" preceded by a consonant becomes "i" before a suffix.
2. If the "y" at the end of a word has a vowel in front of it, keep the "y" when adding suffixes.
3. When adding a suffix beginning with a vowel or with "y," drop the final "e."
4. Form the plural of most nouns by adding an "s" to the singular form.
5. Words ending in an "o" preceded by a vowel form their plural by adding "es."

Answer: 5.

16. Take advantage of chronobiology.

You probably know that "chronos" refers to time. And you know that "biology" refers to the study of plants and animals (including man). "Chronobiology" is the study of the effect of time on plants and animals. It's an emerging science, but a useful one. Among its findings: We all have certain hours during which we operate at peak proficiency. And, for each of us, there are times when we simply are not as efficient as we could be.

If you don't yet know what those hours are for you, find out. And then schedule your most intense or difficult studying to be done during that time.

Brainteaser: Which of the following is *not* a legitimate rule for dividing words in a line of type or hyphenating?

1. Divide a word between syllables only.
2. Divide a one-syllable word after the first letter.
3. Divide compound words at the hyphen.
4. Divide words with a double final consonant at the double letters.
5. Do not divide between double consonants that form the ending of a root word.
6. Hyphenate compound numbers from twenty-one to ninety-nine.

Answer: 2.

17. Make discuss-able notes.

Apart from the notes you are making in the text, have a separate list of notes regarding the most interesting fact you found on each page of your reading. As soon as possible after your study time, show that list of notes (at least one note per page of text) and discuss it at length with someone whose opinion matters to you.

Brainteaser: Which of the following is *not* a legitimate rule for capitalization?

1. Capitalize a title preceding a name.
2. Capitalize the first word and all nouns in the salutation of a letter.
3. Capitalize the first word only in the complimentary closing of a letter.
4. Capitalize the first letter of abbreviated words.
5. Capitalize the pronoun "I."
6. Capitalize geographic regions.
7. Do not capitalize the word depicting a family member when the word is used in direct address.
8. Capitalize nouns that have been personified.
9. Do not capitalize compass directions.

Answer: 7.

18. Make your learning murally visible.

Tape a large sheet of paper to a wall. After 15 or 20 minutes of study, walk over to it and write on it the main points you've understood. When you return to the material you've been studying, compare what's on the wall-sheet to what's in front of you. If you've omitted any critical points, go back to the sheet and add them.

Brainteaser: Which of the following sentences is correct?

1. It was his first trip to the far east.
2. Susan's notes are more thorough than your's.
3. He lost his luggage in El Paso twenty four days ago.
4. To get ahead, I'm planning to take more after hours classes.
5. Sam Browne, Jr. will join our team next week.
6. In the latest issue of Defense News is an article about heat-seeking devices.
7. As war strode across the stage, peace cowered in the corner as the children gasped in dismay.
8. The ladies room is on the third floor.

Answers: None of the sentences are correct. 1. Far East 2. yours 3. twenty-four 4. after-hours 5. comma not needed before or after "Jr." 6. Defense News should be underlined or italicized 7. War, Peace 8. Think about the male equivalent: you'd never spell it mens room. So, the answer is ladies'.

---

19. Deliver a speech to an empty house.

Prior to taking a break, stand and pretend you are addressing an audience. Imagine that your boss or the school principal has asked for a summary of what you've learned so far. Without referring to the material, try to capture its main points and speak them aloud. When you sit back down, quickly scan the material you have just studied to see if you forgot anything of importance.

Brainteaser: You know E. B. White of *Charlotte's Web* fame. You probably also know him as the co-author of *The Elements of Style*. Here is something you may not have known about him: He was the person who made the statement below. Which set of words best fits the blank spaces in the original statement?

"No one can _____ decently who is _____ of the reader's intelligence or whose _____ is _____."

1. speak   ignorant   mind   superior
2. think   mindful   belief   wavering
3. write   distrustful attitude   patronizing
4. declare warning   value   obnoxious

Answer: 3.

20. Do a soundless, sightless review.

It helps to block out the external environment when studying. (You are used to doing this because you tend to close your eyes when you are really concentrating. Everyone does.) So, at least once during your study session, close your eyes and silently review what stands out in your mind regarding the material. Then make notes of the questions, concerns, and additional ideas that come to you with your eyes closed.

Take action on your notes by getting the questions answered, addressing the concerns, and exploring the relevant ideas that occurred to you.

Brainteaser: Which of the two sentences in each pair is the correct one?

1. a. Shall we order chinese food for the meeting?
   b. Shall we order Chinese food for the meeting?
2. a. George is president of the local Toastmasters Club.
   b. George is President of the local Toastmasters Club.
3. a. I spoke to Shari—what is her last name—just a minute ago.
   b. I spoke to Shari—What is her last name—just a minute ago.

Answers: 1. b   2. a   3. a

---

21. Become a teacher, if only for a day.

When Ernest Boyer was Secretary of Education, he advised parents to ask their children to teach them what they had learned in school each day. "If they can't teach you," he told parents, "they haven't learned it."

Make his advice a staple in your review-refrigerator. After finishing your study for the day, find a friend, neighbor, co-worker, or relative and teach her what you think you've learned. If she seems utterly confused, it probably means that you are, too.

Brainteaser: You've heard of misplaced modifiers and dangling participles, no doubt. Here are some appearing in either the first or the second sentence in each question. Which sentence's modifiers are not doing their jobs correctly?

1. a. Being correctly typed, the boss appreciated my report.
   b. Being correctly typed, my report earned the boss's appreciation.
2. a. Being old and decrepit, I was able to buy the house at a bargain price.
   b. Being old and decrepit, the house sold far beneath its value.

Answers: 1. a   2. a

22. Steal a memory trick from the ancient Greeks.

For thousands of years, people have used this room-of-the-house tool for recalling important information. Visualize your own house or apartment. Jot down the rooms you would encounter as you go through your home.

Example: Foyer, living room, dining room, kitchen, hallway, bathroom, bedroom #1, bathroom, bedroom #2.

The above example has nine separate locations. Using this number, you would divide the material you have studied into nine main points, trying to capture each point with a single word or short phrase. Then, as you think about going through your house, think about each word and make as weird an association as you can.

When you need to recall details of the nine main parts of the chapter or book you studied, all you have to think about is going through your home.

Example for a Leadership class (nine topics in boldface):

FOYER	**Traits** (Imagine adjectives pasted all over the door and the walls of the entryway.)
LIVING ROOM	**Styles** (Imagine a huge stylus writing things all over your living-room walls.)
DINING ROOM	**Power** (Imagine yourself power-walking round and round your dining room.)
KITCHEN	**Language** (Imagine going into your kitchen and finding it filled with a dozen people speaking all at once, and each speaking a different language!)
HALLWAY	**Change** (Imagine yourself walking down the hall without having your feet ever touch the floor at all. Why? Because the floor is littered with all the loose change you have saved for the last ten years.)
BATHROOM	**Ethics** (Imagine yourself going into the bathroom and finding a preacher standing on the toilet and using it as a pulpit from which he is addressing people lined up in your bathtub.)
BEDROOM #1	**Politics** (Imagine yourself going into your bedroom and seeing the President of the United States taking a nap on your bed while members of Congress stand over him, shaking their heads in disapproval.)
BATHROOM	**Liaisons** (Imagine yourself in your bathrobe opening the door of your bathroom, one inch and one minute away from taking a refreshing shower. When you pull back the curtain, a man jumps out, extends his hand in a friendly handshake, and announces, "Hi. I'm Lee Azon.")
BEDROOM #2	**Ability to Inspire** (Imagine going into the guest bedroom and finding that someone has taken church spires and stuck them in the bed, the walls, the closet, and the furniture.)

(continued)

22. **Steal a memory trick from the ancient Greeks.** *(concluded)*

   Brainteaser: Time yourself. How fast can you figure out the antonym of each word? The answer, by the way, must start with the letter "p."

   1. vivid
   2. important
   3. praise
   4. straight
   5. hell
   6. dissimilar
   7. burn
   8. convicted

   Answers: 1. pale 2. paltry 3. pan 4. parabolic 5. paradise 6. parallel 7. parboil 8. pardoned

---

23. # Borrow from the Greeks again: Go mnemonic.

   Let's use a simple but familiar example. Say you had to memorize the names of the Great Lakes for a geography quiz. Rather than attempt to force them into your brain cells with no rhyme or reason, you could use a popular mnemonic device—the word that was created from the first letter of each lake (H-O-M-E-S, standing for Huron, Ontario, Michigan, Erie, and Superior).

   ### Example from Geography:

   Task: To memorize the names of the states that make up New England.

   Mnemonic device: CRY, "New ham...m...m....Vermont!"

   The "C" represents Connecticut. The "RY" represents Rhode Island. (This you had to stretch a bit, but remember that "Y" and "I" often have the same sound.) When you need to pause to figure out an answer, you often make a humming, "mmmmm" sound. These next two "M's" represent Maine and Massachusetts. And then finally, your cry or shout comes out of your mouth: "New Ham 'in (an') Vermont!" Depending on the material you have to study, you will make up appropriate mnemonics. Just remember, the more absurd they are, the easier they are to remember.

24. Create a song.

Ignore the voice inside you that protests that you are not a musician. This is a song for your ears only. It may sound silly, but this study tip really works. Take the main points you have to remember from the material you are studying, and create an upbeat rhythm for it. Then write the lyrics using the subject matter you are studying.

Suggestion: To really deepen your memory-commitment, add some dance steps to go along with the song.

Brainteaser: "Cidio" in Latin means *kill*. How many kill-words can you think of that end in "cide"? The most familiar is probably homicide, but there are dozens of others. Among them is "verbicide"—the distortion or butchering of language. What famous person committed the following verbicidal crimes?

1. Let's have some new cliches.
2. I'll give you a definite maybe.
3. Why name your baby *John*? Every Tom, Dick, and Harry is named *John*.

Answer: Movie mogul Samuel Goldwyn.

---

25. Make a tape recording.

Once you feel you have a handle on the material you are trying to learn, read your notes (better yet, talk through your outline) into a tape recorder. Then, play that tape whenever you can. Many advise playing it as you fall asleep, as well as when you are fully awake. The more you hear the tape, the easier it will be for you to recall the information.

Brainteaser: What is this pompous passage trying to tell you?

> It was the nocturnal segment of the diurnal period preceding the annual celebratory observance of the emergence of a deified individual into the mundane environment, and throughout our place of residence, kinetic activity was not in evidence among the possessors of this potential, including that species of domestic rodent known as Mus Musculus. Hosiery was meticulously suspended from the forward promontory of the wood-burning caloric apparatus, pursuant to our anticipatory pleasure regarding an imminent visitation from an eccentric philanthropist among whose folkloric appellations is the canonization of the figure whose agnomen has a rhyming association with the lead cantor from an assemblage known as the revolving petrous substances.

Answer: "'Twas the night before Christmas and all through the house..."

Chapter 17

25 Ways to Conduct Non-Threatening Competition

Chapter Overview

From the outset of our lives, we learn that sometimes we get what we want and sometimes we don't. In infancy, we learn that if we cry loudly enough and long enough, we can usually get someone to attend to our needs. But once we have passed the infancy stage, we learn all too quickly about success and failure. We stumble as we learn to walk, but we learn to get up again. And, once we learn to use words, we learn the power of the word "no" and its ability to nullify our wishes.

Even though we've become quite familiar with the concepts of winning and losing before we even enter school, some people are still uncomfortable with competition. Personally, I think it adds a dynamic quality to classroom interactions—but only if the competition is non-threatening. Here are 25 ways to make it so.

1. Ask groups to decide if they want to engage in competition.

You can pass out scraps of paper and have individuals vote, or have the group leader ask group members for their preference, or you could ask for a show of hands.

If the majority clearly prefers not to operate on a competitive basis, honor their wishes. However, if you have a fairly even split, arrange to have some groups compete and some not. If there are only one or two people who do not wish to join in the competition, assure them that they have every right *not* to participate in the competition. Do not make them feel isolated or different. Instead, arrange for them to work on assignments individually, instead of with competitive groups.

Brainteaser: Which word in parentheses is the correct word?

1. His retirement had a positive (affect/effect) on staff morale.
2. The new supervisor will (affect/effect) new policies.
3. Psychologists know that psychopaths have a flat (affect/effect).
4. Did the storm (affect/effect) your house at all?

Answers: 1. effect   2. effect   3. affect   4. affect

2. Reward speed at the end of the day.

Competition can come in many different forms. Here's how I use it at the end of the day. Participants should be tired then, because you will have worked them hard. I've learned that to prevent ennui from setting in for the last 15 minutes, I give an assignment (usually a summarizing one) and tell them that one table group will be able to get out ahead of the others—the first team to finish. A transformation overcomes participants as they rush to complete their final assignment.

Brainteaser: The word that belongs inside the parentheses will complete the first word and will start the second.

1. S P (___) O W
2. K E R (_____) T A I N
3. L (___) I R O N
4. R (___) L Y
5. C (___) I S T
6. P (___) G O N
7. T (____) M A K E R

Answers: 1. End 2. Chief 3. And 4. Ear 5. Art 6. Ore 7. Rain

---

3. Announce in advance that group membership will change with every assignment.

To prevent other groups from giving up because one particular group seems to be winning every time, make an announcement once they've voted to compete and have learned what their reward will be. That announcement concerns the changes about to come in the make-up of their groups.

Number the group members from 1 to 5 (or 6, depending on the number of participants). After the first assignment, all the number 1's have to move to the closest table. After the second assignment, all the 2's have to move to the closest table, and so on. This rotation lends a fairness to the competition so that if you have one participant who is extremely knowledgeable, she will be moved around to share her wisdom with others.

Note: You could also have the #1 participants move to the farthest table on the second round and form their own team. For the second round, they will return to their original group. All the #2 participants will sit at the farthest table as a group unto themselves.

4. Compile a list of daily competitions.

It's true that some people freeze when they hear the word "compete." In truth, we face competition every day of our lives. Before engaging in the competitive activity, use the flipchart and ask participants about ways they compete and have competed on a regular basis. Once the list has been written on the flipchart, relate the ideas to the course itself and to the competitive circumstances the future holds in relation to what they are currently learning.

Brainteaser: Find the word that fits in the parentheses and you'll also find the end of the first word and the beginning of the second.

1. R E A (_ _ _) N E T
2. A T (_ _ _ _) E R
3. A P (_ _ _ _) L
4. O (_ _ _) D A N T
5. P (_ _ _) J E T
6. I N (_ _ _ _ _) A T

Answers: 1. Son 2. Tend 3. Pear 4. Pen 5. Ink 6. Habit

---

5. Exonerate the winners from the homework assignment.

The fear and disappointment that are sometimes associated with competition can be reduced, if not altogether eliminated, if the "prize" is something as mundane as exoneration from homework. Knowing that they are not losing much if they lose, the reluctant participants are more likely to engage in this low-stakes competition.

Brainteaser: Studies of male and female drivers reveal that, statistically speaking, more men are involved in accidents each year than women. The only conclusion that can be reached with certainty regarding this statement is:

1. Women are better drivers than men.
2. The commonplace belief that men are better drivers is erroneous.
3. Most truck drivers are men.
4. Men are actually better drivers, but are on the road more than women.
5. There is not enough information to draw any certain conclusion.

Answer: 5

6. Extend favored status to every participant.

One hundred years ago, when I taught junior high, I tried to make every single student feel that she was the teacher's pet. How? By thinking of 30 different ways (per class) to recognize the individual student.

Now that I'm older and wider, I've learned to do the same thing with adult students. The trick is that you cannot be obvious. To illustrate: If everyone is wonderful, no one is wonderful. Compliment one student on her command of pronouns (in a Business Writing class); another, on her team leadership skills; a third on her willingness to assist others. Some of the compliments can be given publicly and others, privately. But before the course is over, every person, ideally, will have been recognized by you.

Brainteaser: Can you put 46 tiny puppies into nine large cages so that each cage holds an odd number of puppies? (Think puppies and think playful.)

Answer: It is possible: Put one puppy into each of the first eight cages and put the remaining 38 into the last cage. "But 38 is an even number," you say. Well, we told you we would be playful with this one. Here's our thinking: 38 is an "odd" (strange) number of puppies to put in a cage.

---

7. Limit the competition.

It's easier to compete against time than against other people. So, for a given activity, heighten the excitement that can surround it by saying, truthfully, "No individual, group, or class has ever solved this problem in less than ten minutes. Let's see how well *you* do." Or "I've given this grammar test to thousands of people. The highest score ever earned was by someone who wasn't even born in this country. William Ho, a student of mine who worked at Lockheed-Martin in Burbank, California, earned a score of 86%. No one has ever surpassed that. Can you break his record?" (The actual test is in the Appendix.)

Brainteaser: Which word in each line comes closest to the meaning of the word in capital letters?

1. USURP
   a) motivate   b) challenge   c) seize   d) waste

2. AFFRONT
   a) insult   b) worry   c) take charge   d) envy

Answers: 1. c 2. a

8. Make it real via reality television.

Force yourself to watch a reality TV program. (You can be sure there are others in your classroom watching it or one like it.) The next day, lead a discussion regarding the nature of competition, the kinds of people who like to compete, the benefits of competing, and the lessons to be learned.

I happen to like The Donald's "The Apprentice" and the short-lived Martha Stewart spin-off. If you can tolerate the host's hubris, you can pick up some great ideas about creativity, marketing, teamwork, and so on. I use these ideas as discussion points in my management classes. I even replicate some of the assignments the teams are given and give them to my own students.

To illustrate, in her debut show, Martha divided the contestants into two groups and asked them to find one thing they had in common (beyond the obvious). You could easily use this assignment to divide your class into teams for a new project or use it to have small groups get to know each other.

Their task was to update a classic fairy tale. One team (the winning one) had Jack's beanstalk going down into the ground instead of up into the air. If you're teaching a problem-solving class, this kind of opposites-thinking (officially "Janusian" thinking) provides the perfect illustration of a creative technique.

Consider the words of Tracy Jacobson, a substitute teacher in Lexington, Kentucky: "Don't underestimate the power of talk shows to help with relationships. For example, Dr. Phil always says, 'You can't change a problem until you acknowledge there is a problem.' Many employees in high-powered positions are good at denying problems or making excuses. Dr. Phil's advice could be very helpful in such workplace situations."

Brainteaser: The answers to these analogies are five-letter words ending in "e."

1. MEDIUM : CHARCOAL : : WRAPPING : _____
2. ERROR : DELETE : : MISTAKE : _____
3. POPULATION : KING : : COMMODITIES :
4. PIE : SLICE : : INCOME :
5. WIN : MEDAL : : WORK HARD :

Answers: 1. Paper   2. Erase   3. Staple   4. Tithe   5. Raise

9. Use job applications as an example.

Life is filled with examples of the need to compete, but let's restrict the competition to the process of trying to land a job. Sooner or later, everyone will have to go through the interview process. Even if your participants already have a job, chances are that before they retire, they will seek a promotion or perhaps a job in a different company, or look for a part-time job.

More people are now competing for a given job than ever before—thanks, in part, to the advent of the Internet. To help narrow the field to find the ideal candidate, organizations are asking very difficult interview questions. Here's a question that has been used by companies like Microsoft:

"How many barbers are there in Chicago?"

I've heard some clever responses when I've shared this question with my own students in Career Development or thinking-on-your-feet classes. To illustrate: "None—they're all hair stylists." I've also heard students say that if they were asked the question, they would get the Chicago phone book and count, or look the information up on the Internet. Alas, during the real interview situation, there are no phone books or computers available. One has to think through the answer and reach an approximate number. (1,700 is the correct answer.)

To reach the answer, you'd have to know the population of Chicago (2.7 million—but not everyone walks around with such statistics in his head. There would be nothing wrong, though, with asking the interviewer for that one number.) Calculate from there. Assume that half the residents in the city are men. Subtract a small number for the hairless (including babies). Then calculate how often a man gets his hair cut. ("Even if you are not a man," I say to my female students, "you know men—fathers, husbands, boyfriends. You have some sense of how often they get their hair cut.") Continue with your calculations, and you'll be able to come up with a number close enough to the correct number to impress your interviewer.

Yes, your students can avoid competition in a classroom, but they can't avoid it in real life. The more opportunities they have to work under pressure, the better equipped they will be to handle pressure when they most need to.

Brainteaser: Can you think of a possible reason why the hair on a man's head gets gray before the hair on his moustache does?

Answer: The hair on his head is 20 years older.

10. Discuss the origin of the word "competition."

It has a non-threatening origin, to be sure. "Petere" is the Latin word meaning "to seek."

"Petition" is derived from this root word. Interestingly enough, so is the word "competent." I like this connection between competent and competition, for the implication is that being able to "seek" "together" (the "com" part of the word) means being able to demonstrate skill or competency with or because of others.

Viewed from an etymological perspective, there's nothing threatening about the word. Share your rationale for using competition in the classroom to enhance the process of seeking knowledge together.

Brainteaser: Can you think of words that contain these letters, in this order?

1. MXMZ
2. DCTN
3. CNDTN
4. TSUR
5. DOLA
6. CTRY
7. PDCRN
8. ANOC
9. ESCBL
10. MDCE

Answers: 1. Maximize 2. Dictionary 3. Condition 4. Thesaurus 5. Dollar 6. Country 7. Pediatrician 8. Announce 9. Respectable 10. Medicine

---

11. Take them to Olympian heights.

There are very few people who don't enjoy watching the Summer or Winter Olympics, and few who do not respond to accounts of the "Miracle on Ice" (the story of the U.S. Olympic hockey team that won the gold medal in 1980). Explain that you like competition because it brings out the best in people. Assure your participants repeatedly, though, that you don't like competition that is so stiff it paralyzes people. Tell them you will always honor their expressed desire *not* to compete.

Note: Think about how many people, all over the world, are inspired by the Lance Armstrong story. (Dozens of other athletes could be used as exemplars as well—competitors who overcame seemingly insurmountable odds. I like the Wilma Glodean Rudolph story and Leroy Satchel Paige's.) How impoverished our lives would be if we had no such stories to inspire us because these individuals shied away from competition and thus away from becoming the heroes and heroines they are.

Brainteaser: What's next in this series? 9, 16, 25, 36, ___

Answer: 49. Each number is the square of consecutive numbers starting with 4.

500 Creative Classroom Techniques for Teachers and Trainers

12. Distance yourself from the decision.

Participants are sometimes reluctant to engage in competition because they don't want to subject themselves to additional scrutiny from the instructor. To circumvent this hesitation, have an outsider make the decision regarding the winner of a particular assignment. To provide an additional layer of protection or privacy, have them submit their ideas, essays, or projects anonymously. You can be sure that when the winning entry is announced, the winner(s) will step up to claim it . . . proudly.

Brainteaser: Remember the mental exercise that asks you to take a word—let's say, "meat"—and make as many words as you can from it? You'd have "a," for example, and "me," and "at," and "tea," and "ate," and so on. Well, this brainteaser does much the same thing, only with numbers instead of words. Given a set of numbers, see how many other numbers you can make, using only the numbers you are given and using them only once. (You could not say, for example, 9 is the product of 3 × 3, because there is only one 3 in the set of numbers in our brainteaser. But you could say 3^2, which would give you 9. You can add, subtract, multiply, or divide. Some possible answers are provided. You'll no doubt find more.

GIVEN NUMBERS: 3   5   8   2

Answers: 3, 5, 8, 2, 15, 2, 15, 24, 6, 16

---

13. Define "winning" and "losing."

Author Sydney Harris once defined a loser as "a winner whom God has asked to wait." Even if you don't believe in a god or God, you probably like the idea that none of us can win *everything* *every* time. Sometimes, we just have to wait our turn before one of our circumventions on life's merry-go-round yields the gold ring.

To offset the agony of defeat, have small groups create their own definitions of the words "winner" and "loser." Invite them to include peripheral considerations such as good sportsmanship (for losers) and non-gloating (for winners). Doing so will help create a climate of non-threatening competition.

Brainteaser: Here are more of those words that have many letters missing. The letters you are given, though, all appear in the word you are seeking, and all appear in the correct order in that word. Can you figure out all six?

1. E A E   2. O O F O
3. U P O   4. A M B G
5. C F F   6. A R G

Answers: (There are many other possibilities.) 1. Heaven 2. Rooftop 3. Coupon 4. Hamburg 5. Chiffon 6. Daring

14. Use the Ben Franklin columns.

Salespeople are very familiar with the Ben Franklin approach. You might even be using it without knowing who originated it. Basically, the approach asks you to take a sheet of paper, draw a line down the middle, and write the pro's on one side and the con's on the other.

When it comes to competition, have each group do a Ben Franklin listing of the pro's and con's relative to engaging in competitive activities associated with the learning under way. After five or ten minutes, ask a spokesperson from each group to tell you the results: how many things were listed in the pro column and how many in the con column. Also ask each spokesperson to share one pro and one con. Comment briefly or lead a short discussion on the spokesperson-reports.

On the flipchart, have two columns. Keep track, as each group reports, of how many pro's they listed and how many con's. Once all the votes are in, decide with the whole group if a competition should be held. Even if they vote not to compete, they will at least have thought about some of the advantages to having a competitive environment.

---

15. Tell some "loser" stories.

Basketball fans know that Michael Jordan's high school coach seldom permitted him to leave the bench. He simply wasn't a good enough player. Being benched was not good enough for the airy one, though, and so he used his second-string status as an improvement goal.

Examples: Of Vince Lombardi, a college administrator wrote, "Lacks motivation, has minimal football knowledge."

> Of Fred Astaire, a movie executive noted, "Can't act, balding, can dance a little."
>
> Of Louisa May Alcott, a teacher wrote, "She should find work as a servant."
>
> On Enrico Caruso, a critic commented, "Has no voice at all. Cannot sing."
>
> To the young Albert Einstein, the school headmaster asserted, "Your mere presence offends me."

If you have an anecdote of your own, now's the time to share it. And most of us have had observations made about our abilities that were very far off the mark, considering our later accomplishments. Ask class members if any one of them has defied some predictor's dismal words.

Here's another person who did not permit failure to determine his future. Setbacks really did not set him back or deter him from reaching his goals. Do you know who he is?

(continued)

15. **Tell some "loser" stories.** *(concluded)*

At age 22, he failed in business.
At age 23, he ran for the state legislature and was defeated.
At age 24, he failed in another business.
At age 25, he was elected to the legislature.
At age 26, the woman he loved died.
At age 27, he had a nervous breakdown.
At age 29, he was defeated in his bid to be the legislative speaker.
At age 31, he was defeated in his efforts to become an elector.
At age 34, he was defeated in his run for Congress.
At age 37, he was elected to Congress.
At age 39, he was defeated in his bid to run again as a congressman.
At age 46, he was defeated in his campaign to serve as a senator.
At age 47, he was defeated in a run for the vice presidency of the United States.
At age 49, he was defeated once again in his efforts to become a senator.
At age 51, he was elected president of the United States of America.

Answer: His name was Abraham Lincoln.

---

16. **Distribute bricks for an educational edifice.**

Give everyone an outlined drawing of the building where the training/teaching is being conducted. Every time the table group gets a correct answer, give them a row of paper bricks. The first team to have enough rows to fill the building wins a prize. (If the class orders pizza for lunch, perhaps the winning team could decide what toppings will go on the pizza.)

Brainteaser: Analogize this:

A. PLUCKY : UNFORTUNATE : : SCARE :
  1. kindness   2. soothe   3. respectful   4. fine
B. PLEASE : OWN : : DANGER :
  1. weather   2. dancer   3. security   4. heel
C. FAIRY : HEAVY : : GAMBLE :
  1. fling   2. blind   3. rush   4. strategy
D. FLOWER : RAISE : : STOP :
  1. start   2. harbor   3. straw   4. bottom

Answers: A. 2 B. 3 C. 4 D. 1 (Remove the first letter from the first word and the second word is the opposite of what remains. "Plucky" becomes "lucky" and "unfortunate" is the opposite of "lucky.")

17. Conduct informational relay races.

Unless you have an assistant, it's best to have only two teams, as you will have to keep up with them by handing out test questions whenever they are ready to pass the baton. Line the two teams up and give a baton to the first person on the team. Also give a question. (The questions will be different for each team in order to prevent cross-pollination as the teams shout out their answers.) If the answer is correct, the team is ready to pass the baton and to receive a new question. If they do not know the answer, they can look it up in their books or course materials. (Of course, doing that will slow them down and might cost them their victory.)

The first team to pass the baton all the way to the end of the line is the winning team.

Brainteaser: Let's try more of that how-many-numbers-can-you-get-from-these-numbers brainteaser. Work with a friend. See who is faster this time.

$$8 \quad 0 \quad 3 \quad 9$$

Possible answers: 8, 0, 3, 9, 80, 30, 90, 93, 39, 38, 89, 24, 72, 72, 6, 5

18. Use the sumo strategy.

At sumo wrestling meets in Japan, someone always emerges victorious. In fact, there are *many* someones. One competitor might receive a trophy for having shown the most heart. Another, for having displayed the most courteous behavior. Another, for showing the greatest fortitude, and so on.

Divide the class into pairs and have certificates ready for the pair that contributed the most, the pair that didn't interrupt others, the pair that showed the greatest team spirit, the one that helped others, the one that asked the most questions, and so on. As fans of the reality TV show "American Idol" know, the designated winners sometimes fail to sell as many records as the runners-up. These certificates are designed to illustrate that the success-diamond has many facets.

Brainteaser: What word do you need here to complete the analogy?

BROOCH : OVAL :: RING :

    1. square   2. parallelogram   3. circle   4. circus

Answer: 3. Circle.

19. Have an ongoing series of challenges.

Ask participants to number a clean sheet of paper from one to twenty. Then, every time they answer a question correctly, they can place an "X" on one of the lines. When they get 20 "X's," they also get a prize.

Options: This competition can also be done with groups. You could also have a few hundred pennies and issue them as tokens whenever someone answers a question correctly.

Brainteaser: The missing word in the middle of each line has some connection (perhaps not a direct one) to the word that precedes it and the word that succeeds it. For example:

    Read   _____   Boy

The missing word is "page." You'd read a page in a book and a page boy (pageboy) is a hair style.

Good luck.

1. Pot   _____   Gamble
2. Prison   _____   Music
3. Sea   _____   Garden

Answers: 1. Luck 2. Bar 3. Weed

---

20. Encourage comparisons to favorite sports teams.

Form small groups of four or five participants and give them about five minutes to talk sports. Then ask the groups to decide on a favorite team from any sport and to tell why this team is so good or so popular. Finally, ask them to find similarities between their classroom teams and their favorite sports team.

Call on a spokesperson from each team to share the similarities.

Brainteaser: Ready for more of those word-in-the-middle challenges? Remember, the connection need not be direct, but rather, relative.

1. blackboard   _____   lion
2. paint   _____   hair
3. police   _____   conductor
4. rabbit   _____   podiatrist
5. question   _____   back
6. mutual   _____   adulation
7. clock   _____   bug

Answers: 1. jungle 2. brush 3. baton 4. foot 5. answer 6. admiration 7. tick

21. Develop self-competition tendencies.

Let this four-word mantra represent the only competition participants are concerned with: "Exceed your personal best." Moving beyond previously established goals should always be the challenge. And this attention to setting and surpassing one's own goals can be addressed in ways both large and small.

Example: This is a fun exercise designed to improve hand-to-eye coordination; really short, short-term memory; concentration; reading speed; and digital dexterity.

From an old phone book, cut strips of names and phone numbers. There are typically four strips or columns to a page; have one strip for each participant. Then ask participants to draw three rows of quarter-sized coins or circles, one beneath each other, on a sheet of 8½-by-11-inch paper. The fourth row will have only one circle, in the middle of the line. Next, have participants number the circles from 1 to 9, with the last circle in the last row getting the number "0." (These circles and their numbers represent the buttons on a typical phone.)

Distribute the strips of names and phone numbers and have participants start at the top of their strip, "dialing" each phone number by touching the proper button or circle on their papers. After two minutes, say "Stop!" and tell them to place an "X" next to the last number they dialed. Talk for a moment or two about exceeding your personal best, and then ask them to start at the top again and to dial for two more minutes. (They might protest that they've already seen the numbers, but there is no way they will have memorized them.)

When you say "Stop!" have them place the "X" next to the last number they "dialed." Ask how many had an "X" lower on the page the second time. Those who did exceeded their personal best and deserve a round of applause.

Brainteaser: There are five possible interpretations for this American (Texan) proverb. Only one is correct. It's up to you to find it.

> "Lick by lick, the cow ate the grindstone."

1. There's more than one way to digest things.
2. The determination of some animals is as strong as stone.
3. Animals will surprise you.
4. Little by little, big things get done, even if it takes a long time to do them.

Answer: 4.

22. Draw the name of a group from a hat and issue a challenge.

This is the challenge: They are to outdo all other groups in giving the next report. Ask them to rise to the occasion and put forth even more effort than they usually do as they plan and then deliver their group work. After all the reports have been given, ask people to vote with a "yes" or "no" (silently and anonymously, on a small scrap of paper): *Did the selected team outperform all others?*

Continue throughout the day whenever a report is required so that every group has a chance to learn what "Herculean effort" really means.

Note: The challenge need not be used with reports. You can apply it to any task, but especially one that is repeated several times during the day so you can avoid charges of *That's not fair. They had an easy task.*

Brainteaser: Which mixed-up word does not belong with the others?

1. Y K K C T N U E   2. M M D E O   3. E E O B S W   4. T T E E N N R I

Answer: 1. Kentucky. The others are all computer terms: Modem, Web site, Internet.

23. Ask them to choose their game preference.

In writing about games, French psychologist and anthropologist Roger Caillois divides these pleasurable activities into five categories:

- **Agon**, which are competitive games
- **Alea**, which are games of chance
- **Flinx**, which are consciousness-altering activities, such as skydiving
- **Mimicry**, which are games that create other realities, such as theater games or role plays
- **Wonder**, which are games that contain seeds of knowledge.

Take a vote and provide the kind of game that participants most want to participate in. If "Flinx" garners the most votes, do something that will "blow their minds." This could be, for example, giving them the Mensa entrance exam. If they opt for "Alea," structure an ordinary classroom activity using a pair of dice.

24. Give the competition a metaphorical twist.

Ask participants to imagine that they are about to enter the metaphorical College of Competition. Then have them work in small groups to ascertain what the "tuition" for that college would be.

Example: In order to get in to this college, one would not need money for the tuition, but rather admirable learning traits, such as self-confidence, a willingness to take risks, a constitution strong enough to accept (potential) rejection, and so on. Don't give too many examples, though; you need to leave some for them to think about.

Brainteaser: Find the missing letters and you'll "get" the word. As usual, the letters given are in the right order. Use them just once and add other letters.

1. E V E R E
2. P H P H Y
3. I T R T R
4. O T O C C
5. S R G
6. N N N
7. D W R
8. T I N

Answers: 1. Beverage 2. Philosophy 3. Literature 4. Motorcycle 5. Strong 6. Invention 7. Dwarf 8. Train

---

25. Have them create a motto.

"Citius, Altius, Fortius." You hear the phrase and see it every two years when the Summer or Winter Olympics are upon us. "Swifter, Higher, Stronger." The words have challenged thousands of athletes for thousands of years to reach beyond mediocrity, beyond the records that have been set by others before them.

Have small groups create their own motto that will serve for the classroom competitions in which they engage. (Latin is not a requirement.)

Brainteaser: Select the line that contains the best words to complete the sentence: "Horace noted that _____ without _____ _____ of its own _____.

1. power   kindness   succeeds   wonder
2. force   wisdom   falls   weight
3. splendor   love   amazes   wonder
4. trust   respect   falls   vacuum
5. property   wealth   destroys   inadequacy
6. honor   faith   tarnishes   age

Answer: 2.

Chapter 18

25 Ways to Make Take-Home Assignments Relevant

Chapter Overview

To paraphrase Colin Powell: "Relevance is a learning-multiplier." The more evidence participants have that what they are learning will actually *help* them in some way, the easier your job will be.

Relevancy comes in many shapes and sizes. In the following pages, you'll find 25 special ways to create deeper connections between homework learning, classroom learning, and the real world.

1. Have them watch television and draw a parallel to class.

Virtually any course you teach can be applied to something that is happening on television on any given night. Admittedly, though, this assignment works best for courses that deal with communication, conflict, interpersonal skills, and so on. Ask participants to find in some program an example of a concept they learned during the day.

Note: Preparing some questions in advance will facilitate the participant's ability to make correlations. To illustrate: For a course dealing with decision-making. they could watch a sit com, the biography channel, the history channel, a drama, or even a reality show. Ask:

What decision had to be made?

What were the circumstances surrounding the decision?

How much time was allocated to it?

What process was used or what steps were taken to reach the decision?

Who was involved?

How important was the decision?

What were the results?

How could the results have been improved?

2. Give them a choice of a homework-discussion partner.

To prevent anyone from feeling that you *made* them give out their phone number or e-mail address, give participants a choice: They can exchange their phone number or e-mail address with someone in the class, or they can find someone outside class with whom to discuss the take-home assignment. Either way, tell them that the opinions of the second person must be mentioned in a report they give in class the following day.

So, they should not only *learn* what the other person's opinion is, they should *make note* of the feedback and include it in their brief report.

Brainteaser: There is a pattern to the letters below. If you can figure it out, you will know what letter belongs in the blank.

B F J M Q ? X

Answer: The pattern records every third consonant in the alphabet. The missing letter is "T."

---

3. Take them one step beyond the reading.

That step is to the Internet or to a library or to a book or magazine in their own home that contains information regarding the subject. Encourage them to cite sources they have used as they prepare the homework assignment. They will share the sources the next day as they make a brief report.

Brainteaser: Put the four-letter word in the parentheses that can be added to any and all of the letters on the left to create a new word with each of them.

T

R

BL   (__ __ __ __)

B

IMP

Answer: e-a-c-h

4. Have them make a game out of the assignment.

Tell them that once they have completed the assigned reading, they are to distill what they have learned into one sentence of 10–15 words. (With younger students, you should ask for shorter sentences.) Then, they are to arrange that sentence on several lines of a sheet of paper, removing one letter that appears repeatedly; removing spaces; and writing some of the words as wraparounds (i.e., hyphenated words that start at the end of one line and continue on to the beginning of the next line.) They should not use hyphens in their wraparounds.

Example for a class on leadership:

Original sentence: *A number of experts agree: the essence of leadership is the ability to effect change.*

Revised sentence with the "E"s and spaces omitted:

ANUMBROFXP
RTSAGRTHS
SNCOFLADR
SHIPISTHEAB
ILITYTOFFCT
CHANG.

Note: You can get a lot of mileage out of this assignment. If the class meets for a whole month, for example, start each class with one participant sentence written on the white board. The first person to figure it out earns points of some kind. If the class is only of one or two days' duration, simply have participants exchange papers and try to uncover the meaning of the letter-omitted sentences.

Brainteaser: Which of the choices (a-d) is right for the next box in the series?

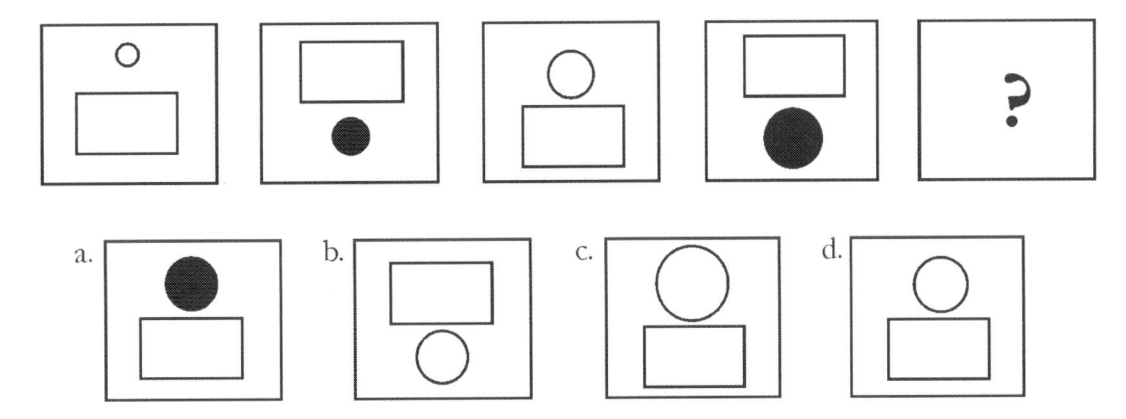

Answer: c. The rectangle remains the same, but the circle gets larger in each box as the positions switch.

5. Have them evaluate the material in a "love-to-hate" vein.

Instead of a report on the reading they did the night before (or the learning they acquired on a given day of the class), have them choose three topics from the list that follows and put them in separate columns. Then have them write five items for each topic. Then, the next day, they can circulate around the room, finding people who had similar feeling- or column-entries.

Column headings:

- Things I didn't understand
- Things I enjoyed learning about
- Things that bored me
- Things worth telling someone else about
- Things I can use in the future
- Things that surprised me
- Things that I'll never forget
- Things not worth remembering
- Things that contradicted what I thought or what I had been taught before

---

6. Have them sum it up in an insect analogy.

You probably have animalistic analogies that you enjoy using in the classroom. For example, to remind students of what a preposition is, I say, "If a rabbit can do it to a hill, it's a preposition. The rabbit can go *in* the hill, *above* the hill, *under* the hill, *to* the hill . . ."

Use insects to help participants escape the tedium of typical reports. Ask them to compare the take-home reading assignment to some insect and to explain the thinking behind their choice.

Procrastination examples: Some people are like fireflies whose light goes out with every interruption. It takes a long time for them to fly again, so they get little work done.

Other people are like ants—they know that nothing is impossible to move. They just keep plodding along, moving anything that stands in their way.

7. Have them interview the first person they see after class (in a safe setting) regarding the upcoming take-home assignment.

With younger students, of course, you'd have to caution that the first person must be someone they know (anyone but the school bus driver, who will be too busy to answer their questions). You may wish to narrow it down a little more to, say, the first person they see when they get home from school. Adult students usually respond well to the quirkiness of striking up a conversation with a stranger. Basically, participants will ask the first person they see what she knows about the subject-matter reading assignment, or what she thinks about the subject, or what use she has for the subject.

The interviewee's opinion is not as important as the effort to take the learning out of the classroom and into the real world.

Brainteaser: Can you figure out the answer to this imagination-stretching exercise? You get in your car, which is facing west on a straight road. You drive for a mile and find you have traveled a mile to the east. How can this be?

Answer: You are driving in reverse!

8. Make the last thing the first thing on the next day.

Start off class on the next day by appointing five people to be group leaders. Have them pick four to six other people with whom they have not yet worked. When the groups assemble, they are to prepare a consolidated report, based on input from each of the group members. Their report reflects what they did the previous evening—scholastically.

Brainteaser: Time yourself on your (correct, ideally) matches of D-words in the first column with their meanings in the second column.

1. doldrums   A. a foolish person
2. dolorous   B. sleeping
3. dolt   C. sullen
4. dormant   D. meaningless talk
5. dotage   E. shabby
6. dour   F. amusing
7. dowdy   G. a period of sadness
8. drivel   H. senility
9. droll   I. sad

Answers: 1. G 2. I 3. A 4. B 5. H 6. C 7. C 8. D 9. A

9. Bring antiques off the road and into the classroom.

This assignment requires some thinking on your part, and it allows you to use ordinary household or hardware-store objects instead of antiques. You will display those objects in the front of the room and encourage people to speculate about their use—much as the producers do on shows like PBS's "Antiques Roadshow."

Select objects that have some relevance to the course, and try to get objects that are not immediately recognizable (the way a can opener would be).

On the table holding the five or six objects, place a big sign that says, "How do these relate to your homework assignment?" As individuals think they have an answer, encourage them to join others and prepare their answer to the question.

Example: A Science student holding a garlic-clove cruncher made this comment: "I never thought the study of plants would interest me, but the more I learn about epicalyxes, the more I realize they have me in their grip."

---

10. Follow the Hans Selye example: Give choices, give control.

The one thing that causes stress is the belief/reality that you are no longer in control. By contrast, whenever you can choose what interests you instead of having someone else's interests foisted upon you, you are exerting control over your circumstances and will be able to play a more active role in the experience. "Ownership" of the material is what we are seeking with the take-home assignments.

During the course of the day, I usually write five or six assignment choices on the board, and let participants choose the one that interests them most. Then, the next day, they form groups based on the choices they made.

Choice possibilities:

- Prepare a one-page summary of what you've learned so far.
- Answer any two of the questions that appear on page 3 of your text.
- Watch a television program, and be ready tomorrow to tell how a character tackled a specific problem.
- Prepare a ten-question quiz based on today's learning.

11. Elicit anonymous feedback for anonymous reports.

Some courses deal with interpersonal skills and thus probe some psychological soft spots. There is value in having participants explore those touchy areas, but there can also be danger, so approach assignments that deal with inner feelings with extreme caution.

Tell participants that for the homework assignment tonight, you don't want them to write their name on the paper. They can either write a phony name or submit a paper with no name. The assignment will ask them to recall a specific incident or a specific person. For example, in a supervision class, they might be asked to describe the most difficult supervisor they ever had and tell how they dealt with that person.

Collect the papers the next morning. Shuffle them repeatedly and then distribute them. (If anyone reports that she received her own paper, be sure to mix it with several others before redistributing the papers.) Each person will then comment on the paper she receives, couching her remarks about the writer in the most positive language possible.

Suggestion: Post a list of positive adjectives to help with the positive feedback, such as these: trusting, artistic, calm, self-reliant, verbal, skeptical, hardworking, witty, humble, goal-setting, adaptable, neat, organized, dramatic, logical, tolerant, strong-willed, creative, consistent, serious, motivated, detailed, analytical, persuasive, compassionate, independent, patient, decisive, friendly, sincere, determined.

Brainteaser: What letter is missing?

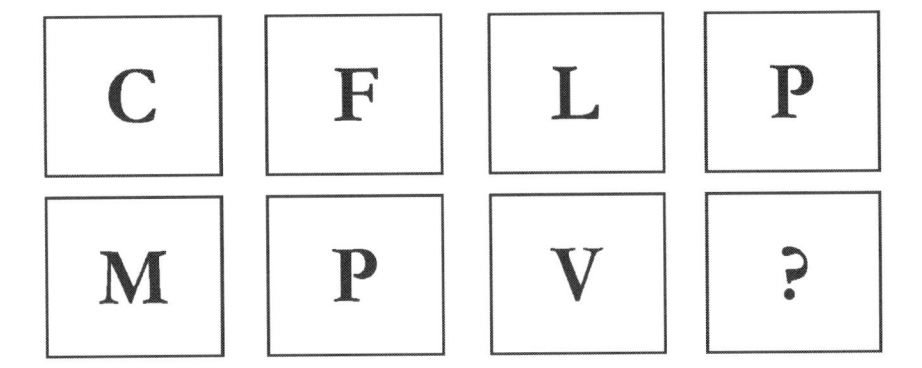

C	F	L	P
M	P	V	?

Answer: Z. Each bottom letter is the tenth letter from the letter directly above it.

12. Use props to help them discuss the assignment and to develop listening skills at the same time.

Prepare ten true-or-false statements about the reading assignment. The next day, distribute a copy of the statements to each person. Have them record their answers individually. As they do this, place a ball (or some other interesting object) at each table.

Next, divide them into groups and have them aim for group consensus regarding which statements are true and which are false. The only proviso: The person who is holding the ball is the only one who can speak. If someone else wants to take over the discussion, she must ask for the ball, paraphrase the preceding speaker's comments (to that speaker's satisfaction), and then and only then, commence speaking.

Brainteaser: Which of the following choices represents the theme of this proverb shared by Germans, Swedes, Spaniards, and Hungarians?

"Good words cost nothing"

a) universality   b) kindness   c) education   d) poverty

Answer: b.

---

13. Pass out puzzle pieces.

Glue a piece of cardboard on the back of a magazine picture or poster that is related to the course. Divide the picture into 20 pieces (more or less, depending on the number of participants.) The pieces don't have to be jigsaw'd—they can be easier-to-cut geometric shapes or simple one-inch by two-inch rectangles. Cut them up and give one puzzle piece to each participant.

They are to write on the back of their puzzle piece how the homework assignment could be important in their future. They can write, for example, one thing they learned that has prompted them to take action.

Then gather participants around a large table in the front of the room and have them begin to assemble the puzzle. Before they can lay down their individual pieces, though, they must read aloud what they've written on the back.

Note: If your class size is greater than 20, you may want to prepare two puzzles.

14. Elicit freely associated words in relation to the take-home assignment.

It's not only psychologists who can take advantage of the revelations evoked by free association. The classroom teacher can as well. Here's what you do the morning after the take-home assignment: Ask one person from each group to stand and leave the room for a moment. (This creates a disequilibrium that is bound to keep students alert.) One at a time, call them in and ask each person to state the first word that comes to mind when she thinks about the homework assignment. Write that word on the flipchart, ask the person to return to her group, and then call in the next person.

Once you have five key words on the chart (one from each of the five group selectees), ask people to shout out other words in a free-association manner. Write them all down. Then task the groups with creating sentences that summarize the homework assignment, using at least five of the words on the flipchart.

---

15. Give them a chance to advocate.

You probably know enough Latin to know that a "vocation" is a calling and an "avocation" is something that calls us *away* from our calling—a hobby, in other words. This assignment asks participants to think about something they like to do when they are not working (or are not in school). They are to write one paragraph telling why they like it, what they know about it, what skills are required for it, et cetera.

That evening, as they do their homework assignment, they are to note at least two ways that their hobby connects to the assignment.

Example: Patience is a trait required by those who enjoy hunting or bird-watching. Someone might note that it took considerable patience to complete the assignment!

Brainteaser: How sharp are your detecting abilities? Figure out what might have happened in this true-crime incident: A man is lying severely injured in the road after deliberately walking in front of a motorcyclist and being hit.

Answer: The man had actually been the driver in a fatal hit-and-run accident. He drove a few miles farther to an isolated area and left the car so it looked as if it had been stolen and abandoned. He phoned police to report a missing car, and then caused the motorcycle accident that injured him. His ploy didn't work, though. Police figured out what he had done and he was arrested.

16. Make use of the titles that rock their worlds.

Begin this assignment by eliciting titles—titles of movies, books, plays, operas, poems, songs. On the flipchart, record as many as you can in a three- or four-minute spurt. Then ask table groups to select one title they are familiar with (a movie they have all seen, for example, or a television program they have all watched) and draw a connection between the title (only) and the homework assignment they completed the previous night.

The connection can be direct—a character in a book had a conflict, for example, and was able to resolve the problem by seeking to understand the other person, just as the reading assignment suggested they do. The connection can also be indirect: Take *The Color Purple*, the movie based on Alice Walker's superb book. A marketing class might relate *The Color Purple* to the Red Hat Society and its phenomenal membership growth and marketing strategies.

Brainteaser: What four-letter word ending in "m" completes the analogy?

VICTORY PARTY : POLITICIAN : : _____ : SENIOR

Answer: Prom.

---

17. Employ circles to summarize.

Ask participants to draw three circles: one representing the homework assignment, a second representing their current lives, and a third representing their future. Then ask for volunteers to analyze the placement and size of those circles. Aid them in their analyses by asking some amateur-analyst questions.

Examples:

Is it significant that your homework circle was so far away from your life and future circles?
What do you think it means that your circles were concentric?
What do you think it means that your circles were not touching?
What do you think it means that your current-life circle was so much larger than the other two?
What do you think it means that the future circle is hardly visible?
What do you think it means that the homework circle is hardly visible?
What do you think it means that your circles are so much larger than anyone else's?

18. Have them design a greeting card.

First, though, they have to discuss the homework assignment with a partner. Then, distribute basic tools (paper and marking pens) and ask individuals to separate and work alone. They will create a clever greeting card for their partner, based on her reaction to the homework. The card could be one of condolence, of congratulations, of empathy, or of invitation. Have them exchange the cards right after the break and ask for volunteers to share what they have received.

Brainteaser: Let's do more testing of your intuitive skills. Below are three words I am fairly certain you have never seen. What does your intuition tell you the meanings of these capitalized words would be? If you missed more than two, you may wish to reconsider your tendency to rely on your intuition.

1. IDIOBLAST
   a) a means of punishment for the slow-witted b) a thick-walled plant cell
   c) a philosophy known for its flexibility d) means of generating ideas rapidly

2. OLEASTER
   a) an ornamental plant b) a smooth plaster-like surface
   c) a weapon that causes erratic movement in those not skilled in its use d) a religious artifact

3. DUUMVIR
   a) an expensive coverlet for a bed b) a mathematical operation
   c) a Roman magistrate d) a celestial formation

Answers: 1. b 2. a 3. c

19. Ask for a midway assessment.

If you are teaching a multi-day course, stop at the halfway point and ask each person to write the one thing she found most valuable so far. Collect the comments and type them. For their homework that day or the next, distribute the typed list and ask participants to work alone to prioritize the items in terms of value. (#1 would be their most valued bit of knowledge and #25 the least valued.)

Collect the prioritized sheets the next morning and hand them to a few people who are to leave the room to prepare a tally of the votes. Briefly discuss the results of that tally, and be sure to save it. Your job is to make the least-valued items more significant the next time they are introduced.

Brainteaser: While on vacation in Mexico, a tourist bought six small, hand-woven baskets for a total of 17 pesos. Some of the baskets cost one peso each; others cost two pesos, while the most expensive one cost ten pesos. How many of each did the tourist buy?

Answer: 6 baskets altogether—one for ten pesos, two for two pesos each, and three for one peso each.

20. Give them assessment choices.

The morning after the homework assignment, have word-pairs written on the flipchart.

Have	Have not
Will	Won't
Do	Don't
Want	Need
Loved	Liked
Learned	Already knew
Agreed	Disagreed

They will work alone at first. Their task: choose one word pair and use it to assess the homework assignment. After five or ten minutes, ask them to form pairs, triads, or groups with others who chose the same word pair. Have them discuss their responses in groups.

Brainteaser: What six-letter word ending in "e" completes the analogy?

DETECTIVE : CRIME : : YOU, AS READER :

Answer: Puzzle.

---

21. Ask them to write a letter.

The recipient of the letter: a student in a future class. The letter should briefly outline the take-home assignment and tell what the participant learned from it. Tell participants that if they would like a response a month or a year hence, they should provide their e-mail address.

Option: Write the name of each class member on a separate sheet of paper. Put the papers with their names into an envelope. Have participants withdraw one name and write a letter to that individual. The letter should tell in positive terms what the letter-writer has observed about that person. It should also include some information about the take-home assignment that represents a novel insight. Have them deliver the letters during class. If time permits, have the recipient write a letter in return.

Brainteaser: What words have these letters, in this order, plus some other letters, now missing?

1. M D M
2. Y P S
3. M D M N
4. A I O

Answers: 1. Medium 2. Typist 3. Madman 4. Radio

22. Garner ideas for a survival kit.

If you teach in California, briefly discuss the earthquake-preparedness kits participants should keep in their cars and homes. If not, lead a brief discussion about such kits for first aid or accidents or camping. Then have them work with a partner or in a triad to describe a metaphorical survival kit, based on their take-home assignment.

Give them free rein. If the assignment made them think about getting ready for a future of learning demands, encourage them to go in that direction. If the pair has a quirky sense of humor and they want to include things like caffeine, permit that. If they want to specify steps the organization or society needs to take to be ready for future crises, let them move in *that* intellectual direction.

In other words, the assignment will yield very different responses. Rest assured, there are no wrong answers.

Brainteaser: How many numbers can you derive from some mathematical operation related to the number 1,302?

Possible answers: 1, 3, 0, 2, 10, 20, 30, 130, 120, 21, 23, 31, 32, 6, 65, 13, 12

---

23. Require them to write two questions.

When you give them the take-home assignment, tell them that in addition to doing the reading or writing or calculating, they will also be expected to write two questions (based on the assignment) for you to answer in class the next day.

Then call on each person for the first question and provide the necessary answers. If time permits, go on to round two.

Brainteaser: Which line contains the best set of words to replace the blank spaces in this statement by actress Helen Hayes?

"The hardest _____ in _____ are those between the _____ of ten and _____."

1. times, existence, periods, death
2. experiences, life, increments, twenty
3. discoveries, journeys, times, destination
4. lessons, learning, grades, twelve
5. years, life, ages, seventy

Answer: 5.

279

24. Provide materials for creating gems of homework-knowledge.

In advance, draw 15 small diamonds on paper. Cut them out and place them in an envelope. Also draw 15 red rubies and 15 green emeralds. Put each batch in its own envelope. On the outside of the appropriate envelopes, write: Diamonds = $500 dollars; Rubies = $300; Emeralds = $100.

The morning after the homework assignment has been done, divide the class into groups. Let them confer for five or ten minutes and to record as many facts as they can about the assignment. Then, in round-robin fashion, call on each group to give you one fact about it. Quickly determine the value of the fact and then instruct them to remove one jewel from your envelopes that matches the value you have established. Do not call on groups in the same order each time to avoid claims of "They took our idea." Explain that you will be as fair as you can, and that if someone took their diamond-idea in the first round, they can go first in the second round to ensure that no one else uses their second diamond-idea.

If you called on groups in 1-2-3 order in the first round, then do 2-3-1 in the second round and 3-1-2 in the third round.

---

25. Challenge them to start a tradition or establish a legend in relation to the homework assignment.

The larger the group size for this assignment, the more creative synergy you are likely to have. And you'll need it, because this assignment really is a challenge. It asks them to derive some future, repeatable action as a result of the homework assignment(s). It can be something frivolous.

Example: "Our group proposes the following tradition for all future classes: When the instructor tells you about this assignment, get on your knees and beg her not to assign it. It really **is** that dull. And if your pleas are earnest enough, you may be able to persuade her, as we did."

The tradition can also be something more serious.

Example: "As a result of what we learned about world hunger, our group would like to establish a tradition of donating to UNICEF whatever loose change we happen to have in our pockets on the day this assignment is given."

Chapter 19

25 Ways to Think on Your Feet

Chapter Overview

This penultimate section differs from all that precede it in that it is designed for two audiences: you *and* your students. All the other chapters of this book are dedicated to the students, but they address you directly as the instructor of those students. The chapter on Study Tips, though, is addressed to the student alone.

Thinking on your feet warrants inclusion of both audiences—the instructor *and* her students. You certainly don't need me to tell you how important it is for an instructor to possess the ability to think well on her feet.

To illustrate, here's a true story of the time when I was most grateful that I was able to apply the skill. I won't mention the organization with which he is associated, but somewhere in a Northeastern metropolis works a man named Oscar. In the first few minutes of the class I was about to teach, I called on him: "Oscar, could you introduce yourself and give us a few words about the kind of work you do?"

He stood. He glared. He pointed his finger at me. He shouted, "It's not 'Oscar.' It's **Doctor** Smith. In fact, twelve of us in here have doctorates. There is very little that *you* can teach *us*!"

Whether your students are applying for part-time jobs, full-time jobs, or college acceptance, whether they are trying to collect their thoughts for an essay exam or for a report, the ability to generate and organize ideas quickly is invaluable, as it was for me in the Oscar situation.

Here's the introduction I use with my students:

> Thinking well on your feet is not a singular skill—it is a composite of multiple skills. The better you are at listening, the more developed your concentrative skills, the more self-confidence you have, the bigger your vocabulary, the more capable you are of creativity, the more reading you do, the more practice you gain, the wider your repertoire of problem-solving skills—all these and more constitute the package of excellence when it comes to thinking and responding both quickly and appropriately.

The world of business makes increasing demands upon our time and upon our ability to make decisions quickly. Witness the "work-out" Jack Welch instituted at General Electric, where participants in this forum-like setting get a mental workout. The process also allows them to remove unnecessary work from their jobs, and they can work out problems together. Here's how Jack Welch set it up: A group of people from all ranks and functions goes to a hotel and is briefly addressed by the boss, who provides an agenda and then leaves the room. The agenda contains problems, issues, concerns, goals—

things, basically, that can be improved. The group breaks into teams and each team tackles one part of the agenda—detailing the topic, proposing solutions, and preparing presentations for the third day, when the boss returns.

The boss has no idea what has been discussed. All he knows as he sits in the front of the room on the third day is that senior executives are there to watch, and that he will be given proposals about which he must make decisions.

Each team makes its proposals. The boss can only do one of three things: agree to the proposal, reject it, or ask for more information by a certain date. That's it. He must explain his responses adequately—not only so his subordinates will be satisfied, but also because the executives in the back of the room will be weighing his words.

These sessions have proven to be highly effective on many levels, not the least of which is the financial: Hundreds of thousands of dollars can be saved because of the ideas presented. So-called work-outs are but one example of the demands placed upon today's executives. The challenges from employees, from the CEO, from stockholders, from the media, from technological developments, and from the competition-driven global environment are enormous.

The past no longer offers the comfort of precedent—not in today's rapidly changing climate. Miles Davis's dictum for musicians "Don't do tomorrow what you did yesterday" applies equally well to businesspeople who are charged with charting new directions for the future. And, of course, it applies to education people as well. Just as companies have come to regard themselves as integrated, highly responsive, and evolving systems, those who lead are expected to integrate diverse elements; to respond easily, clearly, and quickly; and to evolve continuously as learners and leaders.

In the section that follows, you'll find 25 ideas for helping others think on their feet (and keep their feet out of their mouths).

1. Paraphrase.

It's one of the oldest tricks in the verbal-fluidity book: Paraphrase the question or statement that was given to you to buy yourself some thinking time. You can't always do this, of course, because people will begin to think you are dull-witted. But as I used to tell my students in preparation for New York's Regents essay exam, "Restate the essence of the prompt." In so doing, you are organizing your thoughts for the response.

Anti-heckling tip: Let's hope you never have to face an audience containing mean-spirited people, but if someone in a very large room should shout out an unkind remark or an undermining question, try to paraphrase without verbal acidity.

Example:

Undermining statement: "I've read your credentials, and I was wondering what makes you think you are qualified to talk on this subject."

Paraphrased remark: "For those of you who may not have heard the question, let me restate it. The gentleman in the back is asking about my qualifications to speak about this subject. First, allow me to point out that one need not experience death to write about it. In my case, I've done extensive research on the subject of . . ."

---

2. Take note (literally) of classroom interactions.

A class day seldom goes by without someone making a clever remark. When you hear a quip or bon mot or repartee, make note of it. There may be some clues in these remarks that you can use when a similar situation arises sometime in the future.

Brainteaser: Which of the interpretations below fits best with this Yiddish proverb?

"With money in your pocket, you are wise and you are handsome.
And you sing well, too."

1. Others will always envy the successful businessman.
2. Wealthy people usually have many other attributes.
3. When you have money, people will flatter you.
4. A talented singer can sell many platinum records.
5. Good-looking people can parlay their looks into great wealth.
6. Smart people know how to capitalize on their advantages.
7. In terms of good fortune, some people are "Renaissance" people.

Answer: 3.

3. Watch television—especially political debates.

You'll find a wealth of ideas as you listen to politicians respond to reporters' questions. To illustrate, a reporter not long ago asked a Congressman a decidedly challenging question. The politician responded, "What answer would satisfy you?" Now the politician was turning the tables, putting the *reporter* on the spot. I suspect it was not a move designed to create discomfort, but rather a move designed to give the politician time to formulate a response that would not come back to haunt him.

Note: You can pick up some social graces as well when you watch these formal and informal encounters. In a televised documentary I caught that uncovered the machinations of large auction houses, an elegantly dressed woman at a cocktail party was seen approaching another suitably attired guest. "I'd like to introduce myself," she began. I was impressed with the smoothness of the line. It was somewhat assertive, true, but it eliminated the awkwardness associated with introducing yourself to a stranger. It also moved well beyond the cutesy "Hi. I'm Cindy. Who are you?"

Brainteaser: How many numbers can you make from the number 4,672?

Possible answers: 4, 5, 7, 2, 46, 23, 47, 42, 24, 74, 64, 62, 67, 8, 28, 3, 14

---

4. Practice by taking the last word spoken and using it to start your own sentence.

This is not something you would do in real-life circumstances. Rather, it's a practice that will help you respond easily when the real-life situation presents itself. Work with a friend who is as interested as you are in developing the ability to think quickly.

Begin by asking your friend to respond to a question: "What do you think is the biggest problem facing the world today?" When he finishes his response, take the very last word spoken and use it as the first word in your response. Continue in this fashion until you've each had two or three practices. Then change the question.

Challenge yourself: You can really refine your segue skills by not only taking the last word your partner spoke and using it as the first word in your next sentence, but using it to change the topic altogether. It may help to have a third friend put 10 or 20 questions in an envelope. ("Why is grass green?" "Why did Emelda Marcos have so many pairs of shoes?") As soon as you hear the last word, grab a question from the envelope and use the last word you heard as the first word in your response to the new envelope-question.

5. Explain a quote—without hesitating.

Prepare yourself (and a partner, if you'd like to have feedback) by finding quotations and putting them in an envelope. Ideally, you will be using quotes you've never seen before and have not had a chance to think about. Have your partner cut up a batch of individual quotes and put the strips in one envelope. You do the same for him, using a second envelope.

Withdraw a quote, read it, and immediately respond to it. You can interpret it, tell what it reminds you of, discuss how it relates to an actual experience you had, and so on. After your partner has commented on your "performance," it's time for him to pull his own quote from the envelope you provided. You'll provide feedback after *his* performance.

Note: There's a list of quotations in the Appendix. If you choose to copy this page, simply cut off each quote separately and place all of them in the envelope.

Brainteaser: What other words can you think of that are truncated versions of the original word yet mean the same thing, such as "pol" for "politician"?

Possible answers: Celeb for celebrity; deb for debutante; invite for invitation; exec for executive; Dems for Democrats; vets for veterans; bloggers for Web loggers

---

6. Practice having a questions-only conversation.

Here are the rules for this practice. (Again, this is only *practice*—not a technique you would use in a real-life situation.)

1. You begin by asking your partner a question.
2. His response must be another question.
3. That question must bear some relevance to the original question.
4. It cannot take more than a second to formulate.
5. It must be a real question—not a declarative statement with *"isn't it?"* tacked on at the end.

The moment one of these rules is broken, the practice is over.

Note: You may wish to have a third person present to count the number of questions in the exchange. The pair that has reached ten in total has done exceedingly well.

(continued)

500 Creative Classroom Techniques for Teachers and Trainers

6. Practice having a questions-only conversation. *(concluded)*

Example:

Speaker #1: How are you today?
Speaker #2: Why do you ask?
Speaker #1: Does my question offend you?
Speaker #2: Do you know what really offends me?
Speaker #1: Are you about to tell me?
Speaker #2: Would you mind if I did?
Speaker #1: Don't you know I'd rather learn about you than learn about world affairs?
Speaker #2: Don't you think world affairs is a more interesting topic than my list of offensive statements?
Speaker #1: Is it?
Speaker #2: Where are we going with these questions?

Brainteaser: Which of the choices completes the series?

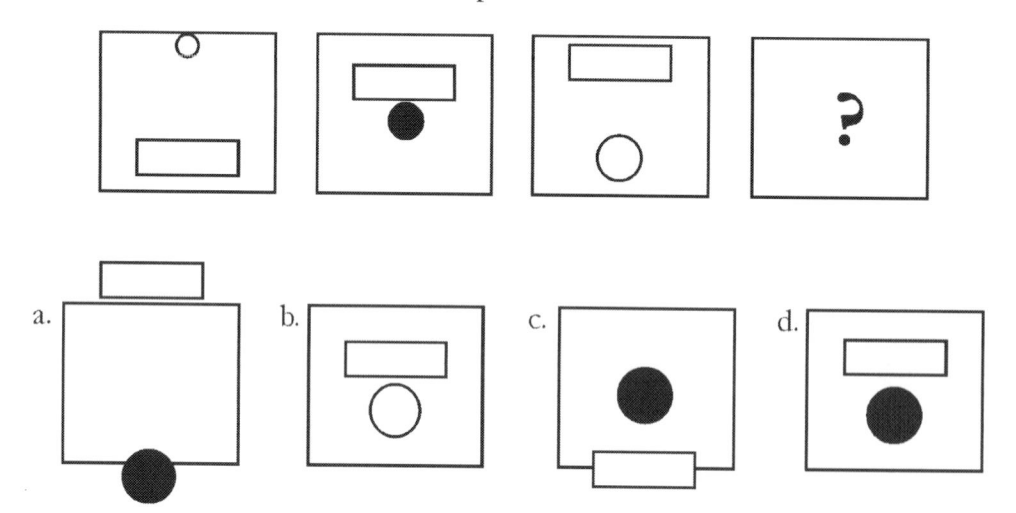

Answer: a. The rectangle is moving from the bottom to the top, while the circle moves down from the top toward the bottom in the first three illustrations. Plus, the circle is going from unfilled to black, then back to unfilled again. Figure (a) continues this pattern by having the rectangle moving up and the circle moving down (so far up and so far down that they go beyond the lines). Plus, the circle turns black again.

7. Take a word and make an association.

When you hear the word "husband," you probably think of the related word "wife." And when you hear the word "write" (or its past tense "wrote"), you probably make an association with the word "read." Keep these two examples in mind as you learn how a realtor and a press secretary used associated words to deliver the perfect comeback.

Judy Columbus is a retired realtor in Rochester, New York. When she was starting her business, she approached a bank's loan officer with her business plan. He reviewed it and then asked, "Does your husband know you are doing this?"

Judy responded with the associated word we mentioned at the outset. To his chagrin, she demanded, "Does your *wife* know you are asking questions like that?"

Our second example comes from the White House. Liz Carpenter served as press secretary to President Lyndon Johnson. Somehow, she also managed to find time to write a book. One day, the historian Arthur Schlesinger delivered her a backhanded compliment: "I read your book, Liz, and really liked it. Who *wrote* it for you?"

Using the associated word we mentioned before, Liz replied, "I'm so glad you liked it, Arthur. Who *read* it to you?"

Caution: Carpenter was perfectly justified in giving a stinging reply, because the question put to her was an offensive one. As a rule, however, I don't recommend using sarcasm. If you must, use it only if you need to defend yourself against someone who has insulted or offended you, as a last resort.

Skillbuilding practice: Have a friend make a comment (and not necessarily a nice one) about you. Try to find some word in his sentence and use it (or a related word) to fashion your reply.

Brainteaser: Each blank needs a computer word to complete it. The words, though, may need some liberties taken with them.

1. So long was the _____, __ _____ was all the musician had time to eat.
2. From the backyard snow _____ _____ three children, eager for lunch.
3. If the _____ _____, the fisherman will be thrilled.

Answers: 1. Gigabyte (gig, a, bite) 2. Fortran (fort, ran) 3. networks (net, works)

500 Creative Classroom Techniques for Teachers and Trainers

8. Circumvent.

You certainly don't have to answer every question that is put to you. Learn to sidestep as graciously as the young lady in the following example did.

Example: A lovely young woman had just been crowned a beauty queen when a reporter tossed an intrusive question at her. "Are you a virgin?" he demanded to know. She thought just a moment and then smiled sweetly, "I don't believe that question is relevant to the duties that await me. May I have the next question, please?"

Caution: You may wish to use a different example more appropriate for the age of your students.

Brainteaser: How do you interpret this amusing bit of Yiddish wisdom?

"The man who marries for money will earn it."

1. You have to work hard when you marry a wealthy woman.
2. It helps to be wealthy before you marry into wealth.

Answer: 1.

---

9. Define.

Especially during interviews, you can gain some thinking time by either giving or asking for a definition. The responses provided below were given by two different quick-thinkers during actual job interviews.

Give-definition examples:

Interviewer: "Tell us about yourself."

Applicant: "If you really want to know who I am, I must tell you that I am a non-conforming conformist. Certainly, I will conform to your rules and regulations. But if I am ever asked to do something I consider unethical, I will not conform!"

- - - - - - - - - -

Interviewer: "How do you know you are intelligent?"

Applicant: "To me, intelligence is knowledge. And I know more today than I knew yesterday."

Seek-definition example:

Interviewer: "What are your views on participative management?"

Applicant: "By that, do you mean 'democratic' management?"

10. Expand your repertoire of examples.

The more you read, the more responses you'll have available. You'll be able to cite other people or sources. Doing so makes you seem intelligent. Further, if you have these people or sources ready, your mind can go on auto pilot as it presents the information, while another part of your mind begins to formulate the real response.

Example:

Interviewer: "What weakness of yours should we know about?"

Applicant: "I tend to agree with Mark Van Doren, who said we should bring ideas in and entertain them royally because one of them may be the king. Like him, I prefer to consider a variety of ideas before making a decision to pursue a particular course of action. I also like to listen to all the ideas of the people on my team. Yes, sometimes that can slow down the process, but I've seen the reverse happen too often. People act in haste and then regret their actions. This willingness to entertain ideas royally could be viewed as a weakness. But it has also proven to be a strength."

Brainteaser: What six-letter word ending in "t" completes the analogy?

DIRT : SUCTION : : FILINGS :

Answer: Magnet.

---

11. Think F-A-S-T.

The next time you are called upon for a verbal contribution and you haven't much time to formulate your response, don't panic. Just think F-A-S-T.

"F" stands for Focus. (You'll state what you will discuss.)

"A" stands for Amplify. (Add a sentence or two to the primary focus.)

"S" stands for Specify. (You'll add a few details or specifics.)

"T" stands for Tie Up. (You'll provide a summarizing sentence at the end.)

(continued)

11. **Think F-A-S-T.** *(concluded)*

   Brainteaser: Using words from the world of computers, can you complete the sentences? (Think word play.)

   1. There were weeds in the grass, but the gardener _____ all down.
   2. The father and the _____ _____ their way through the wood with a drill.
   3. The duck hunter had a _____ _____-ing in the grasses.

   Answers: 1. Modem ("mowed 'em") 2. Motherboard ("mother bored") 3. Web site ("web sighting")

---

12. **Have lines ready for use.**

   Most of us know people who start their privacy-invasion with, "I know it's none of my business…" The next word in their sentence will always be the word *"but."* Then they will go on to ask the question that really *is* none of their business. Yes, you can agree with them; you can say, "You are right! It's none of your business." And you can refuse to answer them. Doing so, however, may alienate someone with whom you have to work every day or sit beside in class.

   To avoid using a caustic reply or to sidestep the question because you can't think of a verbal exit fast enough, have some stock responses ready. For example, "I promised my mother (or boss or husband or partner) that I'd never reveal the answer to that question."

   Historical example: Secretary of the Navy Frank Knox was always being asked by well-meaning, patriotic Americans whether or not the country was going to enter World War II. Secretary Knox would lean down and whisper conspiratorially, "Can you keep a secret?"

   The asker would assure him immediately, "Oh, yes, Mr. Secretary. I can."

   "Good!" Secretary Knox would announce. "So can I!"

   Brainteaser: How good is your geography? You'll need a knowledge of world capitals in order to do well on this puzzle. Each blank requires the name of a city, but the spelling of those capitals may be unusual.

   (continued)

12. **Have lines read for use.** *(concluded)*

    1. The angry, Southern-accented D.A. shouted at the famed forensic pathologist, "Dr. _____, "_____ autopsy report is missing!"
    2. The _____ _____ the plank didn't bother the carpenter in the least.
    3. Buffalo no longer have a range to _____.
    4. She's _____ _____s of laundry.
    5. When the teen was asked by his father if he'd pass his chemistry exam, he replied, "It's in the _____, _____!"
    6. For this _____, _____ whatever they want. It's that fabulous!
    7. Shaq's shoes, not surprisingly, are _____ _____ in width.

    Answers: 1. Lima (Lee, Mah) 2. Berlin (burl in) 3. Rome (roam) 4. Washington (washing, ton) 5. Baghdad (bag, Dad) 6. Taipei (tie, pay) 7. Tripoli (Triple E)

---

13. **Practice with odd questions.**

    You'll need a partner for this practice. Not necessarily an odd partner, but a partner who can ask odd questions in an effort to catch you off guard. Reply immediately to the question he asks. (You see, if you take time to write out a reply, you cannot develop the skill of thinking on your feet.) Return the favor by asking your partner odd questions of your own.

    Examples:

    What's more revolting than a squashed peacock?
    What's a better word for "history"?
    Why don't we have a "Land of the Midnight Moon"?
    How do human beings compare to butterflies?
    What can you do with rubber bands, other than use them to gather things?

    Brainteaser: A famous person has a last name that sounds like the combination of two body parts. (Clue #1: This person is no longer alive. Clue #2: The word describing what this person did for a living lends in the letters "ix.") Can you name that world-respected figure?

    Answer: Amelia Earhart ("aviatrix").

14. Count backwards.

Divide the class into pairs or triads. (If there is a third person, he can serve as the mathematician, advising the speaker if he has made a mistake.) One person counts backwards by sixes, sevens, eights, or nines from 100. (Don't use five: it's too easy.) The second person notes how long it took. Even if the timekeeper is not wearing a watch, he can keep track of time by saying in his head, "*One* one thousand; *two* two thousand, and so on.

Once the time is recorded, then the timekeeper repeats the process. (His partner will now serve as timekeeper and the former timekeeper becomes the backwards-counter.) For the second round, though, the person will count backwards by *sevens*. Ideally, there will be a third and a fourth round, so that each person can compare the time it took for the first and the second attempt.

By forcing yourself to do this quickly more than once, you can track improvements in your score. The less time it takes, the more quickly your mind is working to find the information you need and present it to you. In time, you'll not only enjoy and welcome such challenges, you will realize that they are building your self-confidence.

---

15. Choose a letter and ask for words.

This exercise, too, can be used with pairs or triads, or you can be the timekeeper and have people work alone. If they are working in pairs or triads, one person says to the other, "Give me as many words as you can think of that start with the letter "b." (The letter chosen could be any letter except those that have few words that begin with them. Avoid "q," "x," "y," and "z.")

The speaker states his request, the timekeeper counts for 25 seconds, and the third person writes down all the words he can think of starting with the letter "b." In the second rotation, each person takes a different role, and the same goes for the third rotation. This way, each person has a chance to perform each role once. If time permits, do the exercise again so that each person will have a chance to compare his second total with the first total of recalled words. (Choose a letter other than "b" for the subsequent rounds.)

Option: You can make the assignment even more extreme by narrowing the words to a specific realm. For example, tell me all the words you can think of that start with the letter "l" that pertain to business.

16. Toss it back; gain some time.

Admittedly, it's a stalling technique, a way to buy time until you can formulate your ideas. But it really does work—just don't use it too often. When someone asks a difficult question (one you haven't thought about or one for which you'd had little time to prepare), gain a few needed moments by tossing it back.

(Think spelling-bee contestants.) You can ask for clarification. You can ask for a definition. You can ask a honing question, such as "Would you like me to address that in the context of the individual, or in the context of the organization?"

Example: Journalist Diane Sawyer once asked British Prime Minister Tony Blair, "Who do you think would make the better President—Bill Clinton, or Hillary Clinton?" Talk about being between a rock and a hard place! Given the fact that Bill Clinton held the office, Blair really could not say Hillary. On the other hand, by not doing so, he might offend a large number of people who would like to see a woman running the country.

In a bid for time, Tony Blair smiled at the reporter and declared, "That's naughty." Diane Sawyer sheepishly defended herself, "Well, it really wasn't *my* question," she asserted. "The cameraman wanted to know." The camera shifts to faces other than Blair's (including a switch to the naughty cameraman), giving Blair the time he needed to develop a diplomatic response.

Brainteaser: More vocabulary-opportunities for you. Match the E-words with their definitions in the second column.

1. ebullience		A.	boldness
2. eclat		B.	enormously happy
3. eclectic		C.	public notice
4. ecstatic		D.	brilliant achievement
5. ecumenical		E.	excessive enthusiasm
6. edict		F.	mentally build or develop
7. edify		G.	limp, exhausted
8. educe		H.	lead or draw out
9. effete		I.	general
10. effrontery		J.	chosen from a wide variety

Answers: 1. E 2. B 3. J 4. B 5. I 6. C 7. F 8. H 9. G 10. A

17. Plant red flags.

There's no guarantee that this next technique will prevent the gaffes from ever being expressed, but it will definitely help train the brain to avoid continuing in a direction that might have negative consequences. The exercise forces your brain to find words other than the ones you would naturally speak. (The very words that will get you in trouble—the ones that you are about to send rolling off your tongue without much thought.)

Basically, you take a topic from one envelope and then turn the paper over. On the back side will be a word closely related to the topic—a word that you must avoid saying as you talk about the topic. Tell your listeners both the topic and the word to be avoided. Then start talking about the topic. Your audience (whether it's a helpful friend or an entire class) will let you know if you slipped up and spoke an "avoid-word."

Practice topics or words to avoid:

War/President Bush   Children/Future
Horse/Race   School/Teachers
Food/Restaurant   Crime/Criminals
Computers/Internet   Movies/Hollywood

18. Anticipate objections.

Each person will write (on a sheet of paper) one way to improve the world/school/organization. Collect the papers and give one to each group. Groups, after receiving a sheet, will read the improvement idea and will then ask one person from their group to leave the room. While he is in the corridor, that person is tasked with considering the objections the group is likely to have regarding the improvement suggestion. He is also tasked with thinking of ways to counter or overcome their objections.

While the corridor-person is thinking, the group back in the room will also be thinking—thinking of reasons why the improvement idea won't work or flaws in the design or problems with the design, and so on.

After five or ten-minutes, call the corridor-person back in the room and have his group members explain their opposition while he tries to deflect their criticism of the idea.

Note: Having an observer in each group to record the exchanges between idea-opposers and the idea-defender will deepen the learning to be derived from this exercise.

19. Improve concentration.

You may remember from the Overview that concentration skills are part of the whole rapid-thinking package. There are numerous ways to develop the ability to concentrate, but one that participants truly seem to enjoy requires the formation of four-person groups.

One person is the Speaker, who will talk about something he knows really well—his family, his pet, his hobby, his last vacation.

The second person is the Listener, who will try to remember as many facts as possible from the Speaker's monologue, without taking any notes.

The third person is the Whisperer. He will try to disrupt the Listener's concentration by whispering non-stop into the listener's ear. (With older students, you can heighten the fun by having the Whisperer discuss semi-salacious tidbits. If the Whisperer is talking about the Federal Reserve, for example, it will be easy for most Listeners to tune him out. But if the Whisperer is speculating about Angelina Jolie and her penchant for strange behavior, the Listener will probably be hanging on every juicy word.)

Stop the exercise after three minutes, and ask the Listener to repeat all the facts he can from the Speaker's monologue. The fourth person is the Recorder, who will note the spoken statements and then place a check mark in front of each one that the Listener repeats accurately. (Repeat the exercise if time permits.)

Brainteaser: One abbreviation in this long list does not belong. How quickly can you spot it?

1. NO
2. AM
3. MD
4. LA
5. TH
6. MO
7. K
8. I
9. B
10. C
11. FM
12. O
13. HO
14. Q
15. LI
16. V
17. N
18. PA
19. BA
20. TA

Answer: 14. Q. All the others are listed on the Periodic Table of the Elements.

20. Take ten; give five.

Pairs will work on this exercise, which has one person coming up with a challenge that he will issue to his partner. The challenge is to come up with five correct answers in a ten-second span. Then the roles will be switched: The challenger will now be the one who has to come up with five answers in ten seconds. The challenge can be from any field and can cover any topic.

Example:

You have ten seconds. Give me the names of five world leaders.
You have ten seconds. Give me the names of five European rivers.
You have ten seconds. Give me the names of five titles that contain a woman's name.
You have ten seconds. Give me the names of five opera singers.
You have ten seconds. Give me the names of five basketball stars.
You have ten seconds. Give me the names of five cities that have hosted the Olympics.
You have ten seconds. Give me the names of five Cabinet members.
You have ten seconds. Give me the names of five Ivy League colleges.
You have ten seconds. Give me the names of five famous scientists.
You have ten seconds. Give me the names of five titles that have a geographic reference.
You have ten seconds. Give me the names of five body parts spelled with six letters.

---

21. Elicit prevarications.

If someone asks you a question, your natural reaction is to respond honestly. Such responses require no thinking, really. Our brains work automatically and phenomenally quickly to find the answer in our mental files and offer it to the question-asker. The natural patterns are interrupted, though, when our brains tell us that we cannot go to our usual files. Then, we are forced to come up with an answer different from the familiar and comfortable one we are used to giving.

This exercise is designed to stimulate the brain to go into unexplored territory, and to feel comfortable doing so. (It is *not* designed to encourage lying.) You see, our minds do not "go blank" when we have to deal with familiar and comfortable questions. It's when the *unexpected* hits us that we seem to freeze. Thus, working on exercises that force the brain to move quickly into unknown territory will, in time, increase our comfort level in dealing with the unanticipated.

Someone will ask you a question. It could be as ordinary as "What is your name?" Your job, however, is not so simple. You have to respond, quickly, with an answer other than "John Smith." It doesn't have to be a lie. You could, for example, say, "My name is a common one. In fact, it's so common that it has meanings that go far beyond the name meanings."

(continued)

21. **Elicit prevarications.** *(concluded)*

   Brainteaser: Which two proverbs are essentially saying the same thing?
   1. Silence is not always a sign of wisdom, but babbling is ever a folly.
   2. Better to go to bed supperless than to get up in debt.
   3. Even ill luck itself is good for something in a wise man's hand.
   4. Better a lean peace than a fat victory.
   5. A civil denial is better than a rude grant.
   6. Better slip with foot than with tongue.
   7. Out of the frying pan and into the fire.
   8. Great men must die, but death cannot kill them.
   9. When the well's dry, we know the worth of water.
   10. Where bees are, there is honey.
   11. Little dogs start the hare, but big ones catch it.
   12. He who plants trees loves others besides himself.
   13. A donkey is still a donkey, even though laden with gold.
   14. He jumped in the water to escape the rain.

   Answers: 7 and 14

---

22. **Practice giving impromptu speeches (if only to yourself).**

   If you are a college student, a trainer for a corporate university, or a corporate trainer, you probably spend considerable time on the road. Use that time to hone your quick-thinking skills. Turn on the radio. Take the first word the reporter or disc jockey speaks. Turn off the radio. Use that word as the topic of an impromptu speech. (Granted, other drivers might look over and think you strange as they see you talking to yourself, but you'll never see them again, so it doesn't matter.)

   If you are a high school or college student, you can do the same thing, minus the car. Have someone write 20 or 30 words, each on its own scrap of paper. Put the papers into an envelope, and when you need to practice (alone or with an audience), draw a topic from the envelope and speak intelligently about it for three to five minutes.

   Brainteaser: Even though there are some letters missing, you're expected to figure out the words because some letters, in the correct order, have been provided. (More than one answer is possible.)

   1. N S W   2. R B L E   3. A S W   4. U F L W

   Answers: 1. Answer 2. Problem 3. Cashew 4. Sunflower

23. Expand your vocabulary.

Those who are able to collect and express their thoughts quickly seldom grope for words. It stands to reason: the more words you know, the greater your chances of finding the right one (or the right synonym) when you need it.

There are many ways to expand your vocabulary: calendars, tapes, books, and nightly visits to the dictionary are a few good ones.

You can also receive a word a day on your computer by registering at the following site:

http://wordsmith.org/awad/subscriber.html

Brainteaser: What familiar phrase is to be found in the box?

> COTAXABLEME

Answer: Taxable income.

---

24. Create creative lists.

Work with a partner and do one of these tasks each week. They will challenge your verbal flexibility and convince you that you need not be stumped in your search for words:

Create a list of . . .
- 25 ways to say "no"
- 25 ways to say "It's hot out today"
- 25 ways to say "I don't like this"
- 25 ways to say "In the past . . ."
- 25 ways to say "In the present . . ."
- 25 ways to say "In the future . . ."

(continued)

24. **Create creative lists.** *(concluded)*

Brainteaser: If you are a speed dialer, you'll do well with this challenge.

You can match the number on the left with the business or business people on the right by figuring out the letters contained in the numbers you would dial. The right letters, associated with the numbers, will spell out the business (e.g., 1-800-FLOWER = 1-800-356-9377).

1. 724-6837
2. 738-7467
3. 897-4787
4. 738-7467
5. 227-2377

A. BARBERS
B. TYPISTS
C. PET SHOP
D. BANKERS
E. PAINTER

Answers: 1. E 2. C 3. B 4. D 5. A

---

25. Use the P-P-F Technique.

When you are called upon to share information or to express your views on a particular subject, do a chronological tracking of the past, the present, and the future (P-P-F). Don't, however, be so obvious as to say "In the past . . ." "In the present . . ." "In the future . . ."

Instead, confident in the knowledge that among the one million words in the English language you can find some verbal options, say, "There was a time . . ." or "Years ago . . ." or "Our predecessors used to . . ."

No matter what topic is thrown at you, it will be pretty easy to come up with a cohesive and intelligent response, merely by moving backwards and then forward in time.

Brainteaser: Study these four words:

BOW   STORM   CHECK   DROP

Then decide which of these words belongs in the same category:

FALL   FADE   FAIL   FURY

Answer: Fall. All the words have an association with "rain."

Chapter 20

25 Ways to Develop Self-Confidence

Chapter Overview

Confidence is a theme that runs through a number of courses I teach. I often introduce the topic by telling students an inspirational story. (Newspapers and magazines are filled with them. If you wish, start collecting them and then give a different one to each participant. Of course, you could simply tell the same story to everyone.)

One of my favorite stories, for example, concerns a young woman named Cara Dunne-Yates, who works as a law clerk for the Public Council on Children's Rights while studying for the bar exam. She's also training for the next Paralympic Games. Cara is a new mother, too, who graduated *magna cum laude* from Harvard University. She then went on to UCLA Law School.

An active life? Yes, but in addition to all this, Cara's a downhill skiing legend with ten medals to her credit. Further, she's won both silver and bronze medals in international competitions for tandem bike racing.

Oh, I forgot to mention something: Cara is fighting cancer, and she has been blind since the age of five.

I then move from Cara's story to this question: "What is holding *you* back from achieving your goals?" After hearing or reading eye-opening and spirit-opening stories such as Cara's, the answer is typically, "Nothing!"

In this final chapter are 25 additional ways for you to help students develop self-confidence.

1. Have them describe incremental journeys.

Years ago, a middle school teacher asked me to address students who were frightened about moving on to junior high, having heard tales of somewhat nefarious rites of passage. In my talk, I took the students through a list of the enormous changes they had already made (and survived) in their young lives—from lying helplessly in a crib to crawling, to walking, to running, to leaving home for kindergarten. We talked about all the ways they had gained independence and taken on adult behaviors. Diapers and cribs and baby food were a thing of the past, as were security blankets and teddy bears.

And, while I didn't share Goethe's quote with them, I share it with you to illustrate the benefit of asking participants to record their own incremental journeys toward competence and confidence: "If you treat an individual as he is, he will stay as he is, but if you treat him as if he were what he ought to be, he will become what he ought to be and could be."

Brainteaser: What fraction of 4 equals $\frac{1}{2}$ of 1?

a) $\frac{1}{10}$ b) $\frac{1}{8}$ c) $\frac{1}{4}$ d) $\frac{1}{2}$ e) $\frac{2}{3}$

Answer: b. If 4 is divided into four parts, each part equals the number one. If 4 is divided into eight parts, each part equals half of the number 1.

---

2. Ask them to list who's or what's.

Ask participants to list all the "who's" or "what's" they are. For example, in response to the question "Who am I?" someone might respond, "I am a San Diegan, a Californian, a Native American, a tribal member, a church-goer, a father," and so on. Curiously, asking "What am I?" will often elicit a different set of responses. For example: "A staunch opponent of the war," "an activist," "a proponent of family values."

Award the person with the longest list a token prize. She is usually the person who knows herself best. (Offset any ruffled feathers by saying that the oldest person in the room is often the one who knows herself best, but the winner this time is the exception to the rule.)

Have participants go back to their lists and place the letter "G" next to all the things they are good at. Next, they will place an "S" next to the things that can be described as "so-so" (interests and skills). Finally, they should place a "B" beside the items at which they truly excel, the ones they are best at. Typically, these are their passions. Have partners discuss their "B" entries and the self-confidence they have gained from these achievements.

3. Alter their perspectives.

Ask each person to write down the names of four people they truly admire. The people can be members of their own family—they need not be famous people. Next, ask each person to describe a difficult situation she is facing that may be causing a crisis of confidence.

The third step is to have them complete this sentence: "This is how my father (or other admired person on list) would handle this situation." (If time permits, they can view the situation from more than one perspective.)

Finally, have them specify which actions the admired person would take that the *participant* can take. Ask for volunteers to share not the personal situation, but rather the actions that they can take, based on what their heroes/heroines might do.

Brainteaser: If 9 is 9% of x, then $x =$

a) .01   b) .09   c) 1   d) 9   e) 100

Answer: e.

---

4. Offer leadership opportunities to each participant.

Throughout the course, offer the chance to be a group leader or spokesperson to every single participant. Respect those who decline the offer, but at least make the effort to develop their take-charge capabilities.

Brainteaser: You're familiar with analogies. In the following test, however, the answer will not be expressed in terms of a verbal relationship, but rather in terms of a numerical one. Good luck. The first one is deliberately easy to get you started.

1. TRAMS : SMART : : 69317 :
   a) 31769   b) 73196   c) 71396   d) 91376

2. TEAMS : MATES : : 17432 :
   a) 43127   b) 34172   c) 27134   d) 32741

3. STERN : RENTS : : 64235 :
   a) 32546   b) 52346   c) 25346   d) 42356

4. EVIL : VILE : : 7165 :
   a) 1657   b) 5167   c) 6175   d) 5671

Answers: 1. c   2. b   3. a   4. a

5. Develop "autabe" leaders.

Write several different categories on the flipchart. They could pertain to learning situations (e.g., learning environments); to national situations (e.g., the No Child Left Behind Act); or to world situations (e.g., the growth of terrorism). The categories could also pertain to general topics such as the environment, the economy, foreign relations, et cetera. Ask participants to think about some things that should be changed in at least three of the categories—things that "ought to be," but are not yet in existence.

Then ask if they'd be willing to help create the change they'd like to see. Don't push; gently prod. If no one accepts the leadership challenge, scale it back. If they, for example, don't have time to take an active role in environmental or political issues, would they be willing to write a letter to their Congressional representative urging a certain piece of legislation? Would they be willing to send a contribution to an organization that is actively working to effect the change the participant believes in?

Remind them that whenever they utter the words "There really ought to be . . ." they are outlining a leadership opportunity for themselves. From participation in such opportunities, self-confidence grows.

6. Have them step into the positive (spot) light in which others see them.

Once participants have had a chance to get to know each other, ask them to write their names on a half-sheet of paper. Collect the papers and place them in a box. Then have each person withdraw the name of one class member. She is to write the positive impressions she has of that individual.

Collect the papers. Call off the names and hand each person the paper that has comments about her from another class member. If the group is a lighthearted one or one in which egos abound, ask if anyone would like to share her paper. Ask, too, if anyone is surprised by what was written.

Brainteaser: What familiar phrase is shown in the box?

> BEND
> SDRAWKCAB

Answer: Bend over backwards.

7. Quote Darwin.

Naturalist Charles Darwin observed, "It is not the strongest of the species that survive, nor the most intelligent, but the ones most responsive to change." Remind them of how strong they are, if only because of the things they have survived. In a corporate setting, about half the attendees will have survived divorce. Others will have survived serious illness, perhaps service in a war, perhaps job loss, and so on.

But you will not explore those experiences in this activity. Instead, you will ask them if they are responsive to change and how they can become more responsive. If they *are* responsive, you'd like to know how they *got* that way.

First, ask them to discuss these questions with a partner. Then ask for volunteers to share their insights.

Brainteaser: What is the familiar expression in the box?

> LOFALLVE

Answer: Fall in love.

---

8. Develop their confidence by moving from small to large.

You can spot the shy students immediately. Sometimes, you don't even get a chance to notice them before they approach you, begging you not to call on them. (Of course, you will honor their requests.) With the terminally shy, I move them from the easiest form of classroom participation to the more difficult. Here's a typical "easy" ploy: "Judy, I have a question for you and all I want is a yes or no answer."

Later in the morning, I'll return to Judy and ask a question that requires more than a monosyllabic response (but still, an easy question). Throughout the day, I'll lead the shy person to incrementally more-challenging activities, always giving her the option to decline the invitation if she feels uncomfortable.

Brainteaser: What well-known phrase is contained in the box below?

> MYOWNHEARTAMAN

Answer: A man after my own heart.

9. Give them a chance to self-propel.

As you may know from watching "Jeopardy," the Daily Double permits the contestant to answer a low-value question worth just a few hundred dollars or a high-value question worth much more, or any question in between. Of course, the more value assigned to the question, the more difficult it will be.

With a great many of your activities, you can ask, "Do you want the easy, the medium, or the impossible version?" Ideally, participants will challenge themselves from time to time by going for the virtually impossible-to-answer level of questions.

Brainteaser: Which choice contains the best set of words for filling in the blanks in the following statement?

"_____," Oscar Wilde _____, "is the last _____ of the _____."

1. Fidelity, said, resort, working class
2. Consistency, declared, refuge, unimaginative
3. Trust, opined, exchange, poor
4. Love, yearned, hope, married

Answer: 2.

---

10. Let Friedrich fuel them.

As a prelude to a self-assessment, designed to promote confidence and to encourage action, share this Nietzschean quote: "At bottom, every man knows perfectly well that he is a unique being, only once on this earth; and by no extraordinary chance will such a marvelously picturesque piece of diversity in unity as he is ever be put together a second time."

Ask them to celebrate their uniqueness from time to time. Ask, too, that they call upon that uniqueness to accomplish things they have not yet undertaken. These questions will help in their quest. The answers can be shared with a partner if they elect to do so. Otherwise, the answers should go in a journal.

1. What is my highest priority right now?
2. What is the most constructive action I can take right now on this priority?
3. Which of my strengths can be applied to this priority?
4. Is my best self in charge?
5. How can I make my highest priority most enjoyable?
6. Whom can I count on to help make this priority a reality?

Chapter 20: 25 Ways to Develop Self-Confidence

11. Assign the reading of a biography.

It seems that every famous, wealthy, and/or successful person has had to overcome serious obstacles to achieve what she did. (Lance Armstrong is just one perfect example.) Let participants choose whatever figure interests them, from whatever world intrigues them. Their assignment: to record the strategies employed by the famous person whenever she doubted her own ability to meet a challenge.

Keep a class notebook of these strategies by having each person share one strategy and then recording it in the notebook while the next person is sharing hers.

Note: If you will only see the participants for two or three days, reading a complete biography will be difficult. Suggest instead that they do a quick Google search and read just one article.

Brainteaser: Do you know what this question is asking?

```
N E 1 4 1 0 S
```

Answer: Anyone for tennis?

---

12. Begin emotional self-examinations for them.

Who can argue with the Shakespeare wisdom that commands, "To thine own self be true"? It's hard to be true, though, when you are not sure what your own self *is*. This assignment, which can last a whole year if you wish it to, asks participants to respond to questions about their feelings in specific situations. Even if you only use the assignment once, though, ask participants to share one thing they learned about themselves.*

I feel aggressive when _____.
I feel angry when _____.
I feel annoyed when _____.
I feel anxious when _____.
I feel apathetic when _____.

(continued)

12. **Begin emotional self-examinations for them.** *(concluded)*

Here are additional words you can use for an extended assignment:

> bitter, bored, calm, cautious, combative, confident, confused, crushed, curious, defensive, depressed, determined, disappointed, disgusted, distracted, disturbed, eager, ecstatic, embarrassed, enraged, enthusiastic, envious, excited, exhausted, frightened, frustrated, guilty, happy, helpless, hopeful, hostile, humiliated, hurt, hysterical, infatuated, interested, jealous, joyous, left out, lonely, loved, loving, mischievous, miserable, moody, optimistic, overwhelmed, panicked, paranoid, peaceful, proud, puzzled, rejected, relieved, sad, satisfied, scared, shocked, shy, sorry, stubborn, surprised, suspicious, thoughtful, vulnerable, withdrawn, worried.

***Important note:** The sharing, because it is of a private nature, is optional. If participants don't want to discuss their responses at all, accept that. You might ask, though, if they'd be willing to meet with just one other person—someone they like or think they can trust, or someone with whom they have not yet worked. In a more private setting, most people will feel comfortable opening up. If they do agree to a partnership, advise that when the partner hears positive insights, she should encourage the self-examiner to continue with those behaviors. With she hears negatives, the partner should suggest ways to manage their emotions.

Brainteaser: How quickly can you determine the meaning of what's in the box?

```
    RVE             RVE         RVE
RVE         RVE             RVE
```

Answer: Nerve endings.

---

13. **Adopt the "Fish philosophy."**

Some of you have read about, heard about, or watched a video about the employees of the Seattle Fish Market. The philosophy by which this group of people work (and, I suspect, *live* as well) is a simple one:

- Have a positive attitude.
- Make work seem like play.
- Be there.
- Make someone's day.

(continued)

13. **Adopt the "Fish philosophy."** *(concluded)*

Divide the class into four groups. Assign each group one of the four elements of the philosophy. Ask how they can improve their Attitude; bring Fun to the workplace or the classroom; improve Attendance and/or Attending; and—for the fourth group—make someone else's day special, whether they are in the classroom or in the workplace.

When these four Fish-like actions are put into place, customers benefit. And those customers feel appreciated. In return, when they express that appreciation, the people serving them feel better about their work. All in all, it's a delicious rather than vicious cycle.

Brainteaser: Can you figure out this common phrase?

> THE EN

Answer: Beginning of "the end."

---

14. **Have them go from 0 to 10 within hours.**

Moments after they have assembled, pass out a sheet that you have prepared in advance. The sheet will contain a list of ten course concepts that you are fairly certain they are *not* familiar with. They are to write a number indicating the extent of their knowledge about each topic on a scale of 0–10: "0" = little or virtually nothing; "5" = possessing enough information about the topic to discuss it in a cursory fashion; "10" = a complete understanding of the topic. Ideally, the papers will be filled with 0's. Collect them and hold them until the course is three-quarters complete.

I say "ideally" because near the end of the course, you will distribute a second copy of the list with the same instructions. Then return their first papers to them so they can compare their scores. They should see definite improvements in their knowledge-grasp. And this improvement should deepen their confidence.

Brainteaser: Which of the following fractions is closest to $\frac{1}{2}$?

1) $\frac{1}{3}$ 　　2) $\frac{2}{5}$ 　　3) $\frac{5}{9}$ 　　4) $\frac{6}{11}$ 　　5) $\frac{3}{8}$

Answer: 4.

15. Express appreciation for hard and soft knocks.

Participants sometimes feel distanced from an instructor who, say, has a Ph.D. or has written books. I try to narrow that distance at the very beginning of the class by telling them that the smartest man I know is my father, who has only a fourth-grade education. The most creative woman I know is my mother, who—with only an eighth-grade education—sold an invention to a major manufacturer when she was 70 years old: a drapery rod that eliminates the need for pleats!

Acknowledge that formal training is indeed important, but that *informal* training is equally important. In fact, it may be *more* important, because it is acquired in practice, not in theory, as the need arises—not when an instructor determines. A study by the Xerox corporation found that 87 percent of the knowledge acquired in training sessions or national meetings is forgotten, unless there is some application following the training. So it's not so much the receiving of the knowledge that is valuable, but rather the *application* of the knowledge.

This exercise will help strengthen confidence by recognizing the "smarts" participants possess—informal and formal. It will also help reinforce classroom learning by asking them how they can transfer it to the workplace or how it can be reinforced once class is over. Divide the class into groups of four to six participants. Ask them to list all the ways informal learning occurs. Basically, you'll be asking them how they informally learned what they know (in a one-on-one conversation with a co-worker, in a meeting, on a team, through mentoring, by reading, through a trial-and-error process, via the Internet, by observing, by listening, and so on).

The second step in this process is to list informal-learning methods on the flipchart. Then have groups determine ways they will be able to informally reinforce their learning once the class is over.

F.Y.I. A $1.6 million study funded by the U.S. Department of Labor, the Pew Charitable Trusts, and several state agencies found that informal learning was widespread in the workplace, and that it fulfilled up to 70% of participants' learning needs.

Brainteaser: How sharp are your analytical skills? Try to figure out what the situation is here:

> A small town in upstate New York just built a multi-story building. It has no stairs, elevators, or escalators, and yet it meets all building codes. Why?

Answer: The structure is a library and the stories referred to are literary, not structural.

16. Have them create their own success-formulas.

Everyone's heard of $E = mc^2$. It's Einstein's famous formula, of course. Even though they may not be studying quantum physics, participants can still play with formulas—in this case, one of their own devising:

Begin by asking them what they most want from life. The answers will vary, but list them all on the flipchart. (You may want to start off with a few things of your own.) You'll probably hear Success, Happiness, Good Health, Wealth, Contentment, Joy, Excitement, A Good Job, Education, and Spiritual Growth. Then divide the class into pairs. Have the pairs select two items from the list and write a formula for each that tells how they can obtain what they seek.

Examples:

- Formula for Education: $D = M + Hw^{\infty}$
  To get a Degree: you need Money plus Hard Work (to an infinite degree)

- Formula for Happiness: $C = A \times 365 - I$
  To reach Contentment: Appreciate what you have, every day of the year, and subtract Irritations (the little things that you can upset you).

Note: If the class meets for a whole month, start each class with one of the participants' formulas written on the whiteboard. The first person to figure it out earns points of some kind. If the class is of only one or two days' duration, simply have participants try to uncover the meaning of each other's formula.

Brainteaser: Which of the choices (a through d) is right for the next box in the series?

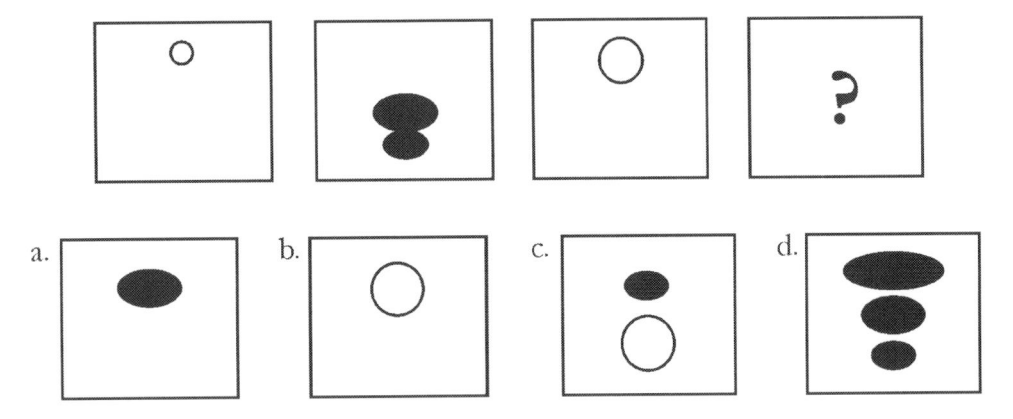

Answer: d. The circle gets larger each time but is alternated with the black oval, which increases in size each time and in number. If there were a fifth box required for the series, it would show one circle, larger than any that preceded it.

17. Encourage collective accomplishment.

Lech Walensa invited nine other leaders to meet with him regarding the need for reform in the Polish government. A month later, that number had grown to 95 million! In the words of cultural anthropologist Margaret Mead, "Never doubt that a small group of thoughtful committed citizens can change the world; indeed, it is the only thing that ever has."

When collective efforts result in positive change, can confidence be far behind? Help participants get at least a taste of such confidence-building experiences by asking for examples of change instituted by a committed individual or a committed group of people. (Be inspired by initiators such as Rosa Parks, Mother Teresa, Princess Diana, Eunice Shriver, JFK, John Walsh, Candy Lichtner [the mother behind MADD], and by programs such as Six Weeks to Wellness, National Secretaries Week, the 4-H Club, and even Ya-Ya sisterhoods.)

Finally, have them speculate regarding group possibilities that would make their small corner of the world—that is, the classroom itself—a better place. Encourage them to undertake a collective project.

Example: That project could be something small but helpful or healthful, such as creating a collection of mental exercises that students can do at their desks to prevent deep-vein thrombosis.

Brainteaser: Which of the choices beneath each capitalized row contains a word that fits with the words that are capitalized?

1. CUTTER / WARE / SAND / AGE
   a) diamond   b) unturned   c) spiral   d) radiance

2. MINDED / STAND / RATED / STATE
   a) taker   b) giver   c) reader   d) listener

3. HOUSE / HEADED / BREEZE / INTO
   a) around   b) between   c) beyond   d) up

4. CATCH / BACK / OFF / ON
   a) into   b) of   c) down   d) holiday

5. ATTENDANT / BAG / DECK / ENGINEER
   a) control   b) war   c) photography   d) show

Answers: 1. b (The original four + "unturned" all relate to "stone")   2. a (All relate to "under")   3. d (All relate to "light")   4. c (All relate to "hold")   5. a (All relate to "flight")

18. Suggest individual projects.

Power does not flow to invisible people. If participants truly want to become more confident, they will have to move out of their comfort zones. They simply cannot cling to the wall like a flower for the rest of their lives. To help them come to the forefront to see and be seen, provide realization-possibilities for them. Distribute copies of the list of possibilities and then have them place a check-mark in front of those projects they believe they can do or those avenues they can pursue in order to execute their own projects.

____ Volunteer for projects that no one else wants or no one else is doing—especially those projects that will get you noticed by those who can help advance your ideas.

____ Write an article about your idea. Yes, you can submit it to the company newsletter. But why not think big? Submit it, for example, to one of Stephen Covey's magazines, or to one of the e-zines that are always seeking submissions.

____ Accept credit (or ask for it) and praise without embarrassment.

____ Make a staff presentation about an idea or plan you have, or present it at the next conference your department is holding.

____ Plan on spending five minutes every Monday morning keeping your supervisor apprised of your plans for the week (other mornings, too, if possible).

____ Become identified with a phrase you coined (the *Czarina of Customer Service*) or a thing you do or an article of clothing you wear. Remember President Reagan's jelly beans? Sally Jesse Raphael's red glasses? Ideally, your hallmark will be related to the passion you feel for your particular project.

____ Develop an expertise, so that when decision-makers and clout-carriers need it, they know where to turn.

____ Show appreciation, if only in the form of a greeting card, to all those who go out of their way to assist you.

____ Develop your network, both inside and outside the company. One of the best ways to do this is to become active in professional associations and in community service.

Other ideas: _____

Have participants discuss with a partner the steps they will take to implement their projects.

Note: These suggestions are clearly directed to employees of an organization. Provide age-appropriate examples if you teach in a high-school or middle-school setting.

19. Write a note to each person.

If you have a big class and little time, you may not be able to execute this possibility. However, few things reach an individual's inner core like a handwritten note, and when that note expresses admiration, you will have given a boost to the recipient's self-confidence.

Caution: Make certain that no two notes sound alike.

Brainteaser: Although the categories are not labeled, you should be able to figure out which diagram best reflects the capitalized words.

ANIMALS   TWO-LEGGED ANIMALS   FOUR-LEGGED ANIMALS

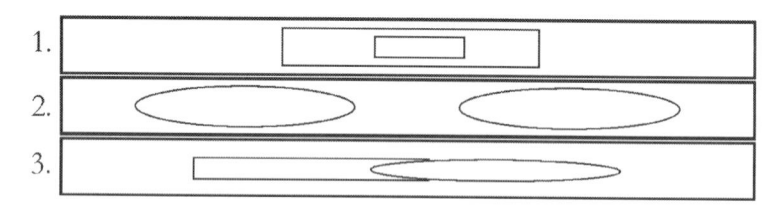

1.
2.
3.

Answer: 2. The large rectangle represents the broad category of animals. Within that broad division are two other small, separate divisions: two-legged and also four-legged creatures. The first diagram is wrong because it suggests that one division is contained within the other, which is not the case. The last answer is also wrong, because the categories do not overlap.

---

20. Give clues to a mystery to the quietest members.

This confidence-building exercise has a dual purpose—it serves to remind the quieter students that they have an important contribution to make to the team's success. It also serves to remind the more active students that they have a responsibility to include all members of the team.

Recommendation: If your students are younger than college-age, change the story details to eliminate the references to violence and drugs. You could make the crime a simple theft of a video game, for example.

Instructions to the class:
>"Your task is to solve a mystery. How quickly you solve the problem will depend on your ability to assume leadership, to work with one another, to listen, and to organize information. To solve the mystery, you must determine: Who? When? Where? Why? and Weapon."

[**Note to instructor:** It is critical that you say "Who the murderer was" when you write the word "Who?" on the flipchart. If they are listening well, they will realize that they need to discover who the murderer was—*not* who was killed. Say the phrase "Who the murderer was" just once. Write all five W-words on the flipchart, and explain that you need to know **when** the murder occurred, **where** it occurred, **why** it occurred, and what **weapon** was used to commit the murder.]

(continued)

20. **Give clues to a mystery to the quietest members.** *(continued)*

   Instructions, continued:

   "All the clues you need will be distributed in a few moments. The answers to these five questions are within your group. You may organize yourselves in any way to solve this mystery. The people who have cards may read their cards out loud if they wish. The only rule is that you cannot exchange cards. You are welcome to use the flipchart if you need it."

[**Note:** Let them use a second flipchart. If none is available, take the five W-word questions off the chart and tape the paper to the wall, thus giving them access to the flipchart if they need it.]

   "Take as much time as you need. When the group has voted unanimously on an answer to one particular question, that answer will be listed here on the flipchart. When you have all five questions answered and written on the flipchart next to the Who, Where, When, Why, and Weapon questions, then I will tell you if all five answers are correct. If any answer is wrong, you have not solved the mystery. I will tell you *only* whether or not you have solved the mystery. I will *not* tell you which answer(s) is wrong.

   If you have no questions, we can get started. Ask now, though, because I will not give you any further information."

[**Note to the instructor:** You may repeat any information you have already shared, but do not tell them that they are looking for the murderer and not the victim, *unless you are specifically asked*. This exercise is also a test of their listening ability.]

   Procedure:

   1. Distribute the clue strips. Some people will receive none, some just one, some will receive two. The strips should be mixed up before you distribute them. The first five on the Clue Strips page are the most critical; note that they are written in the upper case, so you can identify them quickly. These critical five clue strips should be given to the six members of the class who are *least likely* to speak up.
   2. Who? When? Where? Why? Weapon? Write these words on the board or flipchart. Add the answers to these questions as the participants respond.
   3. If they have not given the correct answers in 25 minutes, conclude the exercise and share the answers. Discuss where they went astray, how well they listened, how leadership emerged, how they reacted, how well they worked as a team, how conflicts were resolved, how the people with the critical information dealt with that "power," et cetera. Here are the answers:

      | Who? | Michael Nottingham |
      | When? | 7:30 p.m. |
      | Where? | Celana's apartment |
      | Why? | She threatened to report Nottingham's drug dealing to the police. |
      | Weapon? | Typewriter |

(continued)

20. **Give clues to a mystery to the quietest members.** *(concluded)*

CLUE STRIPS

MICHAEL NOTTINGHAM STRUCK HIS DATE OVER THE HEAD WITH A TYPEWRITER.

MICHAEL NOTTINGHAM PICKED UP THE TYPEWRITER AT 7:29 P.M.

MICHAEL NOTTINGHAM PICKED UP CELANA KIMBER AT HER APARTMENT FOR A DINNER DATE.

CELANA KIMBER DIED AS A RESULT OF SEVERE BLOWS TO THE HEAD, CAUSED BY A HEAVY OBJECT.

CELANA KIMBER WAS DEAD AT 7:30 P.M.

Celana Kimber's teenage brother died of a drug overdose.

Celana Kimber had learned that the drug lord who was supplying drugs to high school students was Michael Nottingham.

Celana Kimber was a model with a deep streak of jealousy.

Celana Kimber's roommate was a world-famous model named Slink.

Slink was having a secret affair with Michael Nottingham.

Slink left the apartment with her date, Geoffrey Tempos, at 7:05 p.m.

Michael Nottingham arrived at the apartment at 7:10 p.m.

Celana Kimber had learned from a former boyfriend (who was still in love with her) that Michael Nottinghan was a drug lord.

Michael Nottingham, still enraged, drove a knife through Celana Kimber's heart at 7:35 p.m.

Neighbors heard screams and called the police, who arrived at 7:45 p.m.

The police dusted for fingerprints until 8:30 p.m.

Geoffrey Tempos, junk bond king, had met Slink when she was shooting an ad on Wall Street.

Geoffrey Tempos arrived at Slink's apartment at 7:00 p.m.

Slink served Geoffrey Tempos a scotch and soda at 7:05 p.m.

Celana Kimber quarreled with Michael Nottingham over his drug dealing.

Slink and Geoffrey Tempos arrived at La Cote Basque at 7:35 p.m.

Celana Kimber suspected that Slink was having an affair with Michael Nottingham.

Geoffrey Tempos punched a member of the paparazzi who tried to photograph Slink at 7:33 p.m.

Celana Kimber's former boyfriend, Lieutenant Sax of the N.Y.P.D., was jealous of Michael Nottingham.

21. Nominate yourself or others for a standing "O."

From Biblical days to the present, wise men and women have acknowledged the importance of not hiding our special lights beneath a bushel. If and when participants do or say something that moves well beyond mediocrity, ask them to stand for an ovation. Encourage them to ask for such if they feel they deserve the accolades.

Brainteaser: What common expression is contained in the box?

```
T
H
E
O
C
E
A
N
at the
```

Answer: At the bottom of the ocean.

---

22. Delineate serve-possibilities.

Everyone knows the most famous of Martin Luther King's words, but there are so many other inspirational words this fine man spoke. Among them are these: "Everybody can be great, because anybody can serve."

You can encourage a small measure of greatness (and the self-confidence that is bound to accompany it) by generating a list of ways participants can serve their school or organization, their peers, their community, their country, their places of worship, their political parties, those in dire circumstances in foreign countries, and so on.

(continued)

500 Creative Classroom Techniques for Teachers and Trainers

22. Delineate serve-possibilities. *(concluded)*

Ask for a volunteer to discuss ways that she is already serving. Then have each person partner up with someone to share why they might be able to serve one of these causes at this time (or why not).

Brainteaser: Can you figure out the familiar phrase in the box below?

> WILWEEPLOW

Answer: Weepin' willow.

---

23. Compile a list of shatter-able myths.

Take charge of a discussion of myths. Note that I've used the words "take charge" rather than simply "lead." You need to make sure that the discussion does not veer off into areas that are prejudicial or stereotypical. You could help guarantee the limits within which you want the discussion to center by writing the myths on the flipchart.

Examples: Women should stay home and raise the children.

Girls are not good at sports.

Men don't like to ask for directions.

Men are not good at the culinary arts.

Men are not nurturing.

Girls are not good at math.

Boys are not creative.

Women have no head for business.

Men have a hard time communicating.

Women let petty issues prevent them from moving ahead.

Others: _____

_____

_____

Then ask each person to think about a way that she has shattered a myth. If any participants wish to share their myth-shattering experiences with others, allow time for this and thank the volunteers. Point out that such myth-busting goes a long way toward developing the self-confidence that allows us to take carefully weighed risks.

(continued)

23. Compile a list of shatter-able myths. *(concluded)*

Finally, ask each person to put on paper some of their thoughts from the earlier discussion on shattering myths. (Note: They should not write their names, but should note their gender: male or female.) Encourage them to recall a time when they went against the predicted grain, or to recall any situations that led them to dispel a myth. Collect the papers and read them aloud, commenting where warranted.

Brainteaser: Here's another of those diagrams, unlabeled. Which one correctly represents the divisions listed in capital letters?

CONGRESS

LEGISLATIVE BRANCH

SENATOR

SENATE

HOUSE OF REPRESENTATIVES

Answer: 1. The legislative branch of our government, the biggest entity of those listed here, is represented by the large rectangle in Figure 1. Congress is contained within that branch and is shown by a large circle. Within that circle (or within Congress) are two entities: the Senate and the House of Representatives, represented by the two small rectangles within the large circle. A Senator is just one person within one of those rectangles, represented by a small circle.

---

24. Take (and give) lessons from parenting texts.

Much of the best advice that is given to adults is the very same advice that is given to children. If you have a parenting text, look for a confidence-building example that pertains to both adults and children. Share it with the class. If you don't have access to such a text, ask the class for suggestions: "How did your parents develop self-confidence in you?" And "What are you doing to develop self-confidence in yourselves (or in your own children)?" (Note: Some participants are not parents and some of you are dealing with younger students, so you could also ask, "What can parents do to develop self-confidence?") List ideas on the flipchart.

Then ask them to work in pairs to discuss one thing on the list that they can do or do more of in order to increase their self-confidence. (For those who already seem quite confident, point out that no one is confident about *everything*. Modify the assignment for these individuals: "What can you do to increase your self-confidence in areas where it is lacking?")

Brainteaser: Although Sue wore a size 3 dress, people were always amazed at what she weighed. Why?

Answer: She worked at a deer-weighing station during hunting season.

25. Use the government's list of competencies.

The United States Office of Personnel Management (OPM) developed a list of competencies that supervisors, managers, and executives must possess if they are to be effective in their job roles. Most of the competencies are important to success in life, as well as in work.

Show participants the list, and ask them to rate themselves on a scale of 1 (low) to 5 (high) on each of the competencies. Then have them total their scores.

Next, form triads. Each person will share some of his lowest scores and solicit ideas from the other two triad members regarding ways to improve those areas.

Oral communication _____
Leadership _____
Listening _____
Flexibility _____
Written communication _____
Interpersonal skills _____
Ability to make decisions _____
Self-direction _____
Technical competence _____
Working with diverse groups _____
Knowledge (acquire/manage) _____
Conflict management _____
Teambuilding _____
Influencing/Negotiating _____
Optimizing human resources _____
Planning/Evaluating _____
Customer orientation _____
Internal controls/Integrity _____
Vision _____
External awareness _____
TOTAL: _____

(continued)

25. **Use the government's list of competencies.** *(concluded)*

Suggestion: If time permits, have each person also share a strength from the list with the other triad members and explain how she acquired her expertise in that particular arena.

(Note: The list has since been revised. Instead of a prioritized list that begins with supervision skills and leads up to executive skills, the list now has five equal categories: Leading Change; Leading People; Building Coalitions/Communication; Being Results-Driven; and Having Business Acumen. Each category has several subsets of related skills.)

Brainteaser: These circles are all the same size. How many more circles of this size are needed to make a complete ring around the black circle?

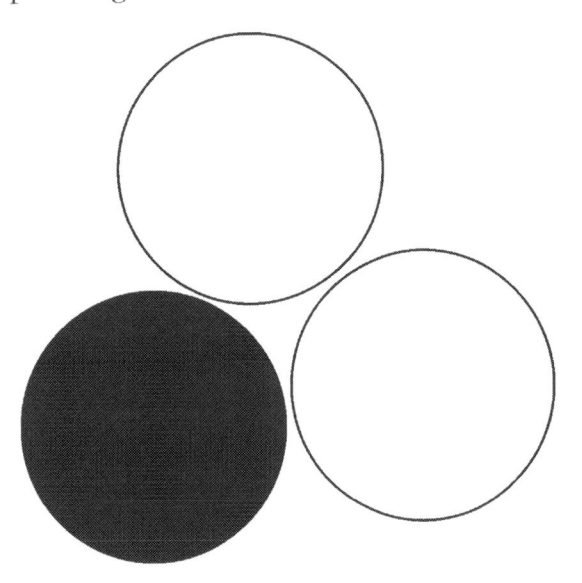

Answer: Four more are needed, as shown in this diagram:

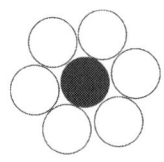

Appendix

Collective Nouns 325

Discussion Questions About Feedback 327

Sample Grammar Test 329

Sample Intuition Quiz 331

Selected Quotations on Leadership 333

Thought-Provoking Proverbs 335

Sample Letters of Commendation 337

A Training Checklist 339

About the Author 343

List of Collective Nouns

The most-effective teachers are able to use humor in the classroom. Chapter 3 presents twenty-five ways to do that. Activity #21 suggests using collective nouns. If you want examples to show participants, here's an irresistible collection of traditional and more-imaginative forms:

An agenda of tasks
An armada of ships
An army of ants
An army of caterpillars
An army of frogs
An audit of bookkeepers
An aurora of polar bears
A balance of accountants
A bale of turtles
A band of gorillas
A band of jays
A bank of monitors
A barren of mules
A bed of clams
A bed of snakes
A belt of asteroids
A bevy of swans
A blessing of unicorns
A bouquet of pheasants
A brace of grouse
A brigade of soldiers
A brood of hens
A bunch of things
A bury of conies
A business of ferrets
A business of flies
A cast of actors
A cast of falcons
A cast of hawks
A cavalcade of horsemen
A chain of islands
A charm of finches

A chattering of choughs
A chorus of angels
A class of students
A cloud of gnats
A clowder of cats
A cluster of grasshoppers
A clutch of chicks
A clutch of eggs
A clutter of cats
A collective of nouns
A colony of ants
A colony of bats
A colony of beavers
A colony of gulls
A colony of penguins
A colony of rats
A company of parrots
A company of soldiers
A conflagration of arsonists
A congregation of plovers
A congress of baboons
A conspiracy of ravens
A constellation of satellites
A convocation of eagles
A cover of coots
A covey of grouse
A covey of partridges
A covey of pheasants
A covey of quail
A cowardice of curs
A crash of rhinoceroses
A crowd of onlookers

A cry of hounds
A culture of bacteria
A deceit of lapwings
A descent of woodpeckers
A dissimulation of birds
A division of soldiers
A donut of data
A down of hares
A draught of fish
A dray of squirrels
A drift of swine
A drove of cattle
A duel of doves
An exaltation of larks
A field of racehorses
A fistful of dollars
A flange of baboons
A fleet of ships
A flight of cormorants
A flight of goshawks
A flight of swallows
A flink of cows
A flock of sheep
A flock of tourists
A flotilla of ships
A gaggle of geese
A galaxy of stars
A galaxy of starlets
A gam of whales
A gang of elk
A gang of hoodlums
A geek of engineers

A giggle of girls
A grove of trees
A heap of trash
A herd of elephants
A hill of beans
A hive of bees
A horde of gnats
A host of angels
A host of sparrows
A hover of trout
A huddle of lawyers
A husk of hares
A kettle of hawks
A kindle of kittens
A knot of toads
A leap of hares
A leap of leopards
A leash of foxes
A litter of pigs
A mob of kangaroos
A murder of crows
A murmuration of starlings
A muster of peacocks
A muster of storks
A mute of hounds
A nest of mice
A nest of rabbits
A nest of vipers
A network of computers
A number of mathematicians
A nye of pheasants
An ostentation of peacocks
A pack of hounds
A pack of rats
A pack of wolves

A paddling of ducks
A pair of horses
A parliament of owls
A peep of chickens
A piteousness of doves
A pitying of turtledoves
A plague of locusts
A platoon of soldiers
A plump of waterfowl
A pod of seals
A pod of whales
A pod of dolphins
A ponder of philosophers
A prickle of hedgehogs
A pride of lions
A rabble of rats
A rafter of turkeys
A range of mountains
A richness of martens
A ring of keys
A rout of wolves
A school of fish
A sedge of cranes
A set of mathematicians
A shoal of bass
A shrewdness of apes
A siege of herons
A singular of boars
A skein of geese
A skulk of foxes
A slew of homework
A slither of snakes
A sloth of bears
A sneak of weasels
A party of jays

A patch of flowers
A sord of mallards
A sounder of swine
A spring of seals
A spring of teal
A squad of soldiers
A staff of employees
A stand of trees
A streak of tigers
A string of ponies
A stud of mares
A swarm of bees
A swarm of rats
A team of athletes
A team of ducks
A team of horses
A tiding of magpies
A tribe of goats
A tribe of monkeys
A tribe of natives
A troop of kangaroos
A troupe of performers
A tumult of tubas
A vagary of impediments
A volery of birds
A walk of snipe
A watch of nightingales
A wealth of information
A wedge of geese
A wedge of swans
A whistle of modems
A wisdom of grandparents
A wisp of snipe
A woop of gorillas

Discussion Questions About Feedback

Feedback plays an important role in learning. The introduction to Chapter 4 on feedback suggests that teachers and trainers use discussion questions for personal and professional growth. They can be used for more-specific purposes as well. The first five in the following list, for example, can be quite useful for team leaders.

1. What is the relationship between leadership and feedback?
2. What general questions ("Does anyone really care what we think?") do employees have?
3. Give an example of how feedback, in answer to these two questions, can also provide some assurance to the person asking the questions.
4. Research by Bruce Tulgan reveals that when it comes to feedback, people make critical mistakes. He calls them the "seven sins of feedback." The first two are "Not enough feedback" and "Too much feedback." What do you think the additional five "sins"* are?
5. Which, if any, of the seven are you guilty of? How about your manager?
6. Discuss the role of feedback in delegation and in empowerment.
7. What are the consequences of providing poor feedback or poorly delivered feedback?
8. Discuss the pro's and con's of rehearsing in advance of delivering feedback.
9. What suggestions can you give to someone who has to give feedback to an individual who is more verbal/powerful/experienced/educated than the feedback provider?
10. What might be some causes underlying a manager's poor feedback process?
11. Draw parallels between outstanding feedback-givers and outstanding teachers.
12. Discuss the pro's and con's of the "sandwich" approach to delivering feedback (starting and ending on a positive note, with negative feedback sandwiched in the middle).
13. What role, if any, does emotion play in providing effective feedback?
14. What's the most difficult part of providing negative feedback, in your opinion?
15. How do the best coaches employ feedback?

*The other five involve feedback that is negative, rushed, inaccurate, vague, and delayed.

Sample Grammar Test

Chapter 6 presented twenty-five ways to use non-threatening competition. In the sixth activity, we suggested giving a quiz and mentioning that no one has ever scored higher than 86%. Believing that it will be nearly impossible to do really well on the test, participants will feel that a load has been taken off their shoulders. Perhaps among your students is a grammar guru who can shatter the previously held "national" record.

Directions: The following sentences may or may not contain errors. If you believe that corrections are needed, indicate where the punctuation marks should be inserted or removed.

1. Any boss who gives expensive birthday gifts will be popular.
2. "Are you?" she demanded "the one in charge.
3. George Bush president of the United States addressed the press corps yesterday.
4. The trainers network which has an international membership provides many opportunities.
5. While the year end report was being prepared the meeting was going on.
6. She is definitely a "tweener
7. Michael Jordan declared "I'm not out here to say, I'm perfect.
8. Do you know any "dinks
9. "We're having an earthquake he screamed"
10. I need Mr. Jones a new desk a new typewriter and a new desk chair.
11. June is without a doubt the most accurate typist in the department.
12. Therefore I think we should consider a Southern state next year the committee agrees.
13. The organization of the firm is simple everyone reports to one person.
14. Mr. Henry will use the famous "I have a dream line in his remarks today."
15. The names of the members are: Lin Day, EEO officer, Susan Black, vice president in charge of international trade, and Anthony Trollop, public relations officer.
16. The fixed price proposal—see Appendix II—includes the changes required for production.
17. Mr. Fujitani despite what you may think is actually the most committed team member.
18. His article, The Impact of Interim Funding will appear in the Subcontractors Quarterly.
19. She asks everyone, Have you read Browning's poem How Do I Love Thee.
20. The womens room is cleaned as well as the mens room.
21. He once wrote a letter to the Prince of Whales sic.
22. She has visited the place where Poe wrote his poem "The Raven."
23. Parent's may watch their children swim only during the Spring Fling, not during practices.
24. The whole unit all 16 of us is going to see "Ragtime."

Sample Grammar Test
Answers

1. Any boss who gives expensive birthday gifts will be popular.
2. "Are you," she demanded, "the one in charge?"
3. George Bush, president (lower case when the title comes after the name) of the United States, addressed the press corps yesterday.
4. The Trainers Network, which has an international membership, provides many opportunities.
5. While the year-end report was being prepared, the meeting was going on.
6. She is definitely a "tweener."
7. Michael Jordan declared, "I'm not out here to say 'I'm perfect'."
8. Do you know any "dinks"?
9. "We're having an earthquake!" he screamed.
10. I need, Mr. Jones, a new desk, a new typewriter, and a new desk chair.
11. June is, without a doubt, the most accurate typist in the department. (There are other correct variations.)
12. Therefore, I think we should consider a Southern state next year. The committee agrees.
13. The organization of the firm is simple: everyone reports to one person. (A semi-colon is also correct, but a colon is better.)
14. Mr. Henry will use the famous "I have a dream . . ." line in his remarks today.
15. The names of the members are Lin Day, EEO officer; Susan Black, vice president in charge of international trade; and Anthony Trollop, public relations officer. (Note: Titles after names are not capitalized.)
16. The fixed (hyphen here) price proposal (see Appendix II) includes the changes required for production.
17. Mr. Fujitani—despite what you may think—is actually the most committed team member.
18. His article, "The Impact of Interim Funding," will appear in the <u>Subcontractors Quarterly</u>. (Italics are better if you have them. Underline only when computer is not available.)
19. She asks everyone, "Have you read Browning's poem 'How Do I Love Thee?'" (Question mark inside the single quote. The poem's title includes the question mark.)
20. The women's room is cleaned as well as the men's room.
21. He once wrote a letter to the Prince of Whales [sic].
22. She has visited the place where Poe wrote his poem "The Raven."
23. Parents may watch their children swim only during the Spring Fling, not during practices.
24. The whole unit—all 16 of us—is going to see <u>Ragtime</u>. (italics preferred)

Sample Intuition Quiz

The second activity in Chapter 1 dealing with ways for participants to introduce themselves suggests giving an intuition quiz. This technique can be used in a number of other ways. For example, ask participants in a course on Decision Making how often they make decisions intuitively. Then ask how successful are the results of those decisions. (Chances are, most people don't track the results.) Assure them that intuition is a valuable tool—*if* they truly possess it. Then give the following test to help determine if they do. The directions to students are provided for your use, via quotations.

Directions: Don't waste time thinking too hard or trying to calculate. This is, after all, a test of your intuitive abilities. To make it easy, you can provide a range within which you believe the correct answer will fall. But don't be ridiculous with it: If I asked you to estimate my age, for example, and you gave a range of 0 to 100 years, you'd be technically correct. But we are trying to learn if you have intuitive powers—if you can "guesstimate" with some degree of precision. So, a more acceptable answer would be 'between 50 and 65.' Keep your range narrow enough to reflect the precision we are seeking.

1. How many muscles does a cat have in one ear?

2. What is the life span (in seconds or minutes or hours) of a dragonfly?

3. For how long (in days, months, or years) can a snail sleep?

4. How many different vocal sounds can a cat make?

5. How many different vocal sounds can a dog make?

6. How many new animals have been domesticated in the last 4,000 years?

7. How far does the ocean liner QE2 move after burning one gallon of fuel?

8. How many ways are there to make change from a dollar?

9. In a lifetime, how long does the average American spend waiting at red lights?

10. There are a million words in the English language. How many end in "dous"?

Answers: 1. 32 2. 24 hours 3. 3 years 4. 100+ 5. 10 6. none 7. 6 inches 8. 93 9. 6 months 10. Only four: stupendous, horrendous, tremendous, and hazardous

Selected Quotations on Leadership

Activity #5 in Chapter 19 about thinking on your feet and Activity #14 in Chapter 9 about ways to select group leaders both encourage the use of quotations. We also devote a whole chapter to outlining the many benefits derived from using quotations in the classroom (Chapter 6). Lists of quotations are readily available from the library or Internet, but what follows are some of *my* favorites.

The bravest are surely those who have the clearest vision of what is before them, glory and danger alike, and yet, notwithstanding, go out to meet it.   —Thucydides

The point of wisdom is not simply to do well . . . it is to do good.   —Patricia Monaghan

Any fool can criticize, condemn, and complain, and most fools do.   —Benjamin Franklin

The greatest lesson in life is to know that even fools are right sometimes.   —Churchill

Do what you can, with what you have, where you are.   —Theodore Roosevelt

You can only lead others where you yourself are prepared to go.   —Lachlan McLean

To wear your heart on your sleeve isn't a very good plan; you should wear it inside, where it functions best.   —Margaret Thatcher

The first rule of any technology used in a business is that automation applied to an efficient operation will magnify the efficiency. The second is that automation applied to an inefficient operation will magnify the inefficiency.   —Bill Gates

Intelligence is what we use when we don't know what to do, when we have to grope rather than using a standard response.   —Jean Piaget

People rise to the challenge when it is *their* challenge.   —James Belasco and Ralph Stayer

The good judgment we have as human beings provides the best judgment for what we need in business.   —John Dalla Costa

Thought-Provoking Proverbs

Chapter 3 focuses on using humor in the classroom, and activity #20 in that chapter endorses the use of proverbs. Of course, proverbs can be used for purposes other than the comedic. To illustrate, in a class on influence, I emphasize the importance of communication in career advancement. A strong element in influence is being able to make transitions—that is, to bridge disparate concerns. Then I cite this Scottish proverb: "Who would be a leader must also be a bridge." Challenge participants to develop a verbal bridge between opposing forces. (The opposition may be between the old and the new ways of doing things; it could be between the creative and the logical, the traditional and the emerging, and so on.)

You'll find numerous opportunities to put proverbs like these to good classroom use.

Idleness is the holiday of fools.
Laziness travels so slowly that poverty soon overtakes him.
In a calm sea, every man is a pilot.
He has good judgment who relies not wholly on his own.
The gown is hers that wears it, and the world is his that enjoys it.
Anger is often more hurtful than the injury that caused it.
Hunger is the best pickle.
He has need of a long spoon that eats with the devil.
He who listens to what people say of him shall never have peace.
Cast no dirt into the well that gives you water.
No one knows the weight of another's burden.
'Tis easier to prevent bad habits than to break them.
If your head is wax, don't walk in the sun.
Wealth is not his that has it, but his that enjoys it.
A fog cannot be dispelled by a fan.
Adversity makes a man wise, not poor.
There was never a good knife made of bad steel.
A harvest of peace is produced from a seed of contentment.

Sample Letters of Commendation

Chapter 14 presents twenty-five ways to encourage participant learning after the course has ended. The second technique in that chapter proposes writing letters to the managers of participants who have volunteered or done especially well on some aspect of the course. Here are examples for you; adapt them to your own purposes.

(Sample Letter of Commendation for a student who volunteered)

Center for Professional Development
11 Fetzner Square; Rochester, NY 14613 (585) 222-6565; mccpd@frontiernet.net

June 8, 2005

Josephine Barker
OFFICE OF THE STATE COMPTROLLER
Department of Human Resources
110 State Street, 12th Floor
Albany, NY 12236

Re: Commendation for Tracy L. Smith

Dear Ms. Barker:

Despite the popular admonitions regarding volunteering, your employee Tracy L. Smith nonetheless offered to assist her co-learners in our recent "Enhancing Interpersonal Relations" session, presented at the OSC Conference this past week.

Of all the individuals present, Tracy was the first (and only person) whose hand went up when I asked for a volunteer. Her actions show both self-confidence and an eagerness to do more than is asked of her. Her task is to assemble the ideas/discussion points generated in the session and share them with other class members. Thus, she is extending the State's investment in training programs and in the employees being trained.

I find this leadership quality most commendable and wanted you to know of my admiration for Tracy's professionalism, enthusiasm, and organizational skills. You are indeed fortunate to have someone of her caliber on your staff.

Please join me in commending Tracy for her special qualities and for her willingness to help others in our continuous-learning efforts.

Regards,
(signature)

**(Sample Letter of Commendation for a student
who excelled in a given exercise)**

Center for Professional Development

11 Fetzner Square; Rochester, NY 14613 (585) 222-6565; mccpd@frontiernet.net

January 7, 2005

767 Franklin Avenue
Naval Air Station
Lemoore, CA 93246-5011

Dear LCDR Barker:

I wish to commend your employees W. G. Austin and Mary Simpson, who were part of a team that earned the highest number of points on extremely challenging exercises in our recent "Effective Business Writing" class. These points were allocated whenever a team demonstrated the first and most-accurate response to assignments related to grammar, verbal economy, and the ability to write quickly and accurately.

The exercises were developed in places like UCLA's Graduate School of English, Stanford University's Executive Development program, and from my own 40 years of experience teaching communication skills.

Class participants learned linguistic and syntactical concepts such as indefinite antecedents; dangling participles; the correct usage of *that* and *which;* weak verbs, which govern subject-case pronouns; prepositions, which govern object-case pronouns; ways to bring variety to sentence structure (including the gerund and the infinitive), and a host of other techniques designed to increase both productivity and professionalism in business writing.

You are indeed fortunate to have employees like Gail and Mary, who possess the intelligence and insight that virtually guarantee success in all they do. They not only functioned admirably on the team, they also evinced a remarkable ability to work well under pressure. Please join me in acknowledging the talents of these remarkable women, whose intellectual gifts make them valuable and, I trust, valued employees.

Regards,
(signature)

A Training Checklist

Included here is a list of responsibilities/recommendations that bespeak both professionalism and an ethical commitment to the profession. Even if you are only an occasional trainer, I think you'll find this self-assessment helpful.

☐ I know this subject well enough to be considered something of an expert in it.

☐ I get to the room at least half an hour early to set it up and to greet early arrivals.

☐ I do all I can to make participants feel welcome, such as putting a welcome sign on the door or writing the word "Welcome" on the flipchart.

☐ I make a sincere effort to learn about my participants, their work, their goals, their environments, and their strengths and weaknesses.

☐ I begin with an introduction to the course, and provide an outline of my objectives and my credentials for teaching the course. Then I follow with introductions of the participants themselves.

☐ I take care of "housekeeping" items at the beginning of class.

☐ I make participants aware of ground rules.

☐ I try to have all their names memorized before the first break.

☐ I am familiar with Howard Gardner's seven intelligences and/or J.P. Guilford's 124 intelligences and applaud more than the verbal or mathematical proficiency of participants.

☐ I work to learn (and post) participants' expectations for the course.

☐ I make sure there's a relevant reason behind all tasks.

☐ I try to structure courses according to a philosophy like Jesse Jackson's: "Put a floor beneath each learner and a ceiling above none." In other words, I make sure everyone possesses the basics before moving on to more-sophisticated concepts.

☐ I actively work to make the learning experience an enjoyable one.

☐ I can integrate their views into the course material.

☐ I try hard to keep discussions on target.

☐ I present an overview or agenda of what the course entails.

☐ I benchmark with other teachers/trainers to ensure that I am providing the most valuable information in the most relevant way.

(continued)

A Training Checklist *(continued)*

☐ I am sensitive to diversity issues, including diversity in learning styles.

☐ I take pride in the professional look of my materials.

☐ I make deliberate efforts to structure activities to optimize the ABC's—the Affective realm, the Behavioral realm, and the Cognitive realm.

☐ I am aware of the "glazed-over" look characteristic of participants who are confused or overwhelmed by the material, and make adjustments when I see it.

☐ I debrief after content-rich activities.

☐ I use anecdotes and continuously refine my raconteur abilities.

☐ I actively work to make the learning environment one of comfort and inclusion.

☐ I seek feedback throughout the session—not just at the end.

☐ I frequently invite participants to discuss their real-world situations in light of the learning that is occurring.

☐ I make myself available to participants before and after the class, as well as during breaks.

☐ I periodically review the material or provide summaries.

☐ I consciously avoid sarcasm, vulgarity, inappropriate humor, and references that may be offensive.

☐ I anticipate questions that will arise and prepare responses to them.

☐ I employ anecdotes to illustrate points.

☐ I assure participants that they will never be made to feel uncomfortable.

☐ I never lecture for more than 15 minutes at a stretch.

☐ I incorporate humor into the presentation.

☐ I include relevant news events and statistics in my presentation.

☐ I am "physical" with the information—i.e., I make dramatic gestures from time to time.

☐ I provide a change of pace on a regular basis.

☐ I consciously think about ways to make the presentations interactive.

☐ I encourage participants to meet and work with others in the room.

(continued)

A Training Checklist *(concluded)*

- ☐ I invite feedback about the presentation.
- ☐ I strive to relate the material to participants' jobs, goals, and lives.
- ☐ I schedule breaks as needed.
- ☐ I make sure that the screen and flipchart can be seen by every participant.
- ☐ I keep abreast of developments in the field.
- ☐ I am familiar with Bloom's Taxonomy and ask questions on all five levels.
- ☐ I revise my materials on a continual basis.
- ☐ I use media effectively.
- ☐ I have not stopped honing my communication skills.
- ☐ I employ a wide variety of methodologies.
- ☐ I evaluate learning comprehension in a variety of ways.
- ☐ I invite questions and feedback on my presentation.
- ☐ I invite (but put limits on) the telling of "war stories."
- ☐ I provide ways for participants to be continuous learners.
- ☐ I design effective closings.

About the Author

After earning her doctorate in education at the University of Rochester, Marlene Caroselli left the public classroom and her native New York State in 1980 and headed to the West Coast. She soon began working as a manager for Trizec Properties, Inc. and as an adjunct professor at UCLA and National University. She has also conducted programs for Clemson University, University of Rochester, Michigan State University, and Southwest Missouri State University. Her university work led to training contracts with the Department of Defense and with such Fortune 100 firms as Lockheed Martin, Northrop Grumman, TRW, Hughes Aircraft, and Allied-Signal.

In 1984, she founded the Center for Professional Development, adding books to her list of professional achievements. Her first book, *The Language of Leadership*, was chosen a main selection by Newbridge's Executive Development book club. Since that publication, she has written fifty-four additional books. (See Amazon.com.) A recent book, *Principled Persuasion: Influence with Integrity, Sell with Standards*, was named a Director's Choice by Doubleday Book Club. Her latest book, *One-to-One for Managers*, has been selected by Barnes and Noble for an online course.

Dr. Caroselli writes frequently for Stephen Covey's *Executive Excellence* publications, for Lakewood's many publications, and for the *National Business Employment Weekly*, as well as for numerous other print and electronic publications.

She has conducted training in more than half the states in the U.S., and has presented programs in Guam, Singapore, Montreal, and Sao Paolo, Brazil. Her corporate clients include Eastman Kodak, Xerox, Bausch & Lomb, Mobil, Chevron, Rockwell, Hughes Aircraft, and Magnavox. Federal agencies with which she has worked include the U. S. Departments of Defense, Labor, Transportation, Agriculture, and Interior, the General Services Administration, and the Bureau of Indian Affairs.

She makes presentations for such organizations as The Executive Committee, Delta Kappa Gamma, the Mortgage Bankers Association, The Institute for International Research, the American Society for Training and Development, the Public Relations Society of America, and Professional Secretaries International.

She can be contacted at the following address: Marlene Caroselli
Barker Square Park
80 Greenwood Park
Pittsford, New York 14534
mccpd@frontiernet.net.

Made in the USA
San Bernardino, CA
15 May 2015